p.85 → p.90

Tenth Edition

ASSESSMENT OF STUDENT ACHIEVEMENT

D0141473

WITHDRAWN

WITHDRAWN

Tenth Edition

ASSESSMENT OF STUDENT ACHIEVEMENT

C. Keith Waugh
Southern Illinois University Carbondale

Norman E. Gronlund
Late of the University of Illinois

TOURO COLLEGE LIBRARY
Kings Hwy

PEARSON

Boston Columbus Indianapolis New York San Francisco Upper Saddle River
Amsterdam Cape Town Dubai London Madrid Milan Munich Paris Montréal Toronto
Delhi Mexico City Sao Paulo Sydney Hong Kong Seoul Singapore Taipei Tokyo

KH

Vice President and Editorial Director: Jeffery W. Johnston
Vice President and Publisher: Kevin Davis
Editorial Assistant: Lauren Carlson
Vice President, Director of Marketing: Margaret Waples
Senior Marketing Manager: Joanna Sabella
Senior Managing Editor: Pamela Bennett
Senior Project Manager: Mary M. Irvin
Production Manager: Laura Messerly

Senior Art Director: Jayne Conte
Cover Designer: Suzanne Duda
Cover Art: Fotolia
Full-service Project Management: Jyotsna Rishi, Element LLC
Composition: Element LLC
Printer/Binder: Courier/Westford
Cover Printer: Courier/Westford
Text Font: ITC Garamond Light

Credits and acknowledgments for materials borrowed from other sources and reproduced, with permission, in this textbook appear on the appropriate page within the text.

Every effort has been made to provide accurate and current Internet information in this book. However, the Internet and information posted on it are constantly changing, so it is inevitable that some of the Internet addresses listed in this textbook will change.

Copyright © 2013, 2009, 2006, 2003, 1998 by Pearson Education, Inc. All rights reserved. Printed in the United States of America. This publication is protected by Copyright and permission should be obtained from the publisher prior to any prohibited reproduction, storage in a retrieval system, or transmission in any form or by any means, electronic, mechanical, photocopying, recording, or likewise. To obtain permission(s) to use material from this work, please submit a written request to Pearson Education, Inc., Permissions Department, One Lake Street, Upper Saddle River, New Jersey 07458 or you may fax your request to 201-236-3290.

Library of Congress Cataloging-in-Publication Data

Waugh, C. Keith
  Assessment of student achievement / C. Keith Waugh, Norman E. Gronlund.—10th ed.
    p. cm.
  Prev. ed. cataloged under author Norman E. Gronlund.
  Includes bibliographical references and index.
  ISBN-13: 978-0-13-268963-2
  ISBN-10: 0-13-268963-4
    1. Achievement tests—Design and construction.   2. Examinations—Design and construction.
I. Gronlund, Norman Edward, II. Title.
  LB3060.65.G766 2013
  371.26'1—dc23

                                                                                        2011032279

2 3 4 5   V088   14 13 12

ISBN 10: 0-13-268963-4
ISBN 13: 978-0-13-268963-2

8/28/13

PREFACE

Assessment of Student Achievement emphasizes the principles and practices of achievement assessment that contribute to more effective classroom instruction and improved student learning.

Effective instruction includes: (1) clarifying what students are expected to learn, (2) planning instructional activities that provide for the intended learning, and (3) using assessment procedures that are in harmony with the intended learning outcomes and the instructional activities. This book focuses on achievement assessment, but it views assessment as an integral part of the instructional process. It can aid in determining learning readiness, in monitoring and improving learning, and in grading or certifying student achievement. If assessment planning is done at the same time as instructional planning, the two can work together to help students achieve the intended learning outcomes of the instruction.

The first two chapters describe the assessment process, its role in instruction, and the historical and legislative influences on assessment in the United States. The third and fourth chapters present the use of taxonomies when planning assessments and the methods to establish the validity and reliability of assessment tools. The remaining chapters cover how to prepare tests and performance assessments, how assessments are conducted in distance education courses, how to grade and report student achievement, how to interpret standardized achievement test scores, and how assessment is used when conducting education action research.

NEW TO THIS EDITION

- A new chapter (Chapter 10) discusses the types of assessment methods used in distance education, how these methods assist in the assessment process, and how to curb cheating.
- A new chapter (Chapter 13) explains the use of action research in education, sampling methods and approaches to data analysis, and how action research is conducted.
- A new section in Chapter 1 discusses the influence of events in U.S. history and legislation on assessment in public education.
- Chapters 9 and 10 have been combined to improve the continuity of discussion about performance assessment processes and procedures.
- The learning outcomes that begin revised chapters have been updated accordingly.
- Questions have been added to the end of each chapter, along with an answer key in the appendices, so that students can assess their learning progress.
- The References and Additional Reading section has been updated in selected chapters.

The book is written in a simple and direct manner, using frequent examples and illustrations to clarify important points. It provides a well-balanced treatment of testing and performance assessment, each to be used where most appropriate. In short, it is a practical guide for those who want to learn how to prepare valid assessment instruments that contribute to effective instruction and student learning.

We would like to thank the following reviewers for their time and input: Fred Hammond, III, University of Central Oklahoma; Michael Ramsey Smith, University of North Florida; and Lou H. Sanders, Jackson State University.

We would also like to thank the authors and publishers referred to in the book, Pearson editorial staff, all others who contributed to the production of the book, and our wives, Marie and Billie Jo, for their support during work on this revision.

C. Keith Waugh

Norman E. Gronlund

BRIEF CONTENTS

CONTENTS

Tenth Edition

ASSESSMENT OF STUDENT ACHIEVEMENT

1 ACHIEVEMENT ASSESSMENT AND INSTRUCTION

Studying this chapter should enable you to[1]

1. Explain why both testing and performance assessment are important in achievement assessment.
2. Write a definition of achievement assessment.
3. Describe the relationship between instruction and assessment.
4. Distinguish among the various roles of assessment in the instructional process.
5. List the ways that assessments can directly aid learning.
6. Describe the historical events and legislation that have influenced assessment.

All of us have taken various types of paper-and-pencil tests during our many years of schooling. Some of these were teacher-made tests requiring us to select an answer (e.g., true-false, multiple choice, or matching) or to supply an answer (e.g., short answer or essay). Others were standardized tests of aptitude or achievement, primarily using multiple-choice items. The widespread use of paper-and-pencil testing in the schools was due, at least in part, to the efficiency with which they could measure a large number of learning outcomes and the ease of scoring and recording the results.

In recent years there has been a reaction to the heavy emphasis on paper-and-pencil testing. Some critics have contended that there should be more emphasis on the assessment of **authentic**, "real-life" tasks (e.g., solving problems that exist in the real world). Others have contended that paper-and-pencil testing should be replaced, at least in part, by **alternative** types of assessment (e.g., oral presentations, demonstrations, portfolios). Some reactions have been extreme but they highlight the importance of focusing

---

[1]Space does not permit using the preferred two-step method of stating intended learning outcomes described in Chapter 3. These statements, however, should provide a focus for your study and for application of the content in each chapter.

BOX 1.1   Commonly Used Assessment Terms

Performance Assessments	Assessments requiring students to demonstrate their achievement of understandings and skills by actually performing a task or set of tasks (e.g., writing a story, giving a speech, conducting an experiment, operating a machine).
Alternative Assessments	A title for performance assessments that emphasizes that these assessment methods provide an alternative to traditional paper-and-pencil testing.
Authentic Assessments	A title for performance assessments that stresses the importance of focusing on the application of understandings and skills to real problems in "real-world" contextual settings.

---

more attention on the actual performance of students (see Box 1.1). If you want to determine whether students can write, have them write something. If you want to determine whether students can operate a machine, have them operate the machine. If you want to determine whether students can conduct an experiment, have them conduct an experiment. In short, if you want to determine whether they can perform a task, have them perform the task. There is little doubt that more emphasis on performance assessment in the schools would improve the assessment of our intended learning outcomes. However, paper-and-pencil testing still has an important role to play, even as we focus more directly on performance-based tasks.

Most types of performance have a knowledge component that is important to the performance. Good writing includes such factors as knowledge of vocabulary, grammar, and spelling. These are not well sampled by a writing task because we tend to use only the words we know, use sentence structures that we can punctuate easily, and substitute words we can spell for those we can't spell. Thus, in writing, we can structure it to conceal our weaknesses. A separate test of vocabulary, grammar, and spelling can identify these weaknesses and be used to improve writing skill. Just don't interpret the test results as measures of "writing ability." The tests measure knowledge useful in writing but writing ability is determined by assessing the actual writing (**performance assessment**). Similarly, in operating machinery, the actual operation of the machine is the ultimate goal, but tests measuring knowledge of how to operate the machine and the safety precautions to follow may be needed before the hands-on performance assessment. Likewise, before conducting an experiment, tests can be used to determine how well students know the information needed for a well-controlled experiment.

Throughout this book, the emphasis will be on achievement assessment that includes both paper-and-pencil testing and performance assessment. Tests can provide direct measures of many important learning outcomes, ranging from simple to complex, and they can provide needed information for assessing and improving actual performance tasks. Thus, although we should strive for as authentic assessment as we can obtain, within the constraints of the school setting, both tests and performance-based tasks are needed for a complete assessment of student achievement.

As used in this book, **achievement assessment** is a broad category that includes all of the various methods for determining the extent to which students are achieving the intended learning outcomes of instruction. Because we are limiting our concern to achievement assessment, the single term *assessment* is used throughout the book as a matter of convenience.

RELATIONSHIP BETWEEN INSTRUCTION AND ASSESSMENT

In preparing for any type of instructional program, our main concern is "How can we most effectively bring about student learning?" As we ponder this question, our attention is naturally directed toward the methods and materials of instruction. However, at the same time we should also consider the role of assessment in the instructional process. When properly designed and appropriately used, assessment procedures can contribute to more effective instruction and greater student learning.

The close relationship between instruction and assessment can be seen in Table 1.1. Both require that we clearly specify the learning outcomes to be achieved by students, and the provisions of well-designed assessments closely parallel the characteristics of effective instruction. This relationship

TABLE 1.1 Relationship Between Instruction and Assessment

Instruction	Assessment
Instruction is most effective when	**Assessment is most effective when**
1. Directed toward a clearly defined set of intended learning outcomes.	1. Designed to assess a clearly defined set of intended learning outcomes.
2. The methods and materials of instruction are congruent with the outcomes to be achieved.	2. The nature and function of the assessments are congruent with the outcomes to be assessed.
3. The instruction is designed to fit the characteristics and needs of the students.	3. The assessments are designed to fit the relevant student characteristics and are fair to everyone.
4. Instructional decisions are based on information that is meaningful, dependable, and relevant.	4. Assessments provide information that is meaningful, dependable, and relevant.
5. Students are periodically informed concerning their learning progress.	5. Provision is made for giving the students early feedback of assessment results.
6. Remediation is provided for students not achieving the intended learning.	6. Specific learning weaknesses are revealed by the assessment results.
7. Instructional effectiveness is periodically reviewed and the intended learning outcomes and instruction modified as needed.	7. Assessment results provide information useful for evaluating the appropriateness of the objectives, the methods, and the materials of instruction.

highlights the importance of broadening instructional planning to include assessment planning. The typical procedure of limiting instructional planning to the teaching–learning process is inadequate. Effective instruction requires that we expand our concern to a teaching–learning–assessment process, with assessment as a basic part of the instructional program. As with all instructional activities, the main function of assessment is to improve learning, and it can contribute to this end in a number of ways.

ASSESSMENT IN THE INSTRUCTIONAL PROCESS

To be fully integrated with instruction, plans for assessment should be made during the planning for instruction. From the beginning of instruction to the end there are numerous decisions that teachers need to make. Carefully planned assessment procedures can improve the effectiveness of many of these decisions by providing more objective information on which to base judgments. Let us consider some of the decisions teachers need to make (1) during the planning of instruction, (2) at the beginning of instruction, (3) during instruction, and (4) at the end of instruction.

Planning of Instruction

Before the construction of a building begins, considerable thought and work go into developing a blueprint that provides direction and defines what the building should look like once completed. This blueprint serves as a guide and ensures quality during construction. Before constructing a course (lecture materials, student activities, lesson plans, etc.), teachers need to have a blueprint that defines what the students should *look like* once they have completed the course. Teachers need to answer the following two questions:

1. What are the intended learning outcomes of instruction?
2. How will we know whether students have achieved the learning outcomes?

Within the public education system, the answers to these questions are provided by the school's respective state through established **content standards**. Content standards describe what students should know and be able to do at the end of a specified period of learning (e.g., a grade or series of grades). They provide a framework for curriculum development, instruction, and the assessment of student achievement. Various professional organizations have also developed sets of content standards in their particular subject areas. It is hoped that the use of such standards will raise achievement expectations, increase the quality of public education, provide a better informed citizenship, and make the country more competitive with other countries.

Content standards consist of statements that specify in a general way what students should learn. Each standard is then followed by a number of *benchmarks* that clarify what students know or can do when they have achieved the content standards. The following standard and benchmarks illustrate a possible standard for the early elementary level.

Understands the methods of measurement.

1. Knows the tools and units used in our daily measurements.
2. Knows the relationship of units for each measurement tool.
3. Applies the measurement tools and units in solving measurement problems.

Many of the standards use such terms as *knows, understands,* and *applies,* as shown in this illustration. Thus, content standards are typically not at the level of instructional objectives and, therefore, do not describe how the student will demonstrate achievement of the learning outcomes. In preparing relevant objectives, we need to clarify in specific terms what is meant by *knows* (e.g., *identifies, describes*), *understands* (e.g., *explains, gives examples*), and *applies* (e.g., *computes, converts*). The following list of instructional objectives might be used to put our sample standard into usable form for instruction and assessment.

1. Understands the methods of measurement.

   1.1 Identifies the tools and units used in measuring distance, time, weight, temperature, and volume.
   1.2 Describes the relationship of units for each measurement tool (e.g., inches, feet, yards).
   1.3 Converts from one unit to another for a given measurement (e.g., inches to feet).
   1.4 Measures an amount in a given situation (e.g., length of a line).
   1.5 States examples of the use of each measurement tool in daily life.
   1.6 Solves measurement problems using the appropriate tools and units.

When the standards are converted to instructional objectives, they provide guidelines (a blueprint) for planning instructional activities and preparing assessment instruments. For instance, given objective 1.1 above, the teacher would be guided to include activities and assessment items that require students to identify from a list the correct tools and units used in measuring distance, time, weight, temperature, and volume. See Gronlund and Brookhart (2009) for how to write instructional objectives for teaching and assessment.

Beginning of Instruction (Placement Assessment)

There are two major questions that teachers need to answer before proceeding with the instruction:

1. To what extent do the students possess the skills and abilities that are needed to begin instruction?
2. To what extent have the students already achieved the intended learning outcomes of the planned instruction?

Information concerning the first question is frequently obtained from *readiness* pretests. These are tests given at the beginning of a course or unit of instruction that cover those prerequisite skills necessary for success in the planned instruction. For example, a test of computational skill might be given at the beginning of an algebra course, or a test of English grammar might be given at the beginning of a German course. Students lacking in prerequisite skills could be given remedial work, or they could be placed in a special section that had lower prerequisites.

The second question is frequently answered by a *placement* pretest covering the intended learning outcomes of the planned instruction. This might very well be the same test that is given at the end of the instruction; preferably it should be another form of it. Here we are interested in determining whether students have already mastered some of the material we plan to include in our instruction. If they have, we might need to modify our teaching plans, encourage some students to skip particular units, and place other students at a more advanced level of instruction. The function of placement assessment is summarized in Figure 1.1.

In addition to the use of pretests, performance-based tasks may also be useful for determining entry skills. In the area of writing, for example, obtaining writing samples at the beginning of instruction can establish a base for later assessments of progress. This type of preassessment would be especially valuable if portfolios of student work were to be maintained during the instruction.

The contribution that preassessment can make to instruction depends on the nature of the instruction, how well we know students, and how the results are to be used. A pretest in arithmetic may be quite useful at the beginning of an algebra course, whereas a pretest in a course that lacks a clearly defined set of prerequisite skills (e.g., social studies) may be of little value. Similarly, the results of a test of basic skills may be of great value to a new teacher unfamiliar with the students and of less value to an experienced teacher familiar with the students' backgrounds. In addition, preassessment

FIGURE 1.1 Simplified Model for the Instructional Role of Placement Assessment.

will contribute little to the instructional program unless plans are made to remedy deficiencies, place students in the most beneficial position in the instructional sequence, or use the results as a base for assessing future progress. To be most effective, the use of preassessment should be considered during the instructional planning stage.

During Instruction (Formative and Diagnostic Assessment)

During the instructional program our main concern is with the students' learning progress. Questions such as the following must be answered:

1. On which learning tasks are the students progressing satisfactorily? On which ones do they need help?
2. Which students are having such severe learning problems that they need remedial work?

Tests used to monitor student progress during instruction are called *formative* tests. Formative tests are typically designed to measure the extent to which students have mastered the learning outcomes of a rather limited segment of instruction, such as a unit or a textbook chapter. These tests are similar to the quizzes and unit tests that teachers have traditionally used, but they place greater emphasis on (1) measuring all of the intended outcomes of the unit of instruction and (2) using the results to improve learning (rather than to assign grades). The purpose is to identify the students' learning successes and failures so that adjustments in instruction and learning can be made. When the majority of students fail a test item, or set of items, the material is typically retaught in a group setting. When a minority of students experience learning failures, alternate methods of study are usually prescribed for each student (e.g., reading assignments in a second book, computer instruction, and visual aids). These corrective prescriptions are frequently keyed to each item or to each set of items designed to measure a separate learning task, so that students can begin immediately after testing to correct their individual learning errors.

Formative assessment using performance-based tasks may involve periodic assessments of a product (e.g., writing sample, drawing) or of a process (e.g., giving a speech, operating a machine) with feedback to students concerning strengths and weaknesses. The aim here, as with formative testing, is to monitor learning progress and to provide corrective prescriptions to improve learning.

When a student's learning problems are so persistent that they cannot be resolved by the corrective prescriptions of formative assessment, a more intensive study of the student's learning difficulties is called for. It is here that *diagnostic* assessment is useful. Diagnostic assessment attempts to answer such questions as the following: Are the students having difficulty in addition because they don't know certain number combinations or because they don't know how to carry? Are the students' difficulties in reading German due to their inadequate knowledge of vocabulary or to their poor grasp of certain elements of grammar? Are the students unable to apply scientific principles to new situations because they don't understand the principles, because their knowledge of particular concepts is weak, or because the new situations are too unfamiliar to them? Thus, diagnostic assessment focuses on the common sources of error encountered by students, so that the learning difficulties can be pinpointed and remedied.

Diagnostic assessment can frequently be aided by the use of diagnostic tests. These tests typically include a relatively large number of test items in each specific area with slight variations from one set of items to the next so that the cause of specific learning errors can be identified. In detecting errors in the addition of whole numbers, for example, we might construct a test that includes a set of items requiring no carrying, a set that requires simple carrying, and one that requires repeated carrying to determine whether carrying is the source of the difficulty. Unfortunately, diagnostic tests are difficult to construct in most areas of instruction. Therefore, we must depend more heavily on observation and judgment.

Diagnosing learning problems is a matter of degree. Formative assessment determines whether a student has mastered the learning tasks being taught and, if not, prescribes how to remedy the learning failures. Diagnostic assessment is designed to probe deeper into the causes of learning deficiencies that are left unresolved by formative assessment. Of course, this is not to imply that all learning problems can be overcome by formative and diagnostic assessment. These are simply methods to aid in the identification and diagnosis of specific learning difficulties so that appropriate remedial steps can be taken. Diagnosing and remedying severe learning problems frequently require a wide array of assessment procedures and the services of specially trained personnel. All we are attempting to do here is to show how formative and diagnostic assessment can contribute to improved student learning during instruction. The model presented in Figure 1.2 summarizes the process.

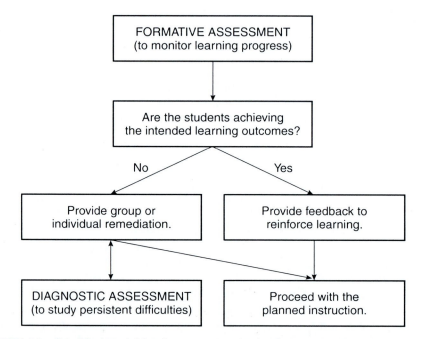

FIGURE 1.2 Simplified Model for the Instructional Role of Formative Assessment.

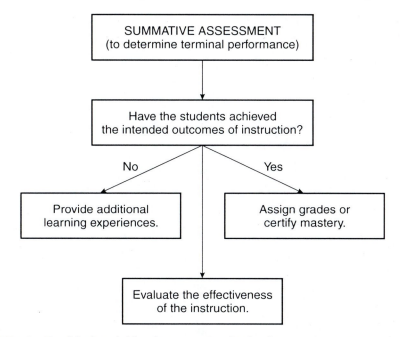

FIGURE 1.3 Simplified Model for the Instructional Role of Summative Assessment.

End of Instruction (Summative Assessment)

At the end of a course or unit of instruction we are concerned primarily with the extent to which the students have achieved the intended outcomes of the instruction. Questions such as the following must be answered:

1. Which students have mastered the learning tasks to such a degree that they should proceed to the next course or unit of instruction?
2. What grade should be assigned to each student?

Achievement assessment at the end of instruction for the purpose of certifying mastery or assigning grades is called *summative* assessment. This assessment is typically comprehensive in coverage and includes both tests and performance assessments. Although the results are used primarily for grading, there should be some feedback to students and the results should be used for evaluating the effectiveness of the instruction. See Figure 1.3 for the summative assessment model.

OTHER WAYS ASSESSMENTS CAN AID LEARNING

As noted in the previous section, assessments can aid the teacher in making various instructional decisions having a direct influence on student learning. In addition, assessments can aid student learning in a number of other ways.

Student Motivation

A carefully planned assessment program can have a direct influence on student learning by (1) providing students with short-term goals, (2) clarifying the types of tasks to be learned, and (3) providing feedback concerning their learning progress. Short-term goals are more motivating than telling students "Some day you will find this knowledge or skill useful." An expected assessment stimulates learning activity and directs it toward the learning tasks to be assessed. Its contribution to learning depends to a large extent on how faithfully our assessments reflect all of the important outcomes of the instruction and how we use the results. For example, if the application of principles is stressed in our assessment as well as in our teaching, we can expect students to direct greater efforts toward learning how to apply principles. Also, if the assessment results are reported to students as soon as possible, this feedback concerning their strengths and weaknesses in the application of principles will further clarify the nature of the task and indicate what changes are needed for effective performance. Thus, properly used assessments can motivate students to work toward the instructional objectives of a course by arousing greater learning activity, by directing it toward the intended learning outcomes, and by providing prompt knowledge of results.

Retention and Transfer of Learning

Because assessments tend to direct students' learning efforts toward the intended outcomes of instruction, they can be used as tools for increasing the retention and transfer of learning. In general, learning outcomes at the understanding, application, and interpretation levels are likely to be retained longer and to have greater transfer value than outcomes at the recall level. By including assessments of these more complex learning outcomes, we can direct attention to their importance and provide reinforcing practice in the skills, applications, and interpretations we are attempting to develop. Thus, assessments can be used to supplement and complement our teaching efforts in these areas and thereby increase the likelihood that the learning will be of greater permanent value to the students.

Student Self-Assessment

All instruction should be directed toward helping individuals better understand themselves so that they can make more intelligent decisions. Periodic assessment and feedback of the results can help students gain insight into what they can do well, the misconceptions that need correction, and the degree of skill they have in various areas. Such information provides the students with a more objective basis for assessing their own strengths and weaknesses. Properly used assessments tend to provide evidence of learning progress in such an objective and impartial way that the results can be accepted with little resistance or distortion. This assumes, of course, that the assessments are properly prepared and are being used to improve learning rather than to threaten or label students. In the latter instance, self-assessment is apt to be distorted by the psychological defense mechanisms an individual uses to maintain a positive self-image.

Evaluation of Instructional Effectiveness

Assessment results can be used to evaluate the effectiveness of various aspects of the instructional process. For example, they can help determine the extent to which the instructional objectives were realistic, whether the methods and materials of instruction were appropriate, and how well the learning experiences were sequenced. When the majority of the students do poorly on an assessment, it may be the fault of the students, but the difficulty is more likely to be found in the instruction. The teacher may be striving for learning outcomes that are unattainable by the students, using inappropriate materials, or using ineffective methods for bringing about the desired changes. An analysis of the students' responses and a class discussion of the results should provide clues to the source of the instructional difficulty so that corrective steps can be taken.

HISTORICAL AND LEGISLATIVE INFLUENCES ON STUDENT ASSESSMENT

The influences of historical events and legislative policies on assessment practices in U.S. public schools have been profound. The beginnings of formal assessment can be traced to Boston when, in the 1840s, Horace Mann began using student test scores to evaluate schools in Massachusetts. This was the first instance in which the wide-scale testing of students for evaluation purposes was made mandatory, and it set in motion the reliance of assessment in education nationwide. However, it wasn't until the early 1900s that educational testing flourished, due in large part to the contributions of E.L. Thorndike. Considered widely as the "father of the measurement movement," E.L. Thorndike championed the use of standardized, norm-referenced testing in the military, private industries, and schools. By the 1940s, roughly half of the schools in the United States were using standardized tests as a means to assess academic achievement. Developing standardized tests became a big industry.

During the Great Depression, President Roosevelt's New Deal established a multitude of federal programs designed to jumpstart the economy. Federal agencies were created to provide oversight of programs, including education, and federal grants were distributed locally to school systems. The result was a growing emphasis on assessment and evaluation in which the impact of these programs on the performance of students and schools became the focus of study. Over the next three decades assessments began to shift toward an objectives-based approach. Guided by the development of the cognitive domain of Bloom's taxonomy (Bloom, Engelhart, Furst, Hill, & Krathwohl, 1956) and the affective domain of the taxonomy (Krathwohl, Bloom, & Masia, 1964), teachers, administrators, and accreditation bodies created learning outcomes and educational objectives. Student achievement and the success of a program, then, were contingent on meeting those stated outcomes and objectives.

In 1957, Russia launched the Sputnik I satellite. Following the launch, the United States was gripped by fear that the Russians were becoming more technologically advanced, and that our inability to match their advancements was a threat to national security. In direct response to that threat, the federal government enacted in 1958 the National Defense Education Act (NDEA) and poured millions of dollars into creating new curricula for math and science public school programs. Funds to conduct objectives-based assessments of students and evaluations of programs quickly followed.

Over the two decades after the launching of Sputnik I, the federal government continued to provide funding for public education. However, the focus on education seemed to wane a bit over the years. Then in 1983 the National Commission on Excellence in Education published *A Nation at Risk.* The report illuminated the inadequacy of the nation's public education system, concluding that the system was broken. To fix the system, the commission recommended that the federal government would need to be more directly involved in overseeing the development of state-established education standards and holding schools accountable when standards aren't met. What followed was legislation that provided funding incentives for states to develop education standards and monitor school performance using standardized achievement tests. The most notable of these is the No Child Left Behind (NCLB) Act that was signed into law by President George W. Bush in 2001.

The overarching purpose of the No Child Left Behind Act is to hold public schools accountable for the academic achievement of their students. States are required to establish their own education standards, and each state must assess its students against the standards by administering a standardize test developed by the state. The percentage of students who meet the standards is then reported to the federal government. If an unacceptable percentage of students within a school fail to meet the standards, then the school may receive sanctions in the form of less funding and/or replacement of teachers and administrators.

The No Child Left Behind Act has created considerable controversy. Many parents and teachers feel that there is too much emphasis on testing, and that teachers are being forced to spend instructional time on rote memorization of content and repetition to prepare students for the test. They argue that this time should be spent teaching students how to think critically and solve problems. Further, the added pressure of testing creates unhealthy stress for students. While these concerns are prevalent, most will agree that assessment is necessary and accountability is needed.

TEACHERS' STANDARDS FOR STUDENT ASSESSMENT

It is generally agreed that student assessment plays an important role in effective teaching. A committee made up of representatives of the American Federation of Teachers, the National Council on Measurement in Education, and the National Education Association considered it so important that they came out with a report entitled *Standards for Teacher Competence in Educational Assessment of Students* (1990). In the report, they review the teacher's responsibilities for student assessment and summarize them by listing seven standards for teacher competence in student assessment. The following list, with abbreviated description of each standard, is taken from the report.

1. **Teachers should be skilled in choosing assessment methods appropriate for instructional decisions.** Skill in choosing appropriate, useful, administratively convenient, technically adequate, and fair assessment methods are prerequisite to good use of information to support instructional decisions.

2. **Teachers should be skilled in developing assessment methods appropriate for instructional decisions.** While teachers often use published or other external assessment tools, the bulk of the assessment information they use for decision making comes from approaches they create and implement.

3. **The teacher should be skilled in administering, scoring, and interpreting the results of both externally produced and teacher-produced assessment methods.** It is not enough that teachers are able to select and develop good assessment methods; they must also be able to apply them properly.

4. **Teachers should be skilled in using assessment results when making decisions about individual students, planning teaching, developing curriculum, and school improvement.** Assessment results are used to make educational decisions at several levels: in the classroom about students, in the community about a school and a school district, and in society, generally, about the purposes and outcomes of the educational enterprise. Teachers play a vital role when participating in decision making at each of these levels and must be able to use assessment results effectively.

5. **Teachers should be skilled in developing valid pupil grading procedures that use pupil assessments.** Grading students is an important part of professional practice for teachers. Grading is defined as indicating both a student's level of performance and a teacher's valuing of that performance. The principles for using assessments to obtain valid grades are known and teachers should employ them.

6. **Teachers should be skilled in communicating assessment results to students, parents, other lay audiences, and other educators.** Teachers must routinely report assessment results to students and to parents or guardians. In addition, they are frequently asked to report or to discuss assessment results with other educators and with diverse lay audiences. If the results are not communicated effectively, they may be misused or not used. To communicate effectively with others on matters of student assessment, teachers must be able to use assessment terminology appropriately and must be able to articulate the meaning, limitations, and implications of assessment results.

7. **Teachers should be skilled in recognizing unethical, illegal, and otherwise inappropriate assessment methods and uses of assessment information.** Fairness, the rights of all concerned, and professional ethical behavior must undergird all student assessment activities, from the initial planning for and gathering of information to the interpretation, use, and communication of the results.

The complete report of *Standards for Teacher Competence in Educational Assessment of Students* is presented in the Appendix of Linn and Gronlund (2000). The report is not copyrighted and reproduction and distribution of it are encouraged.

Summary of Points

1. In recent years there has been a reaction to the heavy emphasis on paper-and-pencil testing with a plea for more realistic and meaningful performance assessment.
2. A well-balanced assessment program should include both testing and performance assessment, with each used where most appropriate.
3. *Achievement assessment* is a general category that includes a broad range of methods for determining the extent to which students are achieving the intended learning outcomes of instruction.
4. Instruction is more effective when well-designed assessments are an integral part of the instructional process.
5. Assessment procedures can be used for measuring entry performance (placement assessment), monitoring learning progress (formative and diagnostic assessment), or measuring end-of-instruction achievement (summative assessments).
6. Achievement assessments can contribute to student motivation, the retention and transfer of learning, student self-evaluation skills, and an evaluation of instructional effectiveness.
7. Historical events (e.g., launch of Sputnik I) and federal legislation (e.g., No Child Left Behind Act) have profoundly influenced the assessment of public school students.
8. Teachers' standards for student assessment focus on their competence in selecting assessment methods, developing assessment methods, administering and scoring them, interpreting and using assessment results, preparing valid grades, communicating assessment results, and recognizing inappropriate assessment methods and uses of assessment information.

References and Additional Reading

Airasian, P.W. *Classroom Assessment*, 4th ed. (New York: McGraw-Hill, 2001).

Bloom, B. S., Engelhart, M. D., Furst, E. J., Hill, W. H., & Krathwohl, D. R. *Taxonomy of Educational Objectives: Handbook I. Cognitive Domain* (New York: David McKay, 1956).

Bloom, B. S., Madaus, G. T., & Hastings, J. T. *Evaluation to Improve Learning* (New York: McGraw-Hill, 1981).

Gronlund, N. E., & Brookhart, S. M. *Gronlund's Writing Instructional Objectives*, 8th ed. (Upper Saddle River, NJ: Pearson/Merrill/Prentice Hall, 2009).

Krathwohl, D. R., Bloom, B. S., & Masia, B. B. *Taxonomy of Educational Objectives: Handbook II. Affective Domain* (New York: David McKay, 1964).

Linn, R. L., & Gronlund, N. E. *Measurement and Assessment in Teaching*, 8th ed. (Upper Saddle River, NJ: Merrill/PrenticeHall, 2000).

McMillan, J. H. *Classroom Assessment: Principles and Practices for Effective Instruction*, 3rd ed. (Boston: Allyn and Bacon, 2004).

Popham, W. J. *Classroom Assessment: What Teachers Need to Know*, 3rd ed. (Boston: Allyn and Bacon, 2002).

Stiggins, R. J. *Student-Involved Classroom Assessment*, 3rd ed. (Upper Saddle River, NJ: Merrill/PrenticeHall, 2001).

Self-Assessment

MULTIPLE CHOICE

DIRECTIONS: Select the best answer for each item by circling the corresponding letter.

1. Which type of assessment is most suitable for evaluating a student's level of knowledge?
   (a) process checklist
   (b) product review
   (c) questionnaire
   (d) paper-and-pencil test

2. Assessments used to monitor student progress during instruction are called
   (a) placement assessments
   (b) criterion assessments
   (c) formative assessments
   (d) summative assessments

3. Summative assessments are concerned with
   (a) certification of mastery
   (b) diagnosis of errors
   (c) entry learning skills
   (d) progress during learning

4. Formative testing is used primarily for
   (a) grading students
   (b) monitoring student progress
   (c) forming students groups
   (d) placing students in groups

5. The extent to which achievement tests contribute to improved learning and instruction is determined largely by the principles underlying their
   (a) development and evaluation
   (b) development and use
   (c) research and development
   (d) use and evaluation

TRUE-FALSE

DIRECTIONS: Read each statement and record as true or false on the lines provided.

6. _____ A summative test evaluates terminal achievement of students.

7. _____ A formative test is designed to cover a wide range of content in a unit.

8. _____ An achievement test used to measure entry performance is called a diagnostic test.

9. _____ Formative testing is used primarily for grading students.

Restricted-Response Essay

10. The authors of your textbook discuss the other ways assessment can aid learning. List and describe how each of these "other ways" can aid student learning. Confine your answer to one page.

2 NATURE OF STUDENT ASSESSMENT

Studying this chapter should enable you to

1. Describe a situation where both testing and performance assessment are needed and indicate why.
2. Describe the major types of assessment methods and give an example of each.
3. Distinguish between tests and performance assessments in terms of realism of tasks, complexity of tasks, assessment time needed, and judgment in scoring.
4. List the guidelines for effective student assessment.
5. Distinguish between norm-referenced and criterion-referenced assessments.

As noted in the first chapter, *assessment* is used as a broad category that includes all of the various methods used to determine the extent to which students are achieving the intended learning outcomes of instruction. This includes both testing and performance assessments. To assess a student's driving ability, for example, an **objective test** is used to measure knowledge of how to drive and follow the rules of the road, and driving over a prescribed course (performance assessment) is used to determine skill in driving the automobile. The test on rules of the road covers a much larger sample of driving rules than are likely to be encountered in the driving performance, but skill in driving can only be determined by sitting behind the wheel and driving. Both are important. The knowledge test tells how well the student knows what to do and the performance assessment tells how skillfully the student can do it.

Teachers have tended to favor selection-type tests (e.g., multiple choice, true-false, matching) because many questions can be asked in a relatively short time, they are easy to administer and score, and the results can be expressed in numbers that are easily recorded, compared, and reported to others. Unfortunately, teachers have also limited selection-type tests almost entirely to remembering facts and terms. Various studies have shown that between

80 and 90 percent of teacher-made tests focus on retention of knowledge. There is little doubt that this overemphasis on selection-type tests and simple knowledge outcomes has led to the movement toward assessment techniques that measure more complex learning outcomes in realistic settings. The fact that paper-and-pencil tests can be designed to measure a wide array of complex learning outcomes has frequently been overlooked in the movement toward performance assessment. It is our contention that education is best served by using both paper-and-pencil testing and the assessment of actual performance, with both focusing on more complex learning tasks than typically has been the case in the past.

MAJOR TYPES OF ASSESSMENT METHODS

Assessment methods vary widely but they can be summarized in four major categories as shown in Table 2.1. Selected-response tests require the student to choose the correct or best answer, as in multiple-choice, true-false, and matching tests. Supply-response tests require students to respond with a word, short phrase, or complete essay answer. Restricted performance assessments are concerned with the performance of a limited task that is highly structured, such as writing a brief paragraph on a given topic, selecting laboratory equipment, measuring humidity, or locating information with a computer. Extended performance assessments involve more comprehensive and less structured performance tasks, such as writing a short story, conducting a laboratory experiment, predicting weather, or using a computer to solve a problem. Besides requiring more extended performances, the assessment typically requires students to integrate and apply knowledge and skills to performance tasks in a realistic setting. If there is a product involved (e.g., a short story), students may also be expected to review and revise the product before submitting it, to add greater realism to the task.

These major types of assessment can be further clarified by reviewing some of the characteristics that are typical of each. These have been summarized in Table 2.1.

TABLE 2.1 Summary Comparison of Assessment Methods

Testing		Performance Assessment	
Selected Response	Supply Response	Restricted Performance	Extended Performance
LOW	←	REALISM OF TASKS →	HIGH
LOW	←	COMPLEXITY OF TASKS →	HIGH
LOW	←	ASSESSMENT TIME NEEDED →	HIGH
LOW	←	JUDGMENT IN SCORING →	HIGH

Realism of Tasks

By realism of assessment tasks, we mean the extent to which they simulate performance in the real world. Traditional selection-type tests are low in realism because they involve selecting a response from a given set of possible answers. The response is limited to the listed alternatives, and such highly structured problems seldom occur in the real world. The extended performance assessment is high in realism because it attempts to simulate performance in the real world. Assessing how well a student can drive an automobile, operate a machine, give a speech, or apply knowledge and understanding to a real-life problem (e.g., how to protect the environment) requires comprehensive sets of responses that approximate those occurring in the real world. In between these extremes are the supply-type tests (e.g., short answer and essay) and the restricted-response performance assessments that provide a moderate amount of structure but greater freedom of response and thus more realistic type problems than the selection-type tests.

In addition to the movement to increase realism in assessment by moving toward extended performance assessment, there has also been a trend toward making traditional paper-and-pencil tests more authentic (i.e., have greater realism). This has resulted in the designing of tests to measure more complex learning outcomes and in the use of problems and procedures more like those in the real world. In a math problem, for example, students may be given more facts than are needed to solve the problem to see if they can select the facts needed to solve it. In solving a science problem, students might be given the freedom to select the procedure for solving the problem and be asked to justify the procedure used. In some cases this involves a shift from selection-type items to supply-type items, but in others it may be a combination of the two items types (e.g., explain why the selected answer was chosen).

Complexity of Tasks

Selected-response items tend to be low in the complexity of the problem presented and in the nature of the expected response. Although items can be designed to measure understanding and thinking skills, they typically present a single, limited problem and require choice of the correct or best answer. Extended performance problems, on the other hand, typically involve multiple learning outcomes, the integration of ideas and skills from a variety of sources, the availability of various possible solutions, and the need for multiple criteria for evaluating the results (e.g., preparing a plan for reducing drug traffic in the United States). Similarly, performance of a hands-on nature involves complex movement patterns that are guided by the integration of information and specific skills from various learning experiences (e.g., playing a musical instrument, operating a machine, repairing electronic equipment). As with the realism category, supply-type tests fall in between the two extremes. Essay tests, for example, can be designed to measure the ability to select, integrate, and express ideas, but the tasks are usually more limited and structured than in performance assessments.

Assessment Time Needed

A large number of selected-response items can be administered to a group of students in a relatively short time, and the results can be quickly scored by hand or by machine. This efficiency has no doubt been a major factor in their widespread use. Performance assessments tend to be extremely time consuming. Some tasks may require days or even weeks to complete (e.g., conduct an experimental study) and others may require assessing students one at a time (e.g., giving a speech, operating a machine). In most cases, evaluating the process or product of the performance is also difficult and time consuming. Supply-response tests, like the essay test, require more time to score than selected-response tests but less than that of performance assessments.

The greater amount of time needed for performance assessment may result in loss of content coverage because of the limited number of assessment problems that can be included in the instructional program. This raises a question concerning the extent to which the assessment results are generalizable to other comparable tasks. We can present "real-world" problems to students, but problems are frequently unique to a particular contextual setting and the real world changes. Thus, transfer of learning is a key consideration in performance assessment. We can justify the greater time needed only if the assessment is an integral part of instruction and transferable learning outcomes are emphasized (e.g., reasoning, critical thinking, psychomotor skills).

Judgment in Scoring

The amount of judgment involved in scoring varies widely. Each selected-response item is marked right or wrong so the scoring is completely objective (i.e., different scorers will arrive at the same score). The essay test provides more freedom of response, and this introduces greater subjectivity into the scoring. Different scorers can and do arrive at different scores as they weight elements of the answer differently (e.g., completeness, organization, clarity of writing, and the like) and introduce other personal biases into their judgments. As the tasks become more comprehensive and complex, as in performance assessment, the demands on teacher judgment become even greater. Complex performance tasks that involve the integration of various types of information and skill and may have multiple solutions make it difficult, and in many cases undesirable, to have model answers as might be used with essay testing. With performance assessment we are most likely to have to depend on identification of the **criteria** of a quality performance and then apply the criteria by means of a **rating scale** or set of **scoring rubrics**. Each of these steps is based on subjective judgment.

A review of these categories makes clear that each assessment method has its strengths and weaknesses. When we use selected-response tests, we can obtain a comprehensive coverage of a content domain, and can administer, score, and interpret it easily, but we sacrifice realism and some types of complexity. When we use extended performance assessment, we can obtain a high degree of realism and increase the complexity of the tasks we can assess, but the time needed for assessment is frequently excessive and the evaluation of the performance is highly judgmental. A useful rule would be to use the most efficient method as long as it is appropriate for assessing the intended learning outcomes, but don't neglect complex learning outcomes just because the assessment methods are time consuming and the results are difficult to score or judge.

GUIDELINES FOR EFFECTIVE STUDENT ASSESSMENT

The main purpose of a classroom assessment program is to improve student learning. This is most likely to result if assessment is closely integrated with instruction and is guided by a basic set of conditions. The following guidelines provide a general framework for using student assessment effectively.

1. **Effective assessment requires a clear conception of all intended learning outcomes.** During both instructional and assessment planning, we need to ask ourselves—What are the intended learning outcomes of the instruction? What types of knowledge, understanding, application, and performance skills are we willing to accept as evidence that the instruction has been successful? Here, there is always the danger of focusing too narrowly on simple learning outcomes because they are easy to identify, state, and measure. Unless we include the more complex learning outcomes at this stage, they are likely to be neglected during assessment. We need to specify all intended learning outcomes in terms of student performance and make plans to assess them all.

2. **Effective assessment requires that a variety of assessment procedures be used.** The vast array of possible learning outcomes in any particular area of instruction means that various types of assessment procedures must be considered when planning for assessment. Selected-response tests may be used for some learning outcomes and essay tests for others, where ability to express ideas is important. In assessing performance skills, where we must depend largely on judgment, rating scales or checklists may be needed.

    In assessing the more complex learning outcomes, a combination of methods may be most suitable. Solving a complex problem, for example, may involve gathering information from diverse sources, analyzing it, integrating it, writing out a suggested solution, and making an oral presentation to a group. Similarly, locating and correcting a malfunction in a machine may involve reading a technical manual, identifying machine sounds, selecting proper tools, testing machine parts, and making the needed repairs. In addition to correcting the malfunction, speed of performance, following the proper sequence of steps, and similar factors may be an important part of the assessment. In evaluating performance skills, multiple assessment is likely to be the rule rather than the exception.

3. **Effective assessment requires that the instructional relevance of the procedures be considered.** Instructionally relevant assessment means that the intended outcomes of instruction, the domain of learning tasks,

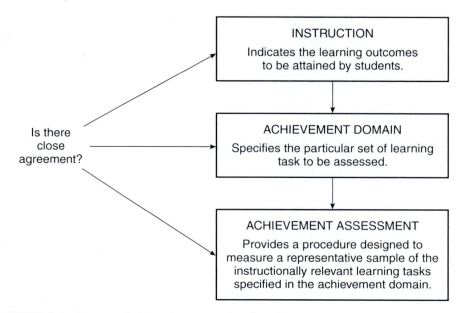

FIGURE 2.1   Sequence in Preparing Instructionally Relevant Assessment.

and the assessment procedures will all be in close agreement, as shown in Figure 2.1. It also means that plans for using the assessment results in the instructional program must be considered. Will the classroom test be sufficiently diagnostic to provide for remedial action? Can the assessment of a complex performance skill be designed as an ongoing activity so that it can contribute directly to the instruction? These and similar questions are needed to obtain maximum integration of instruction and assessment. Remember, the main purpose of both instruction and assessment is to improve student learning. With a well-designed assessment program, assessment activities may become barely distinguishable from instructional activities.

4. **Effective assessment requires an adequate sample of student performance.** Assessment is always a matter of sampling. Our instruction typically covers numerous knowledge and skill outcomes, but because of the limited time available for assessment and other constraints, we can only measure or judge a limited sample of student performance in any particular area. In preparing a classroom test, for example, there may be 100 terms that the students should know but we only have room for 20 terms in our test. Thus, we must select a representative sample from the 100 words because we want to be able to generalize from performance on the 20 terms as to how well students know the 100 terms. If our sample is adequate, we can estimate that 18 correct answers on the 20 terms indicates that a student knows about 90 percent of the 100 terms (with allowance for a margin of error, of course).

Sampling is also a problem in performance assessment. In assessing driving skill, for example, it would be impossible to include all possible driving problems in a brief driving test so we must settle for a representative sample of them. It is interesting to note that, for licensing purposes, some states are now including driving on the expressway to obtain a more adequate sample of driving skill.

In the assessment of performance skills in the classroom there are typically two problems of sampling. In a writing project, for example, we might ask (1) Does the project include a representative sample of the writing skills we are stressing in our teaching? and (2) Does performance on this project represent what writing performance would be like on other similar projects? Because extended performance assessment (e.g., giving a speech, conducting an experiment, applying math to a real-world problem) is so time consuming and context bound, the adequacy of sampling is always an important concern in planning the assessment.

5. **Effective assessment requires that the procedures be fair to everyone.** An assessment program that makes the intended learning outcomes clear to students, that uses assessment procedures that are instructionally relevant and adequately sample student performance, and that uses assessment results to improve learning goes a long way toward creating an atmosphere of fairness. In addition, however, special efforts must be made to eliminate irrelevant sources of difficulty and bias of various types. Student performance may be inadequate because the directions were ambiguous, the reading level was inappropriate, or the performance called for knowledge or skills that were not intended as parts of the assessment task. Similarly, including racial or gender stereotypes in the assessment material may distort the results and create a feeling of unfairness. Fairness requires care in preparing and using assessment procedures, clearly communicating our intentions to students, and using the results to improve learning.

6. **Effective assessment requires the specifications of criteria for judging successful performance.** In the past, success was typically determined by comparing a student's performance to that of others (norm-referenced interpretation). If performance surpassed that of others, it was considered excellent performance. If performance was lower than that of others, it was considered poor performance. Although this method of judging success has its merits and is useful in certain situations, it is not satisfactory as a measure of how well students are learning the intended outcomes of instruction. For this purpose we need *criteria* that describe what students can do when they perform successfully (e.g., type 40 words per minute with no more than two errors).

Establishing performance criteria is difficult in many areas, but, if the intended learning outcomes are clearly stated in performance terms, the criteria for success can be more easily established. In assessing vocabulary, for example, we can describe success in terms of how well students can define each term and use it in a sentence, how well they can distinguish between similar terms, and how well they can use the terms in a writing project. Effective laboratory performance can be described in terms of the selection and manipulation of equipment, the accuracy of measurements, the procedures followed, and the written description and interpretation of results. By specifying success in performance terms, we can describe what students are achieving and how well. The degree of success can be expressed by separate scores, scoring rubrics that describe degrees of effectiveness, rating scales, or whatever means is most useful for describing student performance.

Students should have a clear notion of what is expected of them, and clearly specified criteria of successful performance can be used to clarify the learning tasks. In some cases, students may participate in defining the desired performance. In planning for oral reports, for example, a discussion of criteria and listing them on the board will cause students to focus on the criteria of a good oral report and help them improve their performance. This is one way that instruction and assessment can be blended together to the benefit of students.

7. **Effective assessment requires feedback to students that emphasizes strengths of performance and weaknesses to be corrected.** Feedback of assessment results to students is an essential factor in any assessment program. To be most effective, feedback must meet the following criteria:

   A. Should be given immediately following or during the assessment.
   B. Should be detailed and understandable to students.
   C. Should focus on successful elements of the performance and the errors to be corrected.
   D. Should provide remedial suggestions for correcting errors.
   E. Should be positive and provide a guide for improving both performance and self-assessment.

   In performance assessment, our immediate goal is to improve performance. But if we are to develop self-learners, who will continue to improve performance on their own, then we need to also help them develop self-assessment skills. Thus, feedback must focus on both performance skills and self-assessment skills. For example, we not only suggest how to modify performance but also how to check on the effect of the modifications on performance and ways to determine future improvement. A final question concerning feedback might be, Will this feedback to students make them more dependent on the teacher or will it contribute to more independent learning? The most desirable choice is obvious and is illustrated in Figure 2.2.

8. **Effective assessment must be supported by a comprehensive grading and reporting system.** All too frequently teachers have used various types of assessment procedures and then assigned grades on the basis of scores on an objective test. Instead, we need to have the grading and

FIGURE 2.2   Role of Assessment Feedback.

reporting system reflect the emphasis in our assessments. If half of our learning outcomes are assessed by tests and half by performance assessments, and a single grade is used, the two types of assessment should receive equal weight in the grade. With the recent emphasis on performance assessment, more elaborate grading and reporting systems are needed to describe student performance adequately. Reports based on the intended learning outcomes and portfolios of student work are becoming increasingly important for reporting learning progress to students, parents, and others. These more elaborate reports are in harmony with the more elaborate assessment procedures being used.

Because letter grades are still required for some purposes (e.g., college admission), it may be necessary to use both letter grades and a more elaborate report. In any event, the grading and reporting procedures should reflect and support the assessment procedures, be made clear to students at the beginning of instruction, and provide for periodic feedback to students concerning their learning progress.

NORM-REFERENCED AND CRITERION-REFERENCED ASSESSMENT

An achievement assessment can be used to provide (1) a relative ranking of students or (2) a description of the learning tasks a student can and cannot perform. Results of the first type are interpreted in terms of each student's relative standing among other students (for example, "He is third highest in a class of 35 students"). This method of interpreting student performance is called **norm-referenced interpretation**. Results of the second type are expressed in terms of the specific knowledge and skills each student can demonstrate (e.g., "She can identify the parts of a microscope and demonstrate its use"). This method of interpreting assessment results is called **criterion-referenced interpretation** (see Box 2.1). Both methods of describing assessment results are useful. The first tells how an individual's performance compares with that of others. The second tells in specific performance terms what an individual can do without reference to the performance of others.

Strictly speaking, the terms *norm-referenced* and *criterion-referenced* refer only to the method of interpreting the results. Thus, both types of interpretation could be applied to the same assessment. For example, we might say, "Joan surpassed 90 percent of the students (norm-referenced interpretation) by correctly completing 20 of the 25 chemical equations" (criterion-referenced interpretation). The two types of interpretation are likely to be most meaningful, however, when the assessment is designed specifically for the type of interpretation to be made. In general, norm-referenced interpretation is facilitated by a wide spread of scores so that

---

BOX 2.1   Terms Similar to Criterion-Referenced Interpretation

Domain-Referenced Interpretation	Assessment results are interpreted in terms of a relevant and clearly defined set of related tasks (called a *domain*). Meaning is similar to criterion-referenced interpretation but the term is less used, even though it is a more descriptive term.
Content-Referenced Interpretation	Essentially the same meaning as domain-referenced interpretation when the content domain is broadly defined to include tasks representing both content and process (i.e., reactions to the content). This term is declining in use and being replaced by criterion-referenced interpretation.
Objective-Referenced Interpretation	Assessment results are interpreted in terms of each specific objective that a set of test items represents. This is frequently called *criterion-referenced interpretation*, but the more limited designation is preferable where interpretation is limited to each separate objective.

reliable discriminations can be made among students at various levels of achievement. Criterion-referenced interpretation is facilitated by assessment tasks that provide a detailed description of student performance. In testing, this means a larger number of test items per task. In performance assessment, this means performance tasks that make clear what parts of the task a person can and cannot do.

Although norm-referenced and criterion-referenced interpretations apply to all types of achievement assessments, the differences can be most clearly indicated when applied to testing. A summary of some common characteristics of tests specifically designed for each type of interpretation is presented in Table 2.2. It must be kept in mind, however, that these are primarily matters of emphasis. For example, norm-referenced tests are typically, but not exclusively, used for surveying achievement over a broad range of learning outcomes. By the same token, criterion-referenced tests are typically, but not exclusively, used for **mastery testing**. A review of the characteristics of each testing approach in Table 2.2 will reveal the differences that exist when each test is constructed to serve its principal use. It is not uncommon, however, to view the two test types as the ends of a continuum rather than as discrete categories and to combine the best features of each in constructing achievement tests.

TABLE 2.2 Summary Comparison of Two Basic Approaches to Achievement

	Norm-Referenced Testing	Criterion-Referenced Testing
Principal Use	Survey testing.	Mastery testing.
Major Emphasis	Measures individual differences in achievement.	Describes tasks students can perform.
Interpretation of Results	Compares performance to that of other individuals.	Compares performance to a clearly specified achievement domain.
Content Coverage	Typically covers a broad area of achievement.	Typically focuses on a limited set of learning tasks.
Nature of Test Plan	Table of specifications is commonly used.	Detailed domain specifications are favored.
Item Selection Procedures	Items are selected that provide maximum discrimination among individuals (to obtain a reliable ranking). Easy items are typically eliminated from the test.	Includes all items needed to adequately describe performance. No attempt is made to alter item difficulty or to eliminate easy items to increase the spread of scores.
Performance Standards	Level of performance is determined by *relative* position in some known group (e.g., ranks fifth in a group of 20).	Level of performance is commonly determined by *absolute* standards (e.g., demonstrates mastery by defining 90 percent of the technical terms).

For most instructional purposes, criterion-referenced assessments are to be favored. We can best help students improve learning by determining what tasks they can and cannot perform. Thus, the classroom assessment program should be based on instruments and procedures that provide for this type of interpretation. Norm-referenced interpretation is most useful when we are concerned about the relative ranking of students, as in the selection and classification of students (e.g., advance placement, grouping, giving awards, and relative grading).

Most of the discussions of procedures for constructing tests and making performance assessment will apply to all types of tests and assessments. Where there are significant differences due to the type of interpretation to be made, these will be noted.

Summary of Points

1. Student assessment needs to be expanded to include the assessment of more complex learning outcomes than has been the case in the past.
2. Assessment methods vary widely but they can be classified as selected-response tests, supply-response tests, restricted-response performance assessments, or extended-response performance assessments.
3. Selected-response tests (e.g., multiple-choice tests) are lowest in realism and complexity of the tasks assessed, but require little time to administer and can be scored quickly and objectively.
4. Supply-response tests (e.g., essay tests) are higher in realism and the complexity of tasks they can measure (e.g., ability to originate, integrate, and express ideas) than selected-response tests, but they are more time consuming to use and more difficult to score.
5. Performance assessments, both restricted response and extended response, can be designed with high degrees of realism (i.e., like real-world problems) that focus on highly complex learning tasks, but they require large amounts of time to use and the scoring is judgmental and highly subjective.
6. A sound assessment policy would be to use the most efficient method available for assessing each intended learning outcome as long as it is appropriate, but don't neglect complex learning outcomes just because the assessment methods are more time consuming to use and more difficult to score or judge.
7. Effective assessment requires a clear conception of all intended learning outcomes, a variety of assessment procedures that are relevant to the instruction, an adequate sample of tasks, procedures that are fair to everyone, criteria for judging success, timely and detailed feedback to students, and a grading and reporting system that is in harmony with the assessment program.
8. Assessment results can be interpreted by comparing a student's performance to that of others (norm-referenced) or by describing the student's performance on a clearly defined set of tasks (criterion-referenced).

9. Criterion-referenced interpretation is especially important for instructional uses of assessment results but norm-referenced interpretation may be needed for selection and classification decisions.
10. In some cases both criterion-referenced and norm-referenced interpretation may be used with the same assessment.

References and Additional Reading

Linn, R. L., & Gronlund, N. E. *Measurement and Assessment in Teaching*, 8th ed. (Upper Saddle River, NJ: Merrill/Prentice-Hall, 2000).

McMillan, J. H. *Classroom Assessment: Principles and Practices for Effective Instruction*, 3rd ed. (Boston: Allyn and Bacon, 2004).

Oosterhoff, A. C. *Developing and Using Classroom Assessments*, 2nd ed. (Upper Saddle River, NJ: Prentice-Hall, 1999).

Smith, J. K., Smith, L. F., & DeLisi, R. *Natural Classroom Assessment* (Thousand Oaks, CA: Corwin Press, 2001).

Stiggins, R. J. *Student-Involved Classroom Assessment*, 3rd ed. (Upper Saddle River, NJ: Merrill/Prentice Hall, 2001).

Wiggins, G. P. *Educative Assessment: Designing Assessments to Inform and Improve Student Performance* (San Francisco, CA: Jossey-Bass, 1998).

Self-Assessment

MULTIPLE CHOICE

DIRECTIONS: Select the best answer for each item by circling the corresponding letter.

1. Which of the following is a TRUE statement?
   (a) Paper-and-pencil tests are low in realism of task BUT high in assessment time needed
   (b) Performance assessments are low in complexity of task BUT high in assessment time needed
   (c) Paper-and-pencil tests are high in realism of task AND high in judgment in scoring
   (d) Performance assessments are high in complexity of task AND high in assessment time needed

2. Criterion-referenced assessments provide an indication of a student's
   (a) relative ranking with other students
   (b) ability to perform a task at a specified standard
   (c) attitude toward the training program
   (d) level of knowledge in the subject matter compared with other students

3. Which assessment method is highest in realism?
   (a) Extended performance
   (b) Supply response
   (c) Selected response
   (d) Restricted performance

4. If you have the fourth highest score in the class, which interpretation of your score has been made?
    (a) Criterion-referenced
    (b) Norm-referenced
    (c) Domain-referenced
    (d) Performance-referenced

TRUE-FALSE

DIRECTIONS: Read each statement and record as true or false on the lines provided.

5. _____ Rating scales or scoring rubrics are used when judging performance on a task.

6. _____ Stating that a student completed 8 out 10 steps in a task correctly would be considered a norm-referenced interpretation.

7. _____ Both a norm-referenced and criterion-referenced interpretation may be used with the same assessment.

8. _____ Selected-response items are highest in task complexity.

9. _____ Scores from standardized tests typically are assessed using a criterion-referenced approach.

Restricted-Response Essay

10. The authors of your textbook discuss the ways in which selected response, supply response, restricted performance, and extended performance assessments vary. List and describe each of these four varying characteristics. Confine your answer to one page.

3 | PLANNING FOR ASSESSMENT

Studying this chapter should enable you to

1. Describe the role of instructional objectives in the assessment of student achievement.
2. Describe the revised Taxonomy of Educational Objectives and its usefulness in assessment planning.
3. Describe how instructional objectives should be stated for assessment purposes.
4. Explain the importance of making assessment planning a part of instructional planning.
5. Describe the various assessment methods and their uses in assessing student achievement.
6. Explain why it is important for students to be made aware of the types of test items and assessment instruments to be used in assessing their achievement.
7. Describe the meaning of validity and reliability and the role they play in preparing assessment procedures.

Planning for assessment of student achievement involves a consideration of the following questions.

1. What do we expect the students to learn?
2. What types of student performance are we willing to accept as evidence of learning?
3. What assessment methods will best evaluate the students' performance?

The first question focuses on the goals of the curriculum as set by the school and influenced by the district and state. As noted earlier, most states have developed *content standards* that provide guidelines for determining what students should know and be able to do. This has influenced districts and schools to modify the curriculum and put greater emphasis on the more complex learning outcomes.

The second question focuses on the importance of specifying instructional objectives in performance terms and including all types of desired learning outcomes. These objectives must, of course, be in harmony with the goals of the curriculum and will reflect the state content standards to whatever degree the school curriculum does. In final analysis, the assessment of student achievement is determined by what the students are expected to learn, and this is determined by the goals of the school curriculum. The instructional objectives are simply a means of stating the curriculum goals in more specific terms so that they are useful in both instruction and assessment.

The third question focuses on the match between the instructional objectives and the procedures of assessment. The objectives specify the intended learning outcomes in performance terms and the assessment method is used to determine the extent to which the students' performance is satisfactory. For some performance outcomes, a test will provide adequate evidence. In other cases, some type of observational technique will be needed to evaluate the on-going nature of the performance (e.g., giving a speech) or to evaluate a resulting product (e.g., a written report). The key to effective assessment is to use the most direct and relevant method available.

USING TAXONOMIES AS A GUIDE

A revision of *Bloom's Taxonomy of Educational Objectives* by Anderson and Krathwohl (2001) provides a useful framework for identifying and preparing instructional objectives, instructional activities, and assessment methods. The revised taxonomy is two-dimensional. One dimension includes six cognitive process categories, increasing in complexity, and four knowledge categories, going from concrete to abstract. Thus, the taxonomy framework can be placed in a twofold table, as shown in Table 3.1. The cells where the two dimensions intersect classify the category of learning involved. For example, cell 1A refers to Remembering Factual Knowledge, cell 2B refers to Understanding Conceptual Knowledge, and cell!! refers to Applying Procedural Knowledge. Although a cognitive process may be more closely related to a particular type of knowledge, as illustrated in our examples, use of all cells for each cognitive process must be considered. For example, Remembering Concepts and Procedures may be an important objective, as well as Understanding Facts and Procedures. The cognitive process dimensions and the knowledge dimensions are defined and illustrated, with subcategories and examples, in Appendix A. A review of the subcategories and examples will clarify the various dimensions used in the twofold table and aid in preparing objectives, instructional activities, and assessments.

The Metacognitive Knowledge category may not be as easily related to a specific cognitive process, but it is an important dimension of knowledge that is frequently overlooked. It has to do with knowledge of general and specific strategies used in learning, knowledge about cognitive tasks, and knowledge about one's own learning strengths and weaknesses and the strategies one uses in dealing with cognitive tasks. Having students reflect on what they are learning

TABLE 3.1 Two-Dimensional Table Representing the Revised Edition of Bloom's Cognitive Taxonomy of Educational Objectives

The Knowledge Dimension	The Cognitive Process Dimension					
	1. Remember	2. Understand	3. Apply	4. Analyze	5. Evaluate	6. Create
A. Factual Knowledge						
B. Conceptual Knowledge						
C. Procedural Knowledge						
D. Metacognitive Knowledge						

Source: Adapted from Lorin W. Anderson & David R. Krathwohl, eds., *A Taxonomy For Learning, Teaching, and Assessing: A Revision of Bloom's Taxonomy of Educational Objectives,* © 2001. Published by Allyn and Bacon, Boston, MA. Copyright © 2001 by Pearson Education.

and what strategies work best for them provides an important area of intended learning outcomes. The use of a portfolio (see Chapter 10) is especially useful for assessing Metacognitive Knowledge because it typically includes samples of students' best work, self-assessment results, and students' reflections on the portfolio entries. It also provides evidence for assessing changes in the students' thinking over time.

The Taxonomy table can help broaden the list of objectives being prepared for a unit or course of instruction. All too frequently the remembering of factual material is overused. The table will help you move from this lowest cognitive process to the more meaningful learning covered by the higher cognitive processes. The first step might be to examine the categories Remember, Understand, and Apply. Most content areas include possible objectives in these areas. In fact, many state content standards use Knowledge (Remembering), Understanding, and Application as the main categories for classifying the standards. From this beginning, you might consider Analyze, Evaluate, and Create. In analyzing material or problems in your content area, do the students need to discriminate between the relevant and irrelevant, accurate and inaccurate, cause and effect, facts and opinions, and the like? If so, Analyze should be considered as an area of additional objectives. Similarly, do your students have to make judgments about the appropriateness of a procedure, the quality of a written report, the correctness of a skill, or the like? Do you expect your students to do a research project, write a report, and prepare a chart, graph, poster, or model? If so, objectives in the Evaluate and Create areas are needed. The Knowledge dimensions will then help you complete your objectives. By including the more complex learning outcomes in your list of objectives, you are not only contributing to the transfer of learning but also reinforcing the remembering of facts, concepts, procedures, and strategies.

The Taxonomy can also help select instructional activities that can best achieve the objectives. It helps you shift your focus from the activities to the intended learning outcomes of the activities. Your main concern should not be what the students are doing during an activity, but what they are learning from it. The old "learning by doing" philosophy frequently failed to live up to expectations because there was too much emphasis on the doing and not enough on the intended learning outcomes.

The Taxonomy is also useful in preparing assessment procedures and instruments that are in alignment with the objectives and instructional activities. The instructional objectives describe the intended learning outcomes, the instructional activities are designed to provide the relevant learning, and the assessment instruments provide evidence of the extent to which the intended learning outcomes have been achieved. To be effective, all three must be in close harmony and the Taxonomy two-dimensional table (Table 3.1) provides a basis for checking the alignment of the objectives, instructional activities, and assessments.

In planning for assessment, it is important to keep in mind that the assessments designed to measure intended learning outcomes beyond the Remember category must contain some novelty. In assessing Understanding, for example, students might be asked to define terms in their own words or give examples not covered in the textbook or instruction, so that their responses show that they grasp the meaning of concepts rather than simply recall previous learning. Similarly, with Apply, Analyze, Evaluate, and Create, the assessment must call for responses to new material or problems. These higher cognitive processes are concerned with the transfer of learning and not just the retention of learning—that falls in the Remember category.

Tests can be related to the Taxonomy table more easily than performance assessments. A test item usually falls in one or two cells in the table. For example, an item measuring application may measure both remembering procedural knowledge and applying conceptual knowledge. However, a performance assessment may spread across the entire table. For example, a project might require students to select and describe a problem to study, review relevant literature and other sources for answers, analyze the findings, and write a report summarizing the information, prepare a model or poster, present the findings to the class, and reflect on what has been learned from the project. Such an extended project is likely to cover all cognitive procedures and most types of knowledge. The table is still helpful in planning a project, however, by directing attention to the types of process and knowledge outcomes expected. It will also be useful in preparing criteria for evaluating the various phases of the project. Sharing the evaluation form with students before beginning the project will keep both the teacher and the students focusing on the intended outcomes of the project and prevent it from becoming "busy work."

When making decisions during the planning for performance assessments, applying the psychomotor taxonomy described by Bott (1996) is particularly useful. This taxonomy consists of four levels that describe a student's performance capability. The lowest, most rudimentary level is *observation*, in which the student is expected to simply observe the teacher demonstrate the completion of a task and report what the teacher has done. A student capable of performing at the second level, *imitation*, can only complete a task after observing someone else complete the task and following verbal or written instructions. The third level, *practice*, characterizes a student who can correctly complete a task without assistance. *Adaptation*, the fourth level, describes a student who can coordinate and complete multiple tasks, applying skills learned previously to new situations, without assistance. The psychomotor taxonomy, therefore, can be used as a guide to assist teachers when basing decisions about the level of student performance that will be considered acceptable. For instance, if a student is required to conduct a simple chemistry experiment, then the teacher must decide whether the student will be allowed to demonstrate competence with the assistance of written instructions (i.e., imitation) or must complete the task with no instructional aids (i.e., practice).

In summary, the Taxonomy two-dimensional table is useful in (1) identifying a wide array of intended learning outcomes (i.e., instructional objectives) that go beyond the Remember category; (2) planning for instructional activities that contribute to a variety of types of meaningful learning that are relevant to the instructional objectives; (3) planning for assessment methods that are appropriate for the objectives and instructional activities used in the instruction; and (4) checking on the alignment between the objectives, instructional activities, and assessment methods. Unless all three are in close alignment, a valid assessment of the intended learning outcomes will not be attained.

ROLE OF INSTRUCTIONAL OBJECTIVES

Well-stated instructional objectives provide a description of the intended learning outcomes in performance terms—that is, in terms of the types of performance students can demonstrate to show that they have achieved the knowledge, understanding, or skill described by the objective. By describing the performance that we are willing to accept as evidence of achievement, we provide a focus for instruction, student learning, and assessment. Objectives help keep all three in close harmony. For example, for an objective emphasizing problem-solving strategies, students practice applying the strategies, and we assess their skill in applying problem-solving strategies with new problems. Thus, the instructional targets, the learning targets, and the assessment targets are all the same. If the students are made aware of the objectives at the beginning of instruction, both teacher and students are working toward common goals, and instruction and assessment are both part of the same process.

Stating Instructional Objectives

In stating instructional objectives it is helpful to keep in mind that we are not describing the teaching procedures, the instructional activities, or the learning process. We are simply describing the student performance to be demonstrated at the end of the learning experience as evidence of learning. This permits us to use a variety of procedures, materials, and instructional activities to achieve the intended outcomes.

A useful procedure is to state the general objectives that focus on the broader learning outcomes and then define each general objective in more specific terms, as follows:

1. Understands scientific concepts.

    1.1 Describes the concept in his or her own words.
    1.2 Gives an example of the concept [that is new].
    1.3 Distinguishes the concept from similar scientific concepts.
    1.4 Explains the role of the concept in understanding a scientific event.
    1.5 Uses the concept in solving problems.

The specific learning outcomes listed under the general objective are not meant to be exhaustive, but they should provide a representative sample of the types of performance that we are willing to accept as evidence that the objective has been achieved. The specific learning outcomes will also vary, of course, with the achievement domain. For example, listing specific learning outcomes for understanding mathematical concepts, more emphasis would be given to interpreting, classifying, and problem solving. Also, our example is a model, or template, that would become more content-oriented when planning a unit of instruction. In that case, the general objectives and specific learning outcomes would refer to the concepts being studied, and this could modify the set of specific learning outcomes. All we are doing here is presenting a procedure that is useful in preparing objectives. The procedure is summarized in Box 3.1. An example of this procedure in planning an achievement test is presented in the next chapter. A more detailed description of the procedure, with examples from various subject matter areas and grade levels, can be found in Gronlund and Brookhart (2009).

Sources of Help in Locating Sample Objectives

In getting started with the identification and selection of instructional objectives, it helps to review various sources for ideas. The following sources are helpful in this regard.

1. **State content standards.** Content standards provide broad statements of intended learning outcomes that all students are expected to master. The statements typically are too general to be used as instructional objectives, but in a standards-based program it is expected that teachers' instructional objectives will be based on the content standards. If the state content standards are merely suggestive, they can still be reviewed for

BOX 3.1   Stating Instructional Objectives

The following steps provide guidelines for stating instructional objectives that are useful in instruction and assessment.

1. State the general objectives as follows:

    1.1 Write each as an intended learning outcome.
    1.2 State each in performance terms.
    1.3 Start each with a verb (e.g., "remembers," "understands").
    1.4 Write each so it is general enough to identify a domain of specific learning outcomes.

2. List and state the specific learning outcomes as follows:

    2.1 Clarify each general objective with a representative sample of specific learning outcomes.
    2.2 Begin each with an action verb indicating observable student performance (e.g., "selects," "describes").
    2.3 Include a sufficient number to indicate attainment of the general objective.
    2.4 Check to be sure the specific learning outcomes are relevant to the general objectives and that the general objectives are in harmony with the school goals.

---

learning outcomes to consider, to be supplemented by other sources. The extent to which state standards are reflected in the school curriculum will determine the extent to which they should be reflected in the list of instructional objectives.

2. **Revised Taxonomy of Educational Objectives.** The educational objectives described in the Taxonomy fall at an intermediate level between curriculum goals and instructional objectives. But like the content standards, they provide important areas of intended learning outcomes to consider. The subcategories are also useful in stating instructional objectives by suggesting the type of performance that represents the main categories. Understanding, for example, can be shown by interpreting, exemplifying, classifying, summarizing, inferring, comparing, and explaining. Alternate names and examples for these subcategories can further aid in preparing appropriate instructional objectives. A review of all categories in the table (see Appendix A) can be useful in selecting objectives that cover all important learning outcomes and in stating them in clear, consistent language.

3. **Publications of educational organizations.** There are organizations in each of the major teaching areas that publish useful material on instruction that contains suggested objectives. For example, the National Science Teachers Association, the National Council of Teachers of Mathematics, the National Council of Teachers of English, and the National Council for the Social Studies periodically issue yearbooks and other publications in instruction in their content areas. These and other organizations also have

---

BOX 3.2   Examples of Standards by Professional
Organizations

National Council of Teachers of English and the International Reading Association. *Standards for the English Language Arts.* Urbana, IL: National Council of Teachers of English, 1996.

National Council of Teachers of Mathematics. *Curriculum and Evaluation Standards for School Mathematics.* Reston, VA: National Council of Teachers of Mathematics, 1989.

National Council for the Social Studies. *Expectations of Excellence: Curriculum Standards for Social Studies.* Washington, DC: National Council for the Social Studies, 1994.

National Research Council. *National Science Education Standards.* Washington, DC: National Academy Press, 1996.

---

published sets of standards that may be useful in preparing instructional objectives (see Box 3.2).

4. **Instructor's guides accompanying student textbooks.** These guides typically contain objectives, but they frequently focus on lower level learning outcomes, are poorly stated, and are overly specific. However, they are worth a review for ideas on possible learning outcomes to consider. It may be possible to modify or combine them to put them in more usable form.

In selecting and preparing instructional objectives from these various sources, it is important to keep in mind that the final list must be in harmony with the goals of the local school program.

Evaluating the Final List of Objectives

In evaluating a final list of objectives for a course or unit of instruction there are a number of questions that might be asked about the list.

1. **Have all important learning outcomes been included?** Don't neglect the more complex learning outcomes just because they are more difficult to state.
2. **Are the objectives in harmony with the goals of the curriculum?** The list of objectives should represent the state content standards to the same degree the school goals do. Also, if the school goals emphasize self-assessment and independent learning, both the objectives and the planned instruction should have a similar emphasis.
3. **Are the objectives appropriate for the achievement level of the students?** If the objectives are to be achieved by the students, they must have the necessary background to proceed with the instruction. This may require a review of the objectives by teachers of previous courses or lower grade levels. Developing objectives cooperatively with other teachers may be the best solution.

4. **Are the objectives appropriate for the instructional time, materials, and facilities available?** As we move toward emphasis on the more complex learning outcomes, it is important to keep in mind that complex learning outcomes take longer to achieve than the recall of factual knowledge. Also, instructional materials and facilities may place limits on the types of intended learning outcomes it is possible to achieve.

5. **Do the objectives include meaningful learning that is useful in the real world?** The present trend toward more authentic learning can be incorporated into a set of objectives by including at least some intended learning outcomes concerned with problems in the real world (e.g., improving air quality). Using tasks embedded in a realistic context is motivating to students and makes them aware of the transfer value of what they are learning.

PREPARING FOR ASSESSMENT

Planning for assessment should be done at the same time as planning for instruction so that it will be an integral part of the teaching–learning process. Questions such as the following can serve as a guide.

1. **Is there need for pretesting?** By examining the content and methods of instruction, you can judge whether prerequisite learning is necessary. This may be simply determining whether students can count before teaching addition and subtraction or administering a paper-and-pencil test of the required knowledge. For example, before teaching algebra, a test of arithmetic may be desirable. Also, in a mastery program it may be useful to determine what knowledge and skills have already been mastered so that the instruction can be adjusted.

2. **What type of assessment is needed during instruction?** If assessment is to be used to monitor and improve learning, it must be planned during instructional planning. There may be a need for practice exercises, end-of-unit testing, observation and rating of performance, or evaluation of students' products (e.g., writing or a research project). The nature of the assessment will be determined by the instructional objectives, the instructional activities, and the need to provide feedback to students concerning their learning progress. If properly planned, assessment during instruction can provide for the improvement of student learning, which is the primary function of assessment.

   It is not necessary to prepare all assessment instruments during the planning stage, but plans should include their general nature and when they are to be used. Rating scales, checklists, and other means of assessing performance and products should be shared with students in advance, so they can serve as guides during the learning process. This is one example of how instruction and assessment can join together to improve learning.

3. **What type of assessment is needed at the end of instruction?** There is a need to determine the extent to which the instructional objectives have been achieved so that grades can be assigned or mastery certified. This assessment provides little opportunity for improving learning, but feedback can help students understand their strengths and weaknesses, and the information can help you determine whether future instruction needs to be modified.

TYPES OF ASSESSMENT PROCEDURES

An effective classroom assessment program will include a variety of procedures. Some will be based on a teacher's informal observations during instruction, while others provide a more systematic and structured means of obtaining evidence of achievement. Following are some of the more commonly used procedures with an indication of their main function.

1. **Informal observation during instruction.** Classroom observation during instruction alerts the teacher to many specific ways to guide student learning. Students' questions may indicate a need to review the material or may provide an opportunity to correct a simple misunderstanding. Observation may indicate that the pace of instruction is too fast or too slow for some students. Certain students may need special help in solving problems, performing a skill, or completing an assignment. These ongoing observations and instructional decisions are a basic means of improving student learning. The more systematic assessment procedures are merely ways to supplement the teacher's informal observations during instruction.

2. **Classroom achievement tests.** The tests designed for classroom use provide a systematic procedure for determining the extent to which intended learning outcomes have been achieved. If properly made, they can measure a variety of learning outcomes, including remembering factual knowledge, understanding, application, reasoning ability, and problem solving. Unfortunately, they have been used primarily for measuring the recall of factual knowledge and have been widely criticized for the limited measure of achievement they provide. The answer is not to eliminate testing, as some have suggested, but to construct tests that measure a broad band of achievement.

3. **Performance assessment.** Observation and judgment of an ongoing performance skill is usually obtained by using a checklist, rating scale, or holistic scoring rubric. The purpose of the assessment device is to direct the observation toward the most important elements of the performance and to provide a place to record the judgments. Paper-and-pencil tests can be used to determine whether students know what to do, but direct observation of the students' performance is necessary for determining how well a student can perform (e.g., speaking, reading, using a microscope, batting a ball, using a computer).

4. **Product assessment.** Some types of performance result in a product that becomes the focus of the assessment. A written essay, a graph, a map, a painting, a poster, a model, a woodworking project, and a laboratory report are all examples of products that can be assessed directly. Checklists, rating scales, and holistic scoring rubrics are also useful in product assessment. They provide a focus on the key features of the product and a scale for recording the judgments.

5. **Portfolio assessment.** A portfolio is a collection of student work used to show learning progress over a period of time or to show the student's best work. The students typically participate in selecting the portfolio entries in terms of their learning progress. The entries typically include test results, writing samples, drawings, research reports, performance and product ratings, projects, conference reports, and other evidence relevant to the intended learning outcomes of the instruction. The portfolio is viewed as a comprehensive assessment of a student's overall achievement. It provides the student with an opportunity to participate in the assessment process and to reflect on what is being learned.

To be most effective, the selection and use of assessment methods must be planned at the same time as instructional planning. Determining what assessment methods will be used, when they will be used, and how they will be used can best be done at the time instructional activities are being planned. Although all instruments may not be prepared at that time, plans for their use should be made so that they can be fitted into the teaching schedule. Assessment procedures take time, and unless they are planned for early, they are likely to be slighted.

The preparation of classroom tests and performance assessment methods should be done early enough so that sample test items, like those in the tests, and assessment instruments can be shared with students well before their use. This will clarify for students the type of performance expected. Presenting students with sample test items that measure a variety of learning outcomes, such as understanding, application, and evaluation, will make clear to them that memorizing factual information will not be sufficient. Sharing performance assessment instruments with students will provide them with a guide for both learning and self-assessment.

VALIDITY AND RELIABILITY IN ASSESSMENT PLANNING

Two of the most important characteristics of a well-designed assessment procedure are **validity** and **reliability**. These characteristics are of primary concern during assessment planning, and most of the suggestions in this book are directed toward preparing assessments that provide for valid and reliable interpretation of results.

Validity refers to the appropriateness and meaningfulness of the inferences we make from assessment results for some intended use. For example, if we give a vocabulary test, we would like to be able to interpret the scores as a representative sample of the terms we have been teaching. If we do a good job of (1) clearly defining the domain of vocabulary items to be measured, (2) carefully preparing the test specifications, and (3) constructing a representative sample of relevant test items, our interpretations from the results are likely to be valid. We are now able to infer that high scores represent good knowledge of the vocabulary that has been taught. Note that it is the inference that is important. If we infer that high scores indicate good writing ability or good verbal ability, we are generalizing beyond the limited assessment domain being tested and the validity of our inference is in doubt, without further evidence. Thus, it is not the test scores that are valid or invalid but the inferences we make from them.

Performance assessments are typically viewed as providing more valid inferences concerning learning than traditional paper-and-pencil tests because they focus more directly on the types of performance tasks we are teaching. If we want to determine whether students can read, we have them read something. If we want to determine whether students can give a speech, we have them give a speech. If we want to determine whether students can operate a computer, we have them operate a computer. In each case the task has the appearance of being valid (i.e., we have good *face* validity). However, it is not as simple as it seems. In performance assessment, defining the assessment domain, specifying how the performance will be judged, and obtaining a representative sample of performance tasks pose special problems. For example, there are many different types of reading, many different types of speeches, and many different types of problems to be solved on the computer. Each requires its own specifications and scoring rubrics, and because of the time-consuming nature of performance assessment, the sampling tends to be limited. This restricts the extent to which we can infer that performance on one assessment task is generalizable to performance on other assessment tasks in the same area.

With both tests and performance assessments we need to make plans and follow procedures that are most likely to yield valid inferences concerning learning. This involves selecting appropriate procedures, preparing them carefully, applying them effectively, and then interpreting the results within the limits of the particular achievement domain being assessed. In using the results, we are also, of course, concerned about the consequences of the assessment. Did its use contribute to increased student learning, as intended? This is a legitimate validity-related question because our main purpose in assessing student achievement is to improve learning.

Reliability refers to consistency of assessment results. For example, if a student earns a score of 60 on a test, we would like to be able to say that 60 accurately represents the student's test performance. Thus, if we tested the student at a different time or with a different sample of equivalent items, we would expect to obtain a similar score. Similarly, if a student receives a high rating on a writing project, we would like to say that it represents the student's writing skill and that, if others rated the project, the results would be similar. This consistency of results would indicate that they are relatively free from errors and thus we can rely on them (i.e., they have "rely-ability").

We cannot, of course, expect assessment results to be perfectly consistent over different occasions or over different samples of the same achievement domain. Such factors as ambiguities, variations in samples, fluctuations in motivation and attention, and luck can introduce errors that cause assessment results to vary. Likewise, in judging performance tasks, the personal biases of the rater can introduce error into the results. An important goal in assessment is to keep these various types of errors to a minimum so that our results are as reliable as possible.

In addition to being important in its own right, reliability is necessary to obtain valid inferences from assessment results. After all, if an individual's test score fluctuated widely on a given sample of items, we could not expect to draw valid inferences concerning the student's achievement. Similarly, if rating varied widely on a student's writing project, valid inferences could not be made concerning writing skill. Thus, *reliability provides the consistency of results that makes valid inferences possible.* Of course, the consistency of results is just one important requirement for valid inferences. We could be consistently assessing the wrong thing, using inappropriate procedures, or generalizing beyond the achievement domain being assessed. Thus, reliability is a necessary, but not sufficient, condition for making valid inferences.

Both the validity and reliability of assessment results can be provided for during the preparation of assessment procedures. When we clearly specify the intended learning outcomes, define the achievement domain to be assessed, and select a relevant and representative set of assessment tasks, we are providing for valid inferences concerning learning. When we include an adequate number of tasks in our assessment and we use procedures that are free from ambiguity, irrelevant sources of difficulty, unintended clues, and other factors that might distort the results, we are providing for both reliability and validity. In fact, most of the suggestions for constructing achievement tests and preparing performance assessments are directed toward improving the reliability of the assessment results and the validity of the interpretations we make from them.

A more elaborate discussion of validity and reliability and methods for determining them is presented in the next chapter. Although high-quality assessments can be made without a detailed study of validity and reliability, understanding the basic concepts involved can contribute to improved skill in preparing assessment procedures, making appropriate interpretations of the results, and using the results effectively.

Some of the most important features that enhance the validity and reliability of assessment results are presented in Table 3.2. This table makes clear that concern about validity and reliability takes place in the early stages of assessment planning and preparation, not after the assessment results have been obtained. The procedures listed in Table 3.2 will be described in more detail in the chapters on preparing tests and performance-based assessments. Here, we are simply emphasizing their importance in obtaining valid and reliable interpretations of assessment results and the need for early assessment planning to "build in" the desired features.

TABLE 3.2 Desirable Features for Enhancing the Validity and Reliability of Assessment Results

Desired Features	Procedures to Follow
1. Clearly specified set of learning outcomes.	1. State intended learning outcomes in performance terms.
2. Representative sample of a clearly defined domain of learning tasks.	2. Prepare a description of the achievement domain to be assessed and the sample of task to be used.
3. Tasks that are relevant to the learning outcomes to be measured.	3. Match assessment tasks to the specified performance stated in the learning outcomes.
4. Tasks that are at the proper level of difficulty.	4. Match assessment task difficulty to the learning task, the students' abilities, and the use to be made of the results.
5. Tasks that function effectively in distinguishing between achievers and nonachievers.	5. Follow general guidelines and specific rules for preparing assessment procedures and be alert for factors that distort the results.
6. Sufficient number of tasks to measure an adequate sample of achievement, provide dependable results, and allow for a meaningful interpretation of the results.	6. Where the students' age or available assessment time limit the number of tasks, make tentative interpretations, assess more frequently, and verify the results with other evidence.
7. Procedures that contribute to efficient preparation and use.	7. Write clear directions and arrange procedures for ease of administration, scoring or judging, and interpretation.

Summary of Points

1. Assessment planning should be guided by what the students are expected to learn, as specified by the instructional objectives.
2. The instructional objectives should be in harmony with the school goals and reflect the state standards to the same extent the school goals do.
3. Assessment planning requires a consideration of all possible types of learning outcomes in a given content domain.
4. The revised Taxonomy of Educational Objectives provides a useful framework for (1) identifying a wide array of intended learning outcomes; (2) planning instructional activities; (3) planning assessment methods; and (4) checking on the alignment among objectives, instruction, and assessment.
5. Planning for assessment should be part of instructional planning so that assessment methods are in harmony with the instructional objectives and the instructional activities and are allowed for in the teaching schedule.
6. Instructional objectives should be stated in terms of the student performance to be demonstrated at the end of the learning experience as evidence of learning.
7. Classroom achievement tests can be designed to measure all types of learning outcomes ranging from simple to complex. The performance

measured by the test should match the performance described in the instructional objectives.

8. Performance assessment is concerned with observable skills (e.g., speaking) or a product (e.g., writing) and typically requires the use of a checklist, rating scale, or scoring rubric (scoring guide).

9. Portfolio assessment provides a comprehensive assessment of student achievement and provides an opportunity for students to reflect on what is being learned.

10. Students should be given sample test items well before testing, and performance instruments before beginning the performance activities, so they have achievement targets to guide their study. The performance instruments are also useful in developing student self-assessment skills.

11. Validity and reliability are the two most important characteristics of any assessment method and must be considered during the planning and preparation of assessment procedures.

12. Valid and reliable interpretations of assessment results require clearly defined intended learning outcomes, a representative sample of instructionally relevant tasks, a sound scoring system, and freedom from irrelevant factors that introduce error.

References and Additional Reading

Anderson, L. W., & Krathwohl, D. R. (Eds.). *A Taxonomy for Learning, Teaching, and Assessing: A Revision of Bloom's Taxonomy of Educational Objectives* (New York: Longman, 2001).

Bott, P. A. *Testing and Assessment in Occupational and Technical Education* (Boston: Allyn and Bacon, 1996).

Gronlund, N. E., & Brookhart, S. M. *Gronlund's Writing Instructional Objectives,* 8th ed. (Upper Saddle River, NJ: Pearson/Merrill/Prentice Hall, 2009).

McMillan, J. H. *Classroom Assessment: Principles and Practice for Effective Instruction,* 3rd ed. (Boston: Allyn and Bacon, 2004).

Nitko, A. J. *Educational Assessment of Students,* 4th ed. (Upper Saddle River, NJ: Merrill/Prentice Hall, 2001).

Stiggins, R. J. *Student-Involved Classroom Assessment,* 3rd ed. (Upper Saddle River, NJ: Merrill/Prentice Hall, 2001).

Self-Assessment

MULTIPLE CHOICE

DIRECTIONS: Select the best answer for each item by circling the corresponding letter.

1. The two most important characteristics of a well-constructed achievement test are validity and
   (a) reliability
   (b) usability
   (c) difficulty
   (d) maintainability

2. The revised Taxonomy of Educational Objectives is particularly useful when
  (a) administering a paper-and-pencil test
  (b) determining the reliability of an assessment
  (c) developing scoring rubrics
  (d) preparing instructional objectives

3. The selection and use of assessment methods should be planned
  (a) during the planning of instructional activities
  (b) after the instructional activities have been development
  (c) after the instruction has been delivered to the students
  (d) prior to the planning of instructional activities

4. Test items that are unrelated to the intended learning outcomes is a concern related to
  (a) validity
  (b) difficulty
  (c) maintainability
  (d) reliability

TRUE-FALSE

DIRECTIONS: Read each statement and record as true or false on the lines provided.

5. _____ To improve the validity of an assessment, test items should be related to intended learning outcomes.

6. _____ An assessment must be valid to be reliable.

7. _____ Paper-and-pencil tests are the best method to determine how well a student can perform a task.

8. _____ The cognitive process dimension of Bloom's revised taxonomy labeled Remember requires students to only retrieve information from long-term memory.

9. _____ Solving an algebraic equation using a procedure learned in class would be considered an example of Application.

Restricted-Response Essay

10. The authors of your textbook discuss the desirable features for enhancing the validity and reliability of assessment results. List and describe each of these desirable features and the procedures that should be followed to insure valid and reliable assessments. Confine your answer to one page.

4 | VALIDITY AND RELIABILITY

The two most important questions to ask about a test or other assessment procedure are (1) to what extent will the interpretation of the results be appropriate, meaningful, and useful?, and (2) to what extent will the results be free from errors? The first question is concerned with *validity*, the second with *reliability.* An understanding of both concepts is essential to the effective construction, selection, interpretation, and use of tests and other assessment instruments. Validity is the most important quality to consider in the preparation and use of assessment procedures. First and foremost, we want the results to provide a representative and relevant measure of the achievement domain under consideration. Our second consideration is reliability, which refers to the consistency of our assessment results. For example, if we tested individuals at a different time, or with a different sample of equivalent items, we would like to obtain approximately the same results. This consistency of results is important for two reasons. (1) Unless the results are fairly stable, we cannot expect them to be valid.

For example, if an individual scored high on a test one time and low another time, it would be impossible to validly describe the achievement. (2) Consistency of results indicates smaller errors of measurement and, thereby, more dependable results. Thus, reliability provides the consistency needed to obtain validity and enables us to interpret assessment results with greater confidence.

Although it is frequently unnecessary to make elaborate validation and reliability studies of informal assessment procedures, an understanding of these concepts provides a conceptual framework that can serve as a guide for more effective construction of assessment instruments, more effective selection of standardized tests, and more appropriate interpretation and use of assessment results.

VALIDITY

Validity is concerned with the interpretation and use of assessment results. For example, if we infer from an assessment that students have achieved the intended learning outcomes, we would like some assurance that our tasks provided a relevant and representative measure of the outcomes. If we infer that the assessment is useful for predicting or estimating some other performance, we would like some credible evidence to support that interpretation. If we infer that our assessment indicates that students have good "reasoning ability," we would like some evidence to support the fact that the results actually reflect that construct. If we infer that our use of an assessment had positive effects (e.g., increased motivation) and no adverse effects (e.g., poor study habits) on students, we would like some evidence concerning the consequences of its use. These are the kinds of considerations we are concerned with when considering the validity of assessment results (see the summary in Figure 4.1).

The meaning of *validity* in interpreting and using assessment results can be grasped most easily by reviewing the following characteristics.

1. Validity is *inferred* from available evidence (not measured).
2. Validity depends on *many different types* of evidence.
3. Validity is expressed by *degree* (high, moderate, low).
4. Validity is specific to a particular *use*.

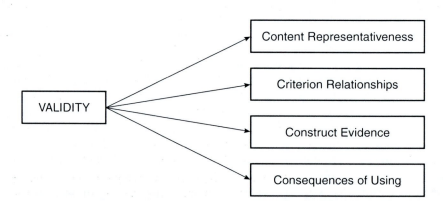

FIGURE 4.1   Types of Considerations in Determining the Validity of Assessment Results.

5. Validity refers to the *inferences drawn*, not the instrument.
6. Validity is a *unitary concept.*
7. Validity is concerned with the *consequences of using the assessments.*

Describing validity as a unitary concept is a basic change in how validity is viewed. The traditional view that there were several different "types of validity" has been replaced by the view that validity is a single, unitary concept that is based on various forms of evidence. The former "types of validity" (content, criterion-related, and construct) are now simply considered to be convenient categories for accumulating evidence to support the validity of an interpretation. Thus, we no longer speak of "content validity," but of "content-related evidence" of validity. Similarly, we speak of "criterion-related evidence" and "construct-related evidence."

For some interpretations of assessment results only one or two types of evidence may be critical, but an *ideal* validation would include evidence from all four categories. We are most likely to draw valid inferences from assessment results when we have a full understanding of: (1) the nature of the assessment procedure and the specifications that were used in developing it, (2) the relation of the assessment results to significant criterion measures, (3) the nature of the psychological characteristic(s) or construct(s) being assessed, and (4) the consequences of using the assessment. Although in many practical situations the evidence falls short of this ideal, we should gather as much relevant evidence as is feasible within the constraints of the situation. We should also look for the various types of evidence when evaluating standardized tests (see Table 4.1).

Content-Related Evidence

Content-related evidence of validity is critical when we want to use performance on a set of tasks as evidence of performance on a larger domain of tasks. Let's assume, for example, that we have a list of 500 words that we expect our students to be able to spell correctly at the end of the school year. To test their spelling ability, we might give them a 50-word spelling test. Their performance

TABLE 4.1 Basic Approaches to Validation

Type of Evidence	Question to Be Answered
Content-Related	How adequately does the sample of assessment tasks represent the domain of tasks to be measured?
Criterion-Related	How accurately does performance on the assessment (e.g., test) predict future performance (predictive study) or estimate present performance (concurrent study) on some other valued measure called a criterion?
Construct-Related	How well can performance on the assessment be explained in terms of psychological characteristics?
Consequences	How well did use of the assessment serve the intended purpose (e.g., improve performance) and avoid adverse effects (e.g., poor study habits)?

on these words is important only insofar as it provides evidence of their ability to spell the 500 words. Thus, our spelling test would provide a valid measure to the degree to which it provided an adequate sample of the 500 words it represented. If we selected only easy words, only difficult words, or only words that represented certain types of common spelling errors, our test would tend to be unrepresentative and thus the scores would have low validity. If we selected a balanced sample of words that took these and similar factors into account, our test scores would provide a representative measure of the 500 spelling words and thereby provide for high validity.

It should be clear from this discussion that the key element in content-related evidence of validity is the adequacy of the *sampling*. An assessment is always a sample of the many tasks that could be included. Content validation is a matter of determining whether the sample of tasks is representative of the larger domain of tasks it is supposed to represent.

Content-related evidence of validity is especially important in achievement assessment. Here we are interested in how well the assessment measures the intended learning outcomes of the instruction. We can provide greater assurance that an assessment provides valid results by (1) identifying the learning outcomes to be assessed, (2) preparing a plan that specifies the sample of tasks to be used, and (3) preparing an assessment procedure that closely fits the set of specifications. These are the best procedures we have for ensuring the assessment of a representative sample of the domain of tasks encompassed by the intended learning outcomes.

Although the focus of content-related evidence of validity is on the adequacy of the sampling, a valid interpretation of the assessment results assumes that the assessment was properly prepared, administered, and scored. Validity can be lowered by inadequate procedures in any of these areas (see Box 4.1). Thus, validity is "built in" during the planning and preparation stages and maintained by proper administration and scoring. Throughout this book we describe how to prepare assessments that provide valid results, even though we do not use the word *validity* as each procedure is discussed.

BOX 4.1   Factors That Lower the Validity of Assessment Results

1. Tasks that provide an inadequate sample of the achievement to be assessed.
2. Tasks that do not function as intended, due to use of improper types of tasks, lack of relevance, ambiguity, clues, bias, inappropriate difficulty, or similar factors.
3. Improper arrangement of tasks and unclear directions.
4. Too few tasks for the types of interpretation to be made (e.g., interpretation by objective based on a few test items).
5. Improper administration—such as inadequate time allowed and poorly controlled conditions.
6. Judgmental scoring that uses inadequate scoring guides, or objective scoring that contains computational errors.

The makers of standardized tests follow these same systematic procedures in building achievement tests, but the content and learning outcomes included in the test specifications are more broadly based than those used in classroom assessment. Typically, they are based on the leading textbooks and the recommendations of various experts in the area being covered by the test. Therefore, a standardized achievement test may be representative of a broad range of content but be unrepresentative of the domain of content taught in a particular school situation. To determine relevance to the local situation, it is necessary to evaluate the sample of test items in light of the content and skills emphasized in the instruction.

In summary, content-related evidence of validity is of major concern in achievement assessment, whether you are developing or selecting the assessment procedure. When constructing a test, for example, content relevance and representativeness are built in by following a systematic procedure for specifying and selecting the sample of test items, constructing high-quality items, and arranging the test for efficient administration and scoring. In test selection, it is a matter of comparing the test sample to the domain of tasks to be measured and determining the degree of correspondence between them. Similar care is needed when preparing and using performance assessments. Thus, content-related evidence of validity is obtained primarily by careful, logical analysis.

Criterion-Related Evidence

There are two types of studies used in obtaining criterion-related evidence of validity. These can be explained most clearly using test scores, although they could be used with any type of assessment result. The first type of study is concerned with the use of test performance to predict future performance on some other valued measure called a *criterion*. For example, we might use scholastic aptitude test scores to predict course grades (the criterion). For obvious reasons, this is called a *predictive* study. The second type of study is concerned with the use of test performance to estimate current performance on some criterion. For instance, we might want to use a test of study skills to estimate what the outcome would be of a careful observation of students in an actual study situation (the criterion). Since with this procedure both measures (test and criterion) are obtained at approximately the same time, this type of study is called a *concurrent* study.

Although the value of using a predictive study is rather obvious, a question might be raised concerning the purpose of a concurrent study. Why would anyone want to use test scores to estimate performance on some other measure that is to be obtained at the same time? There are at least three good reasons for doing this. First, we may want to check the results of a newly constructed test against some existing test that has a considerable amount of validity evidence supporting it. Second, we may want to substitute a brief, simple testing procedure for a more complex and time-consuming measure. For example, our test of study skills might be substituted for an elaborate rating system if it provided a satisfactory estimate of study performance. Third, we may want to determine whether a testing procedure has *potential* as a predictive instrument. If a test provides an unsatisfactory estimate of current performance, it certainly cannot be expected to predict future performance on the same measure. On the other hand, a satisfactory estimate of present performance would indicate that the test might be useful in predicting future performance as well. This would inform us that a predictive study would be worth doing.

The key element in both types of criterion-related study is the *degree of relationship* between the two sets of measures: (1) the test scores and (2) the criterion to be predicted or estimated. This relationship is typically expressed by means of a correlation coefficient or an expectancy table.

CORRELATION COEFFICIENTS. A **correlation coefficient** (r) simply indicates the degree of relationship between two sets of measures. A *positive* relationship is indicated when high scores on one measure are accompanied by high scores on the other; low scores on the two measures are similarly associated. A *negative* relationship is indicated when high scores on one measure are accompanied by low scores on the other. The extreme degrees of relationship it is possible to obtain between two sets of scores are indicated by the following values:

$$1.00 = \text{perfect positive relationship}$$
$$.00 = \text{no relationship}$$
$$-1.00 = \text{perfect negative relationship}$$

When a correlation coefficient is used to express the degree of relationship between a set of test scores and some criterion measure, it is called a *validity coefficient*. For example, a validity coefficient of 1.00 applied to the relationship between a set of aptitude test scores (the predictor) and a set of achievement test scores (the criterion) would indicate that each individual in the group had exactly the same relative standing on both measures, and would thereby provide a perfect prediction from the aptitude scores to the achievement scores. Most validity coefficients are smaller than this, but the extreme positive relationship provides a useful benchmark for evaluating validity coefficients. The closer the validity coefficient approaches 1.00, the higher the degree of relationship and, thus, the more accurate our predictions of each individual's success on the criterion will be.

A more realistic procedure for evaluating a validity coefficient is to compare it to the validity coefficients that are *typically* obtained when the two measures are correlated. For example, a validity coefficient of .40 between a set of aptitude test scores and achievement test scores would be considered small because we typically obtain coefficients in the .50 to .70 range for these two measures. Therefore, validity coefficients must be judged on a relative basis, the larger coefficients being favored. To use validity coefficients effectively, one must become familiar with the size of the validity coefficients that are typically obtained between various pairs of measures under different conditions (e.g., the longer the time span between measures, the smaller the validity coefficient).

A number of statistical software programs and calculators are capable of calculating a correlation coefficient between two sets of measures. However, it is not difficult to calculate a correlation using a simple calculator. It is simply a matter of following a series of steps to arrive at the solution to the following correlation coefficient formula.

$$r = \frac{N(\Sigma xy) - (\Sigma x)(\Sigma y)}{\sqrt{[N(\Sigma x^2) - (\Sigma x)^2][N(\Sigma y^2) - (\Sigma y)^2]}}$$

To illustrate the process, suppose we conduct a predictive study to determine whether students' scores on a paper-and-pencil achievement test predict future performance on a related end-of-course project. Table 4.2 provides each student's score on both the test and the project.

You will note from the table that the test scores, the *predictor*, are labeled *x* and the project scores, the *criterion*, are labeled *y*. As you will see, these labels are necessary in order to calculate the correlation coefficient.

To arrive at the values to place into the correlation coefficient formula, several calculations need to be made first. To make this task much easier, it is helpful to create a new table by adding a few columns to Table 4.2. Table 4.3 shows the existing raw data, as well as derived data from several calculations.

Moving from left to right, the numerator of the correlation coefficient formula begins with N, which refers to the number of students who completed the assessments. In this example, N equals 10 students. The next value in the numerator is the sum of *x* multiplied by *y*, or Σxy. To obtain this number, we must first multiply the *x* and *y* values for each student. For example, as shown in Table 4.3, for student A the test score (*x*) of 15 was multiplied by the student's project score (*y*) of 16, and the product of 240 was placed in the last column, labeled *xy*. This procedure was repeated for the remaining students. The *xy* values were then added, resulting in the sum of *xy* equaling 1787. The two remaining values to be placed in the numerator of the formula are the sum of *x*, or Σx, and the sum of *y*, or Σy. As shown in the table, adding together the test scores (*x*) results in $\Sigma x = 140$. Adding together the project scores (*y*)

TABLE 4.2 Student Scores on Achievement Test and Class Project

Student	Test Scores (x)	Project Scores (y)
A	15	16
B	18	15
C	12	8
D	13	11
E	19	17
F	10	9
G	14	13
H	11	5
I	17	17
J	11	9

TABLE 4.3 Raw and Derived Data

Student	Test Scores (x)	x^2	Project Scores (y)	y^2	xy
A	15	225	16	256	240
B	18	324	15	225	270
C	12	144	8	64	96
D	13	169	11	121	143
E	19	361	17	289	323
F	10	100	9	81	90
G	14	196	13	169	182
H	11	121	5	25	55
I	17	289	17	289	289
J	11	121	9	81	99
Sums (Σ)	140	2050	120	1600	1787

results in $\Sigma y = 120$. Thus, we have calculated all of the values needed for the numerator of the formula.

Again, moving from left to right, the denominator of the correlation coefficient begins with N, which as explained earlier is 10. The next value to be calculated is the sum of x squared, or Σx^2. To obtain this number, we must first square the x values for each student. For example, as shown in Table 4.3, the test score (x) for student A of 15 was squared, and the product of 225 was placed in the third column, labeled x^2. This procedure was repeated for the remaining students. The x^2 values were then added, resulting in the sum of x^2 equaling 2050. Returning to the formula, the next value in the denominator is the sum of x, or Σx, calculated earlier to be 140. Also calculated earlier and included in the denominator is the sum of y, or Σy, which equals 120. Thus, the only value in the denominator that remains unknown is the sum of y squared, or Σy^2. As with the calculation of the Σx^2, we simply square the project scores (y) for each student, place the product of each calculation in the fifth column of the table labeled y^2, and add the values in the column to determine the sum of y squared. In this example, $\Sigma y^2 = 1600$.

Now that all of the needed values have been calculated, we simply place them in the correlation coefficient formula and conduct the calculations. The result is a correlation coefficient of .89.

$$r = \frac{10(1787) - (140)(120)}{\sqrt{[10(2050) - (140)^2][10(1600) - (120)^2]}} = .89$$

This validity coefficient indicates that the degree of relationship between the test scores and project scores is relatively strong, although as noted earlier, the coefficient should ideally be compared with validity coefficients that are typically obtained for these two measures. Given a relatively strong correlation, is it then valid to infer that the test scores will predict performance on the end-of-course project? A relatively strong correlation would support such an inference. Of course, a perfect positive correlation of 1.00 would provide the strongest predictive evidence. But, these correlations are seldom if ever achieved.

EXPECTANCY TABLE. The expectancy table is a simple and practical means of expressing criterion-related evidence of validity and is especially useful for making predictions from test scores. The **expectancy table** is simply a twofold chart with the test scores (the predictor) arranged in categories down the left side of the table and the measure to be predicted (the criterion) arranged in categories across the top of the table. For each category of scores on the *predictor*, the table indicates the percentage of individuals who fall within each category of the *criterion*. An example of an expectancy table is presented in Table 4.4.

Note in Table 4.4 that of those students who were in the above-average group (stanines 7, 8, and 9) on the test scores, 43 percent received a grade of A, 43 percent a B, and 14 percent a C. Although these percentages are based on this particular group, it is possible to use them to predict the future performance of other students in this science course. Hence, if a student falls in the above-average group on this scholastic aptitude test, we might predict that he or she has 43 chances out of 100 of earning an A, 43 chances out of 100 of earning a B, and 14 chances out of a 100 of earning a C in this particular science course. Such predictions are highly tentative, of course, due to the small number of students on which this expectancy table was built. Teachers can construct more dependable tables by accumulating data from several classes over a period of time.

Expectancy tables can be used to show the relationship between any two measures. Constructing the table is simply a matter of (1) grouping the scores on each measure into a series of categories (any number of them), (2) placing the two sets of categories on a twofold chart, (3) tabulating the number of students who fall into each position in the table (based on the student's

TABLE 4.4 Expectancy Table Showing the Relationship Between Scholastic Aptitude Scores and Course Grades for 30 Students in a Science Course

Grouped Scholastic Aptitude Scores (Stanines)	Percentage in Each Score Category Receiving Each Grade				
	F	D	C	B	A
Above Average (7, 8, 9)			14	43	43
Average (4, 5, 6)		19	37	25	19
Below Average (1, 2, 3)	57	29	14		

standing on both measures), and (4) converting these numbers to percentages (of the total number in that row). Thus, the expectancy table is a clear way of showing the relationship between sets of scores. Although the expectancy table is more cumbersome to deal with than a correlation coefficient, it has the special advantage of being easily understood by persons without knowledge of statistics. Thus, it can be used in practical situations to clarify the predictive efficiency of a test.

Construct-Related Evidence

The construct-related category of evidence focuses on assessment results as a basis for inferring the possession of certain psychological characteristics. For example, we might want to describe a person's reading comprehension, reasoning ability, or mechanical aptitude. These are all hypothetical qualities, or *constructs*, that we assume exist in order to explain behavior. Such theoretical constructs are useful in describing individuals and in predicting how they will act in many different specific situations. To describe a person as being highly intelligent, for example, is useful because that term carries with it a series of associated meanings that indicate what the individual's behavior is likely to be under various conditions. Before we can interpret assessment results in terms of these broad behavior descriptions, however, we must first establish that the constructs that are presumed to be reflected in the scores actually do account for differences in performance.

Construct-related evidence of validity for a test includes (1) a description of the theoretical framework that specifies the nature of the construct to be measured, (2) a description of the development of the test and any aspects of measurement that may affect the meaning of the test scores (e.g., test format), (3) the pattern of relationship between the test scores and other significant variables (e.g., high correlations with similar tests and low correlations with tests measuring different constructs), and (4) any other type of evidence that contributes to the meaning of the test scores (e.g., analyzing the mental process used in responding, determining the predictive effectiveness of the test). The specific types of evidence that are most critical for a particular test depend on the nature of the construct, the clarity of the theoretical framework, and the uses to be made of the test scores. Although the gathering of construct-related evidence of validity can be endless, in practical situations it is typically necessary to limit the evidence to that which is most relevant to the interpretations to be made.

The construct-related category of evidence is the broadest of the three categories. Evidence obtained in both the content-related category (e.g., representativeness of the sample of tasks) and the criterion-related category (e.g., how well the scores predict performance on specific criteria) is also relevant to the construct-related category because it helps to clarify the meaning of the assessment results. Thus, the construct-related category encompasses a variety of types of evidence, including that from content-related and criterion-related validation studies (see Figure 4.2).

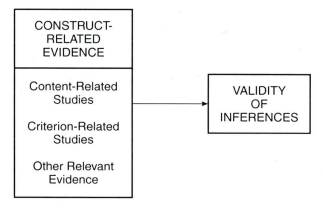

FIGURE 4.2   Construct Validation Includes All Categories of Evidence.

The broad array of evidence that might be considered can be illustrated by a test designed to measure mathematical reasoning ability. Some of the evidence we might consider is the following:

1. Compare the sample of test tasks to the domain of tasks specified by the conceptual framework of the construct. Is the sample relevant and representative (content-related evidence)?
2. Examine the test features and their possible influence on the meaning of the scores (e.g., test format, directions, scoring, reading level of items). Is it possible that some features might distort the scores?
3. Analyze the mental process used in answering the questions by having students "think aloud" as they respond to each item. Do the items require the intended reasoning process?
4. Determine the internal consistency of the test by intercorrelating the test items. Do the items seem to be measuring a single characteristic (in this case mathematical reasoning)?
5. Correlate the test scores with the scores of other mathematical reasoning tests. Do they show a high degree of relationship?
6. Compare the scores of known groups (e.g., mathematical majors and non-majors). Do the scores differentiate between the groups as predicted?
7. Compare the scores of students before and after specific training in mathematical reasoning. Do the scores change as predicted from the theory underlying the construct?
8. Correlate the scores with grades in mathematics. Do they correlate to a satisfactory degree (criterion-related evidence)?

Other types of evidence could be added to this list, but it is sufficiently comprehensive to make clear that no single type of evidence is adequate. Interpreting test scores as a measure of a particular construct involves a comprehensive study of the development of the test, how it functions in a variety of situations, and how the scores relate to other significant measures.

Assessment results are, of course, influenced by many factors other than the construct they are designed to measure. Thus, construct validation is an attempt to account for all possible influences on the scores. We might, for example, ask to what extent the scores on our mathematical reasoning test are influenced by reading comprehension, computation skill, and speed. Each of these factors would require further study. Were attempts made to eliminate such factors during test development by using simple vocabulary, simple computations, and liberal time limits? To what extent do the test scores correlate with measures of reading comprehension and computational skill? How do students' scores differ under different time limits? Answers to these and similar questions will help us to determine how well the test scores reflect the construct we are attempting to measure and the extent to which other factors might be influencing the scores.

Construct validation, then, is an attempt to clarify and verify the inferences to be made from assessment results. This involves a wide variety of procedures and many different types of evidence (including both content-related and criterion-related). As evidence accumulates from many different sources, our interpretations of the results are enriched and we are able to make them with great confidence.

Consequence of Using Assessment Results

Validity focuses on the inferences drawn from assessment results with regard to specific uses. Therefore, it is legitimate to ask, What are the consequences of using the assessment? Did the assessment improve learning, as intended, or did it contribute to adverse effects (e.g., lack of motivation, memorization, poor study habits)? For example, assessment procedures that focus on simple learning outcomes only (e.g., knowledge of facts) cannot provide valid evidence of reasoning and application skills, are likely to narrow the focus of student learning, and tend to reinforce poor learning strategies (e.g., rote learning). Thus, in evaluating the validity of the assessment used, one needs to look at what types of influence the assessments have on students. The following questions provide a general framework for considering some of the possible consequences of assessments on students.

1. Did use of the assessment improve motivation?
2. Did use of the assessment improve performance?
3. Did use of the assessment improve self-assessment skills?
4. Did use of the assessment contribute to transfer of learning to related areas?
5. Did use of the assessment encourage independent learning?
6. Did use of the assessment encourage good study habits?
7. Did use of the assessment contribute to a positive attitude toward schoolwork?
8. Did use of the assessment have an adverse effect in any of the above areas?

Judging the consequences of using the various assessment procedures is an important role of the teacher, if the results are to serve their intended purpose of improving learning. Both testing and performance assessments are most likely to have positive consequences when they are designed to assess a broad range of learning outcomes, they give special emphasis to complex learning outcomes, they are administered and scored (or judged) properly, they are used to identify students' strengths and weaknesses in learning, and the students view the assessments as fair, relevant, and useful for improving learning.

RELIABILITY

Reliability refers to the consistency of assessment results. Would we obtain about the same results if we used a different sample of the same type task? Would we obtain about the same results if we used the assessment at a different time? If a performance assessment is being rated, would different raters rate the performance the same way? These are the kinds of questions we are concerned about when we are considering the reliability of assessment results. Unless the results are generalizable over similar samples of tasks, time periods, and raters, we are not likely to have great confidence in them.

Because the methods for estimating reliability differ for tests and performance assessments, these will be treated separately.

Estimating the Reliability of Test Scores

The score an individual receives on a test is called the *obtained score, raw score,* or *observed score.* This score typically contains a certain amount of error. Some of this error may be *systematic error,* in that it consistently inflates or lowers the obtained score. For example, readily apparent clues in several test items might cause all students' scores to be higher than their achievement would warrant, or short time limits during testing might cause all students' scores to be lower than their "real achievement." The factors causing systematic errors are mainly due to inadequate testing practices. Thus, most of these errors can be eliminated by using care in constructing and administering tests. Removing systematic errors from test scores is especially important because they have a direct effect on the validity of the inferences made from the scores.

Some of the error in obtained scores is *random error,* in that it raises and lowers scores in an unpredictable manner. Random errors are caused by such things as temporary fluctuations in memory, variations in motivation and concentration from time to time, carelessness in marking answers, and luck in guessing. Such factors cause test scores to be inconsistent from one measurement to another. Sometimes an individual's obtained score will be higher than it should be and sometimes it will be lower. Although these errors are difficult to control and cannot be predicted with accuracy, an estimate of their influence can be obtained by various statistical procedures. Thus, when we talk about estimating the *reliability* of test scores or the amount of *measurement error* in test scores, we are referring to the influence of random errors.

Reliability refers to the *consistency* of test scores from one measurement to another. Because of the ever-present measurement error, we can expect a certain amount of variation in test performance from one time to another, from one sample of items to another, and from one part of the test to another. Reliability measures provide an estimate of how much variation we might expect under different conditions. The reliability of test scores is typically reported by means of a *reliability coefficient* or the *standard error of measurement* that is derived from it. Since both methods of estimating reliability require score variability, the procedures to be discussed are useful primarily with tests designed for norm-referenced interpretation.

As we noted earlier, a correlation coefficient expressing the relationship between a set of test scores and a criterion measure is called a *validity coefficient*. A *reliability coefficient* is also a correlation coefficient, but it indicates the correlation between two sets of measurements taken from the same procedure. We may, for example, administer the same test twice to a group, with a time interval in between (*test-retest* method); administer two equivalent forms of the test in close succession (*equivalent-forms* method); administer two equivalent forms of the test with a time interval in between (*test-retest with equivalent forms* method); or administer the test once and compute the consistency of the response within the test (*internal-consistency* method). Each of these methods of obtaining reliability provides a different type of information. Thus, reliability coefficients obtained with the different procedures are not interchangeable. Before deciding on the procedure to be used, we must determine what type of reliability evidence we are seeking. The four basic methods of estimating reliability and the type of information each provides are shown in Table 4.5.

TEST-RETEST METHOD.   The test-retest method requires administering the same form of the test to the same group after some time interval. The time between the two administrations may be just a few days or several years. The length of the time interval should fit the type of interpretation to be made from the results. Thus, if we are interested in using test scores only to group students for more effective learning, short-term stability may be sufficient. On the other hand, if we are attempting to predict vocational success or make some other long-range predictions, we would desire evidence of stability over a period of years.

TABLE 4.5 Methods of Estimating Reliability of Test Scores

Method	Type of Information Provided
Test-retest method	The stability of test scores over a given period of time.
Equivalent-forms method	The consistency of the test scores over different forms of the test (that is, different samples of items).
Test-retest with equivalent forms	The consistency of test scores over *both* a time interval and different forms of the test.
Internal-consistency methods	The consistency of test scores over different parts of the test.

Note: Scorer reliability should also be considered when evaluating the responses to *supply-type* items (for example, essay tests). This is typically done by having the test papers scored independently by two scorers and then correlating the two sets of scores. Agreement among scorers, however, is not a substitute for the methods of estimating reliability shown in the table.

Test-retest reliability coefficients are influenced both by errors within the measurement procedure and by the day-to-day stability of the students' responses. Thus, longer time periods between testing will result in lower reliability coefficients, due to the greater changes in the students. In reporting test-retest reliability coefficients, then, it is important to include the time interval. For example, a report might state: "The stability of test scores obtained on the same form over a three-month period was .90." This makes it possible to determine the extent to which the reliability data are significant for a particular interpretation.

EQUIVALENT-FORMS METHOD. With this method, two equivalent forms of a test (also called **alternate forms** or **parallel forms**) are administered to the same group during the same testing session. The test forms are equivalent in the sense that they are built to measure the same abilities (that is, they are built to the same set of specifications), but for determining reliability it is also important that they be constructed independently. When this is the case, the reliability coefficient indicates the adequacy of the test sample. That is, a high reliability coefficient would indicate that the two independent samples are apparently measuring the same thing. A low reliability coefficient, of course, would indicate that the two forms are measuring different behavior and that therefore both samples of items are questionable.

Reliability coefficients determined by this method take into account errors within the measurement procedures and consistency over different samples of items, but they do not include the day-to-day stability of the students' responses.

TEST-RETEST METHOD WITH EQUIVALENT FORMS. This is a combination of both methods. Here, two different forms of the same test are administered with time intervening. This is the most demanding estimate of reliability, since it takes into account all possible sources of variation. The reliability coefficient reflects errors within the testing procedure, consistency over different samples of items, and the day-to-day stability of the students' responses. For most purposes, this is probably the most useful type of reliability, since it enables us to estimate how generalizable the test results are over the various conditions. A high reliability coefficient obtained by this method would indicate that a test score represents not only present test performance but also what test performance is likely to be at another time or on a different sample of equivalent items.

INTERNAL-CONSISTENCY METHODS. These methods require only a single administration of a test. One procedure, the *split-half* method, involves scoring the odd items and the even items separately and correlating the two sets of scores. This correlation coefficient indicates the degree to which the two arbitrarily selected halves of the test provide the same results. Thus, it reports on the internal consistency of the test. Like the equivalent-forms method, this procedure takes into account errors within the testing procedure and consistency over different samples of items, but it omits the day-to-day stability of the students' responses.

Since the correlation coefficient based on the odd and even items indicates the relationship between two halves of the test, the reliability coefficient for the total test is determined by applying the Spearman-Brown prophecy formula. A simplified version of this formula is as follows:

$$\text{Reliability of total test} = \frac{2 \times \text{reliability for } {}^{1}/_{2} \text{ test}}{1 + \text{reliability for } {}^{1}/_{2} \text{ test}}$$

Thus, if we obtained a correlation coefficient of .60 for two halves of a test, the reliability for the total test would be computed as follows:

$$\text{Reliability of total test} = \frac{2 \times .60}{1 + .60} = \frac{1.20}{1.60} = .75$$

This application of the Spearman-Brown formula makes clear a useful principle of test reliability: The reliability of a test can be increased by lengthening it. This formula shows how much reliability will increase when the length of the test is doubled. Application of the formula, however, assumes that the test is lengthened by adding items like those already in the test.

Another internal-consistency method of estimating reliability is by use of the **Kuder-Richardson Formula 20** (KR-20). Kuder and Richardson developed other formulas but this one is probably the most widely used with standardized tests. It requires a single test administration, a determination of the proportion of individuals passing each item, and the standard deviation of the total set of scores. The formula is not especially helpful in understanding how to interpret the scores, but knowing what the coefficient means is important. Basically, the KR-20 is equivalent to an average of all split-half coefficients when the test is split in all possible ways. Where all items in a test are measuring the same thing (e.g., math reasoning), the result should approximate the split-half reliability estimate. Where the test items are measuring a variety of skills or content areas (i.e., less homogeneous), the KR-20 estimate will be lower than the split-half reliability estimate. Thus, the KR-20 method is useful with homogeneous tests but can be misleading if used with a test designed to measure heterogeneous content.

Internal-consistency methods are used because they require that the test be administered only once. They should not be used with speeded tests, however, because a spuriously high reliability estimate will result. If speed is an important factor in the testing (that is, if the students do not have time to attempt all the items), other methods should be used to estimate reliability.

STANDARD ERROR OF MEASUREMENT.   The standard error of measurement is an especially useful way of expressing test reliability, because it indicates the amount of error to allow for when interpreting individual test scores. The standard error is derived from a reliability coefficient by means of the following formula:

$$\text{Standard error of measurement} = s\sqrt{1 - r_n}$$

where s = the standard deviation and r_n = the reliability coefficient. In applying this formula to a reliability estimate of .60 obtained for a test where $s = 4.5$, the following results would be obtained.

$$\text{Standard error of measurement} = 4.5\sqrt{1 - .60}$$
$$= 4.5\sqrt{.40}$$
$$= 4.5 \times .63$$
$$= 2.8$$

The standard error of measurement shows how many points we must add to, and subtract from, an individual's test score in order to obtain "reasonable limits" for estimating that individual's true score (that is, a score free of error). In our example, the standard error would be rounded to 3 score points. Thus, if a given student scored 35 on this test, that student's *score band,* for establishing reasonable limits, would range from 32 (35 − 3) to 38 (35 + 3). In other words, we could be reasonably sure that the score band of 32 to 38 included the student's true score (statistically, there are two chances out of three that it does). The standard errors of test scores provide a means of allowing for error during test interpretation. If we view test performance in terms of score bands (also called *confidence bands*), we are not likely to overinterpret small differences between test scores.

For the test user, the standard error of measurement is probably more useful than the reliability coefficient. Although reliability coefficients can be used in evaluating the quality of a test and in comparing the relative merits of different tests, the standard error of measurement is directly applicable to the interpretation of individual test scores.

RELIABILITY OF CRITERION-REFERENCED MASTERY TESTS. As noted earlier, the traditional methods for computing reliability require score variability (that is, a spread of scores) and are therefore useful mainly with norm-referenced tests. When used with criterion-referenced tests, they are likely to provide misleading results. Since criterion-referenced tests are not designed to emphasize differences among individuals, they typically have limited score variability. This restricted spread of scores will result in low correlation estimates of reliability, even if the consistency of our test results is adequate for the use to be made of them.

When a criterion-referenced test is used to determine mastery, our primary concern is with how consistently our test classifies masters and nonmasters. If we administered two equivalent forms of a test to the same group of students, for example, we would like the results of both forms to identify the same students as having mastered the material. Such perfect agreement is unrealistic, of course, since some students near the cutoff score are likely to shift from one category to the other on the basis of errors of measurement (due to such factors as lucky guesses or lapses of memory). However, if too many students demonstrated mastery on one form but nonmastery on the other, our decisions concerning who mastered the material would be hopelessly confused. Thus, the reliability of mastery tests can be determined by computing the percentage of consistent mastery-nonmastery decisions over the two forms of the test.

FORM B

		NONMASTERS	MASTERS
	MASTERS	2	30
FORM A			
	NONMASTERS	6	2

FIGURE 4.3   Classification of 40 Students as Masters or Nonmasters on Two Forms of a Criterion-Referenced Test.

The procedure for comparing test performance on two equivalent forms of a test is relatively simple. After both forms have been administered to a group of students, the resulting data can be placed in a two-by-two table like that shown in Figure 4.3. These data are based on two forms of a 25-item test administered to 40 students. Mastery was set at 80 percent correct (20 items), so all students who scored 20 or higher on both forms of the test were placed in the upper right-hand cell (30 students), and all those who scored below 20 on both forms were placed in the lower left-hand cell (6 students). The remaining students demonstrated mastery on one form and nonmastery on the other (4 students). Since 36 of the 40 students were consistently classified by the two forms of the test, we apparently have reasonably good consistency.

We can compute the percentage of consistency for this procedure with the following formula:

$$\% \text{ Consistency} = \frac{\text{Masters (both forms)} + \text{Nonmasters (both forms)}}{\text{Total number in group}} \times 100$$

$$\% \text{ Consistency} = \frac{30 + 6}{40} \times 100 = 90\%$$

This procedure is simple to use but it has a few limitations. First, two forms of the test are required. This may not be as serious as it seems, however, since in most mastery programs more than one form of the test is needed for retesting those students who fail to demonstrate mastery on the first try. Second, it is difficult to determine what percentage of decision consistency is necessary for a given situation. As with other measures of reliability, the greater the consistency, the more satisfied we will be, but what constitutes a minimum acceptable level? There is no simple answer to such a question because it depends on the number of items in the test and the consequences of the decision. If a nonmastery decision for a student simply means further study and later retesting, low consistency might be acceptable. However, if the mastery-nonmastery decision concerns whether to give a student a high school certificate, as in some competency testing programs, then a high level of consistency will be demanded. Since there are no clear guidelines for setting minimum levels, we will need to depend on experience in various situations to determine what are reasonable expectations.

More sophisticated techniques have been developed for estimating the reliability of criterion-referenced tests, but the numerous issues and problems

BOX 4.2 Factors That Lower the Reliability of Test Scores

1. Test scores are based on too few items. (*Remedy:* Use longer tests or accumulate scores from several short tests.)
2. Range of scores is too limited. (*Remedy:* Adjust item difficulty to obtain larger spread of scores.)
3. Testing conditions are inadequate. (*Remedy:* Arrange opportune time for administration and eliminate interruptions, noise, and other disrupting factors.)
4. Scoring is subjective. (*Remedy:* Prepare scoring keys and follow carefully when scoring essay answers.)

involved in their use go beyond the scope of this book. See Box 4.2 for factors that lower reliability of test scores.

Estimating the Reliability of Performance Assessments

Performance assessments are commonly evaluated by using scoring rubrics that describe a number of levels of performance, ranging from high to low (e.g., outstanding to inadequate). The performance for each student is then judged and placed in the category that best fits the quality of the performance. The reliability of these performance judgments can be determined by obtaining and comparing the scores of two judges who scored the performances independently. The scores of the two judges can be correlated to determine the consistency of the scoring, or the proportion of agreement in scoring can be computed.

Let's assume that a performance task, such as writing sample, was obtained from 32 students and two teachers independently rated the students' performance on a four-point scale where 4 is high and 1 is low. The results of the ratings by the two judges are shown in Table 4.6. The ratings for Judge 1 are presented in the columns and those for Judge 2 are presented in the rows. Thus, Judge 1 assigned a score of 4 to seven students and Judge 2 assigned a score of 4 to eight students. Their ratings agreed on six of the students and

TABLE 4.6 Classification of Students Based on Performance Ratings by Two Independent Judges

		Ratings by Judge 1				
	Scores	1	2	3	4	Row Totals
Ratings by Judge 2	4			2	6	8
	3		3	7	1	11
	2	2	6			8
	1	5				5
	Column Totals	7	9	9	7	32

disagreed by one score on three of the students. The number of rating agreements can be seen in the boxes on the diagonal from the upper right-hand corner to the lower left-hand corner. The percentage of agreement can be computed by adding the numbers in these diagonal boxes ($6 + 7 + 6 + 5 = 24$), dividing by the total number of students in the group (32), and multiplying by 100.

$$\text{Rater agreement} = \frac{24}{32} \times 100 = 75\%$$

By inspection, we can see that all ratings were within one score of each other. The results also indicate that Judge 2 was a more lenient rater than Judge 1 (i.e., gave more high ratings and fewer low ratings). Thus, a table of this nature can be used to determine the consistency of ratings and the extent to which leniency can account for the disagreements.

Although the need for two raters will limit the use of this method, it seems reasonable to expect two teachers in the same area to make periodic checks on the scoring of performance assessments. This not only will provide information on the consistency of the scoring, but will provide the teachers with insight into some of their rating idiosyncrasies. See Box 4.3 for factors that lower the reliability of performance assessment.

The percentage of agreement between the scores assigned by independent judges is a common method of estimating the reliability of performance assessments. It should be noted, however, that this reports on only one type of consistency—*the consistency of the scoring*. It does not indicate the consistency of performance over similar tasks or over different time periods. We can obtain a crude measure of this by examining the performance of students over tasks and time, but a more adequate analysis requires an understanding of **generalizability** theory, which is too technical for treatment here.

BOX 4.3   Factors That Lower the Reliability of Performance Assessments

1. Insufficient number of tasks. (*Remedy:* Accumulate results from several assessments. For example, several writing samples.)
2. Poorly structured assessment procedures. (*Remedy:* Define carefully the nature of the tasks, the conditions for obtaining the assessment, and the criteria for scoring or judging the results.)
3. Dimensions of performance are specific to the tasks. (*Remedy:* Increase generalizability of performance by selecting tasks that have dimensions like those in similar tasks.)
4. Inadequate scoring guides for judgmental scoring. (*Remedy:* Use scoring rubrics or rating scales that specifically describe the criteria and levels of quality.)
5. Scoring judgments that are influenced by personal bias. (*Remedy:* Check scores or ratings with those of an independent judge. Receive training in judging and rating, if possible.)

Summary of Points

1. Validity is the most important quality to consider in assessment and is concerned with the appropriateness, meaningfulness, and usefulness of the specific inferences made from assessment results.

2. Validity is a *unitary concept* based on various forms of evidence (content-related, criterion-related, construct-related, and consequences).

3. Content-related evidence of validity refers to how well the sample of tasks represents the domain of tasks to be assessed.

4. Content-related evidence of validity is of major concern in achievement assessment and is built in by following systematic procedures. Validity is lowered by inadequate assessment practices.

5. Criterion-related evidence of validity refers to the degree to which assessment results are related to some other valued measure called a *criterion*.

6. Criterion-related evidence may be based on a predictive study or a concurrent study and is typically expressed by a correlation coefficient or expectancy table.

7. Construct-related evidence of validity refers to how well performance on assessment tasks can be explained in terms of psychological characteristics, or constructs (e.g., mathematical reasoning).

8. The construct-related category of evidence is the most comprehensive. It includes evidence from both content-related and criterion-related studies plus other types of evidence that help clarify the meaning of the assessment results.

9. Consequences of using the assessment are also an important consideration in validity—both positive and negative consequences.

10. Reliability refers to the consistency of scores (i.e., to the degree to which the scores are free from measurement error).

11. Reliability of test scores is typically reported by means of a reliability coefficient or a standard error of measurement.

12. Reliability coefficients can be obtained by a number of different methods (e.g., test-retest, equivalent-forms, internal-consistency) and each one measures a different type of consistency (e.g., over time, over different samples of items, over different parts of the test).

13. Reliability of test scores tends to be lower when the test is short, range of scores is limited, testing conditions are inadequate, and scoring is subjective.

14. The standard error of measurement indicates the amount of error to allow for when interpreting individual test scores.

15. Score bands (or *confidence bands*) take into account the error of measurement and help prevent the overinterpretation of small differences between test scores.

16. The reliability of criterion-referenced mastery tests can be obtained by computing the percentage of agreement between two forms of the test in classifying individuals as masters and nonmasters.

17. The reliability of performance-based assessments is commonly determined by the degree of agreement between two or more judges who rate the performance independently.

References and Additional Reading

American Educational Research Association. *Standards for Educational and Psychological Testing* (Washington, DC: AERA, 1999).

Linn, R. L., & Gronlund, N. E. *Measurement and Assessment in Teaching,* 8th ed. (Upper Saddle River, NJ: Merrill/Prentice Hall, 2000).

Nitko, A. J., & Brookhart, S. M. *Educational Assessment of Students,* 5th ed. (Upper Saddle River, NJ: Merrill/Prentice Hall, Pearson Education, 2007).

Oosterhoff, A. C. *Classroom Applications of Educational Measurement,* 3rd ed. (Upper Saddle River, NJ: Merrill/Prentice Hall, 2001).

Self-Assessment

MULTIPLE CHOICE

DIRECTIONS: Select the best answer for each item by circling the corresponding letter.

1. The appropriateness and meaningfulness of the inferences we make from assessment results refers to a test's
   (a) reliability
   (b) validity
   (c) objectivity
   (d) difficulty

2. To obtain evidence of validity based on content considerations, you would examine the
   (a) expectancy table
   (b) size of the correlation coefficient
   (c) type of criterion used
   (d) table of specifications

3. Interpreting a student's chances of success in college based on the Scholastic Aptitude Test (SAT) requires a
   (a) predictive study
   (b) criterion study
   (c) construct study
   (d) concurrent study

4. External influences such as disruptions during testing that may lower the scores of the students are referred to as
   (a) systematic errors
   (b) standard errors
   (c) random errors
   (d) reliability errors

5. Ensuring an assessment has a good representative sample of relevant test items is a characteristic of
   (a) validity
   (b) referencing
   (c) reliability
   (d) weighting

SUPPLY-TYPE ITEMS

DIRECTIONS: Using the test scores below, calculate the correlation coefficient between test 1 and test 2. Place your answers on the lines provided.

Student	Test 1	Test 2
A	9	10
B	7	6
C	5	3
D	3	6
E	1	3
F	1	3
G	3	5
H	7	6
I	5	1
J	9	7

6. What is the correlation between test 1 and test 2? _____

SUPPLY-TYPE ITEMS

DIRECTIONS: Using the information provided in the paragraph that accompanies each of the following test items, provide an answer on the lines provided.

7. Twenty students are given a 50-item multiple-choice test. To determine the internal consistency of the test, the test has been split and the score based on odd items and the score based on the even items for each student has been calculated. The correlation between the two halves is .82.

   What is the Spearman-Brown reliability coefficient for the test? _____

8. Thirty students are given a 100-item multiple-choice test. The standard deviation of the raw scores is 11 and the Spearman-Brown reliability coefficient for the test is .93.

   What is the standard error of measurement for the test? _____

9. If one of the students in the question above received a raw score of 83, what would be the confidence band around the raw score? _____

Restricted-Response Essay

10. The authors of your textbook discuss the factors that lower the validity of assessment results. Describe each factor. Confine your answer to one page.

5 | PREPARING AND USING ACHIEVEMENT TESTS

Studying this chapter should enable you to

1. List the steps to follow in preparing an achievement test.
2. Prepare a set of specifications for a test.
3. Describe the relative merits of selection-type and supply-type tests.
4. Match test items to the specific learning outcomes they measure.
5. Describe the factors to consider when preparing items for a test.
6. Describe how to arrange items in a test.
7. Write clear directions for a test.
8. Review and evaluate an assembled test.
9. Administer a test properly.
10. Evaluate the effectiveness of a set of test items.

All too frequently teachers prepare a classroom achievement test by reviewing the content covered during the instruction and preparing questions for each area of content. This procedure typically results in a series of questions that measure how well the students can recall what they have learned. This probably accounts for the fact that so many classroom tests are limited to remembering factual knowledge, to the neglect of more complex outcomes such as understanding application, analysis, evaluation, and creating.

The proper preparation and use of an achievement test that measures a broad band of learning outcomes in a balanced manner involves the following steps.

1. Specifying the instructional objectives.
2. Preparing the test specifications.
3. Constructing relevant test items.
4. Arranging the items in the test.
5. Preparing clear directions.
6. Reviewing and evaluating the assembled test.
7. Administering the test and making an item analysis.

Each of these steps will be described in turn.

SPECIFYING THE INSTRUCTIONAL OBJECTIVES

As noted earlier, the first step in preparing instructional objectives is to list the general objectives as intended learning outcomes. The following list illustrates the procedure for a unit on planning an achievement test.

At the end of this unit in achievement test planning the student will demonstrate that he or she

1. Remembers the meaning of common terms.
2. Remembers specific facts.
3. Remembers the basic procedures.
4. Understands the relevant principles.
5. Applies the principles.

Note that these statements of general learning outcomes are drawn directly from Bloom's Cognitive Taxonomy and have been deliberately kept free of specific course content so that with only slight modification they can be used with various units of study. As we shall see later, the test specifications provide a means of relating intended outcomes to specific subject matter topics.

This list of general outcomes could, of course, be expanded by making the statements more specific, and in some cases it may be desirable to do so. The number of general learning outcomes to use is somewhat arbitrary, but somewhere between 5 and 15 items provide a list that is both useful and manageable. Typically, a shorter list is satisfactory for a unit of study, while a more comprehensive list is needed for summative testing at the end of a course.

Defining the General Outcomes in Specific Terms

When a satisfactory list of general learning outcomes has been identified and clearly stated, the next step is to list the specific types of student performance that are to be accepted as evidence that the outcomes have been achieved. For example, what specific types of performance will show that a student "knows the meaning of common terms" or "understands the relevant principles of testing"? For these two areas the specific learning outcomes may be listed as follows:

1. Remembers the meaning of common terms.

    1.1 Identifies the correct definitions of terms.
    1.2 Identifies the meaning of terms when used in context.
    1.3 Distinguishes between terms on basis of meaning.
    1.4 Selects the most appropriate terms when describing testing procedures.

4. Understands the relevant principles.

    4.1 Describes each principle in his or her own words.
    4.2 Matches a specific example to each principle.
    4.3 Explains the relevance of each principle to the major steps in test planning.

4.4 Predicts the most probable effect of violating each of the principles.
4.5 Formulates a test plan that is in harmony with the principles.

Note that the terms used to describe the specific learning outcomes indicate student performance that can be demonstrated to an outside observer. That is, they are *observable* responses that can be called forth by test items. The key terms are listed below to emphasize what is meant by defining learning outcomes in *specific performance terms*.

Identifies	Matches
Distinguishes between	Explains
Selects	Predicts
Describes	Formulates

Action verbs such as these indicate precisely what the student is able to do to demonstrate achievement. Such vague and indefinite terms as "learns," "sees," "realizes," and "is familiar with" should be avoided, since they do not clearly indicate the terminal performance to be measured.

Sample action verbs for stating specific learning outcomes at each level of the cognitive domain of the revised taxonomy are presented in Table 5.1. Although certain action verbs may be used at several different levels (e.g., "identifies"), the table provides a useful guide for defining intended outcomes in performance terms. For more comprehensive lists of action verbs, see Gronlund and Brookhart (2009) listed at the end of this chapter.

In defining the general learning outcomes in specific performance terms, it is typically impossible to list all of the relevant types of performance. All we can do is list a representative sample of them to show what students can do when they have achieved the intended learning outcome.

TABLE 5.1 Illustrative Action Verbs for Defining Objectives in the Cognitive Domain of the Revised Taxonomy

Taxonomy Categories	Sample Verbs for Stating Specific Learning Outcomes
Remember	Identifies, names, defines, describes, lists, matches, selects, outlines
Understand	Classifies, explains, summarizes, converts, predicts, interprets, illustrates
Apply	Demonstrates, computes, solves, modifies, arranges, operates, relates, uses
Analyze	Differentiates, diagrams, estimates, separates, orders, subdivides, distinguishes between
Evaluate	Judges, criticizes, compares, justifies, concludes, discriminates, detects
Create	Combines, creates, formulates, designs, composes, constructs, rearranges, revises

PREPARING THE TEST SPECIFICATIONS

At this point, general outcomes and specific terms have been developed. As stated earlier, these should not relate to specific course content. The writing of test items should be guided by a carefully prepared set of test specifications. The function of the specifications is to (1) describe the achievement domain being measured, (2) link the achievement domains to course subject matter, and (3) provide guidelines for obtaining a representative sample of test tasks. Although the nature and detail of test specifications can be expected to vary considerably, here we shall describe one of the more commonly recommended procedures. In the construction of an **achievement test**, one of the most widely used devices has been a two-way chart called a *table of specifications*.

Building a Table of Specifications

Preparing a table of specifications involves (1) selecting the learning outcomes to be tested, (2) outlining the subject matter, and (3) making a two-way chart. The two-way chart describes the sample of items to be included in the test.

SELECTING THE LEARNING OUTCOMES TO BE TESTED.

The learning outcomes for a particular course will depend on the specific nature of the course, the objectives attained in previous courses, the philosophy of the school, the special needs of the students, and a host of other local factors that have a bearing on the instructional program. Despite the variation from course to course, most lists of instructional objectives will include learning outcomes in the following areas: (1) recall of knowledge, (2) intellectual abilities and skills, (3) general skills (laboratory, performance, communication, work-study), and (4) attitudes, interests, and appreciations. It is in the first two areas covered by the cognitive domain of the taxonomy that achievement testing is most useful. Learning outcomes in the other areas are typically evaluated by rating scales, checklists, anecdotal records, inventories, and similar nontest assessment procedures. Thus, the first step is to separate from the list of learning outcomes those that are testable by paper-and-pencil tests. The selected list of learning outcomes should, of course, be defined in specific terms, as described in the previous section. Clarifying the specific types of performance to be called forth by the test will aid in constructing test items that are most relevant to the intended learning outcomes.

OUTLINING THE SUBJECT MATTER.

The stated learning outcomes specify how students are expected to react to the subject matter of a unit or course. Although it is possible to include both the student performance and the specific subject matter the student is to react toward in the same statement, it is usually desirable to list them separately. The reason for this is that the student can react in the same way to many different areas of subject matter, and he can react in many different ways to the same area of subject matter. For example, when we state that a student can "define a term in her own words," "recall a specific fact," or "identify an example of a principle," these types of performance can be applied to almost any area of subject matter. Since particular types of student performance can overlap a variety of subject matter areas, and vice versa, it is more convenient to list each aspect of performance and subject matter separately and then to relate them in the table of specifications.

The content of a course may be outlined in detail for teaching purposes, but for test planning only the major categories need be listed. The following outline of subject matter topics based on a unit on achievement testing illustrates sufficient detail for the test plan.

A. Role of testing in the instructional process
    1. Instructional decisions and test types
    2. Influence of tests on learning and instruction
B. Principles of achievement testing
    1. Relation to instructional objectives
    2. Representative sampling
    3. Relevance of items to outcomes
    4. Relevance of test to use of results
    5. Reliability of results
    6. Improvement of learning
C. Norm-referenced versus criterion-referenced testing
D. Planning the test
    1. Determining the purpose of the test
    2. Identifying the intended learning outcomes
    3. Preparing the test specifications
    4. Constructing relevant test items

MAKING THE TWO-WAY CHART.   When the learning outcomes have been selected and clearly defined and the course content outlined, the two-way chart should be prepared. This is called a **table of specifications.** It relates outcomes to content and indicates the relative weight to be given to each of the various areas. As noted earlier, the purpose of the table is to provide assurance that the test will measure a representative sample of the learning outcomes and the subject matter topics to be measured.

An example of a table of specifications for a summative test on a unit on achievement testing is given in Table 5.2. Note that only the general learning outcomes and the major subject matter categories have been included. A more detailed table may be desirable for test purposes, but this is sufficient for illustration.

The numbers in each cell of the table indicate the number of test items to be devoted to that area. For example, 15 items in the test will measure knowledge of terms; 4 of them pertain to the "role of tests in instruction," 4 to "principles of testing," 4 to "norm-referenced versus criterion-referenced," and 3 to "planning the test." The number of items assigned to each cell is determined by the weight given to each learning outcome and each subject matter area.

A number of factors will enter into assigning relative weights to each learning outcome and each content area. How important is each area in the total learning experience? How much time was devoted to each area during

TABLE 5.2 Table of Specifications for a Summative Test on a Unit for Achievement Testing

Outcomes Content	Remembers			Understands Principles	Applies Principles	Total Number of Items
	Terms	*Facts*	*Procedures*			
Role of Tests in Instruction	4	4		2		10
Principles of Testing	4	3	2	6	5	20
Norm-Referenced versus Criterion-Referenced	4	3	3			10
Planning the Test	3	5	5	2	5	20
Total Number of Items	15	15	10	10	10	60

instruction? Which outcomes have the greater retention and transfer value? What relative importance do curriculum specialists assign to each area? These and similar criteria must be considered. In the final analysis, however, the weights assigned in the table should faithfully reflect the emphasis given during instruction. In Table 5.2, for example, it is assumed that twice as much emphasis was given to "planning the test" (20 items) as was given to "norm-referenced versus criterion-referenced" (10 items). Similarly, it is assumed that knowledge outcomes were given approximately two-thirds of the emphasis during instruction (40 items) and that understands and application outcomes were each given approximately one-sixth of the total emphasis (10 items each).

In summary, preparing a table of specifications includes the following steps:

1. Identify the learning outcomes and content areas to be measured by the test.
2. Weight the learning outcomes and content areas in terms of their relative importance.
3. Build the table in accordance with these relative weights by distributing the test items proportionately among the relevant cells of the table.

The resulting two-way table indicates the type of test needed to measure the learning outcomes and course content in a balanced manner. Thus, the table of specifications serves the test maker like a blueprint. It specifies the number and the nature of the items in the test, and it thereby provides a guide for item writing.

CONSIDERATIONS IN CONSTRUCTING RELEVANT TEST ITEMS

The construction of a set of relevant test items is greatly simplified if the intended learning outcomes have been clearly defined and the test specifications carefully prepared. The quality of the test will then depend on how closely the test maker can match the specifications. Here we shall confine our discussion to some of the general specifications in preparing test items. More detailed procedures and rules for item writing will be described in the chapters that follow.

Selecting the Types of Test Items to Use

The items used in achievement tests can be classified as either *selection-type* items or *supply-type* items. The selection-type item presents students with a set of possible responses from which they are to select the most appropriate answer. The supply-type item requires students to create and supply their own answers. These two major categories can be used to classify the most widely used item types as follows.

Selection-Type Items
1. Multiple choice
2. True-false
3. Matching
4. Interpretive exercise

Supply-Type Items
1. Short answer
2. Essay (restricted response)
3. Essay (extended response)

These categories are sometimes referred to as *recognition* and *recall* items. This is a case of mislabeling that confuses the method of responding with the mental reaction needed to make the response. When measuring knowledge of facts, test responses might be limited to either the recognition or recall of the answer. However, when measuring complex learning outcomes with selection-type items, the answer is not achieved through mere recognition of a previously learned answer. It typically involves some use of higher mental processes to arrive at a solution (e.g., verbal or mathematical reasoning) before the correct answer can be selected. Similarly, a short-answer item may require reasoning or problem solving rather than simply recalling and supplying factual information. Essay answers, of course, typically require analysis, synthesis, and evaluation skills in addition to recall. Using the *selection* and *supply* labels makes clear how the responses are made but it does not imply limits on the types of learning outcomes that can be measured with each.

In deciding which item types to use in a test, a guiding principle should be: *Use the item types that provide the most direct measures of student performance specified by the intended learning outcome.* Thus, if you want to determine whether students can spell, have them spell from dictation. If you want to determine whether students can solve mathematics problems, have them solve problems and supply the answers. If you want to determine whether students can write, have them write something. Use selection-type items for supply-type outcomes only if there is a compelling reason for doing so (e.g., electronic scoring) and then take into account, during interpretation of the results, that a less direct measure has been used. In some cases, of course, both types of items are useful in the same area. For example, a writing project may provide the best evidence of writing skill, but a selection-type test would provide the most systematic coverage of the elements of grammar needed for effective writing.

There are a number of achievement areas where either selection-type items or supply-type items would measure equally well. In these cases, our choice between them must be based on other item characteristics. The preparation of good selection-type items is difficult, and students can get a proportion of answers correct by guessing. However, these disadvantages are offset by the fact that (1) they can be scored quickly and objectively (i.e., scorers agree on the answers), (2) they eliminate bluffing, (3) they eliminate the influence of writing skill, (4) they provide an extensive sample of student performance (because of the large number of items used), and (5) they provide for the identification of specific learning errors. In comparison, supply-type items are easier to construct (although harder than commonly believed) but more difficult to score. The scoring of short-answer items is contaminated by answers of varying degrees of correctness and by adjustments needed for misspellings. The scoring of essay tests is tedious, time consuming, and influenced by bluffing, writing skill, and the shifting of standards during scoring. Another major shortcoming of supply-type items is the limited sample of learning tasks that can be measured. The short-answer item is restricted primarily to measuring factual knowledge. Although the essay test is especially suited to measuring complex learning outcomes, its sampling is limited by the relatively few questions that can be included in a test.

A summary comparison of the relative merits of selection-type and supply-type items is presented in Table 5.3. Although this should serve as a guide in selecting the types of items to use in a given test, as noted earlier, the most important question to ask is: *Does this item type provide the most direct measure of the intended learning outcome?* If the various item types are equal in this regard, the selection-type items would be favored because of the broad sampling, the objective scoring, and the pinpointing of specific learning errors.

Matching Items to Specific Learning Outcomes

Effective achievement testing requires that a set of test items be constructed that calls forth the performance described in the intended learning outcomes. While we can never be certain of a perfect correspondence between outcome and item, the following examples illustrate how items should be written to measure the specific type of performance stated in the specific learning outcome.

TABLE 5.3 Summary of the Relative Merits of Selection-Type Items and Supply-Type Items

Characteristic	Selection-Type Items	Supply-Type Items Short Answer	Essay
Measures factual information	Yes	Yes	Yes(*)
Measures understanding	Yes	No(**)	Yes
Measures synthesis	No(**)	No(**)	Yes
Easy to construct	No	Yes	Yes
Samples broadly	Yes	Yes	No
Eliminates bluffing	Yes	No	No
Eliminates writing skill	Yes	No	No
Eliminates blind guessing	No	Yes	Yes
Easy to score	Yes	No	No
Scoring is objective	Yes	No	No
Pinpoints learning errors	Yes	Yes	No
Encourages originality	No	No	Yes

(*)The essay test can measure knowledge of facts, but because of scoring and sampling problems, it probably should not be used for this purpose.

(**)These items can be designed to measure limited aspects of these characteristics.

EXAMPLES

Specific Learning Outcome: Defines terms in student's own words.

Directions: Define each of the following terms in a sentence or two.

1. Taxonomy
2. Cognitive
3. Measurement
4. Evaluation

Specific Learning Outcome: Identifies procedural steps in planning for a test.

1. Which one of the following steps should be completed first in planning for an achievement test?

   A. Select the types of test items to use.
   B. Decide on the length of the test.
   *C. Define the intended learning outcomes.
   D. Prepare the test specifications.

Specific Learning Outcome: Distinguishes between sound and unsound principles of achievement testing.

---

*The correct answer is indicated throughout this book by an asterisk.

Directions: Read each of the following statements. If the statement indicates a sound principle of achievement testing, circle the S; if it indicates an unsound principle, circle the U.

    *S   U   1. The specific learning outcomes to be tested should be stated in terms of student performance.

    S   *U   2. Achievement testing should be limited to outcomes that can be measured objectively.

    *S   U   3. Each achievement test item should measure a clearly defined type of student performance.

It should be noted in these examples that each specific learning outcome provides a precise definition of the student performance to be measured, and the test item simply provides a task that makes measurement of the specified performance possible.

Improving the Functioning Content of Items

If test items are to call forth the performance described in the intended learning outcomes, great care must be taken in phrasing the items. We need to eliminate all barriers that might prevent a knowledgeable person from responding and all clues that might lead the uninformed to the correct answer. Only those who have achieved the outcome being measured should get the item right. All others (no matter how intelligent) should miss it.

Some of the common *barriers* to be avoided during test preparation are:

Vocabulary that is unnecessarily difficult.

Sentence structure that is unnecessarily complex.

Statements containing ambiguity.

Unclear pictorial materials.

Directions that are vague.

Material reflecting race, ethnic, or sex bias.

Awareness of such barriers during the planning and preparation of the test is the first step in their elimination. Essentially, we can avoid these barriers by (1) writing each test item so that it presents a clearly formulated task, (2) stating the items in simple, clear language, (3) keeping the items free from biased and nonfunctional material, and (4) using a test format and directions that contribute to effective test taking. Much of the material presented later in this book is directed toward constructing tests that prevent extraneous factors from distorting the test results.

Some of the common *clues* to be avoided during test preparation are:

Verbal associations that give away the answer.

Grammatical inconsistencies that eliminate wrong answers.

Specific determiners that make certain answers probable (e.g., sometimes) and others improbable (e.g., always).

Stereotyped or textbook phrasing of correct answers.

Length or location of correct answers.

Material in an item that aids in answering another item.

Just as in controlling extraneous factors that provide barriers to the correct answer, clues such as these can be eliminated by being aware of them and by following sound principles of test construction. Many of the rules for item writing and test preparation in the chapters that follow provide guidelines for this purpose.

Determining the Number of Test Items to Use

The number of items to use should be indicated in the test specifications, as noted earlier, and is modified by a number of practical constraints, such as the following:

1. Age of the students tested.
2. Time available for testing.
3. Type of test items used.
4. Type of interpretation to be made.

In the testing of elementary school students, the testing time typically should be no more than 20 or 30 minutes so that proper motivation is maintained. At the high school and college levels, students can be given tests lasting several hours (e.g., a final examination), but most tests are limited to a testing time of 40 to 50 minutes because of the length of the typical class period.

In matching the number of items to available testing time, we are faced with the problem of estimating how many items students can complete per minute. Unfortunately, there are no simple answers. The size of the final product depends on the type of test item, the complexity of the learning outcome measured, and the age of the students. As a guideline, high school and college students should be able to answer one multiple-choice item, three short-answer items, or three true-false items per minute when the items are measuring recall of factual knowledge. For measuring more complex learning outcomes such as understanding and application, and for testing younger age groups, more time per item is needed. In estimating the number of items to be used, keep in mind the slower students in the group, because it is desirable to give all students an opportunity to complete the test. Experience in testing a given group of students is frequently the only dependable guide for determining proper test length.

In addition to our concern with total test length, consideration must be given to the number of test items needed for each type of interpretation to be made. This issue is especially crucial in criterion-referenced interpretation, where we want to describe student performance in terms of each intended learning outcome. For this purpose we should use at least 10 items per outcome. Where practical constraints make it necessary to use fewer than 10 items for an intended outcome, only tentative judgments should be made and these should be verified by other means. In some cases it is possible to combine

BOX 5.1   Checklist for Evaluating the Test Plan

1. Is the purpose of the test clear?
2. Have the intended learning outcomes been identified and defined?
3. Are the intended learning outcomes stated in performance (measurable) terms?
4. Have test specifications been prepared that indicate the nature and distribution of items to be included in the test?
5. Does the specified set of items provide a representative sample of the tasks contained in the achievement domain?
6. Are the types of items appropriate for the learning outcomes to be measured?
7. Is the difficulty of the items appropriate for the students to be tested and the nature of the measurement (e.g., mastery or survey)?
8. Is the number of items appropriate for the students to be tested, the time available for testing, and the interpretations to be made?
9. Does the test plan include built-in features that contribute to valid and reliable scores?
10. Have plans been made for arranging the items in the test, writing directions, scoring, and using the results?

items into larger item clusters for a more meaningful interpretation. See Box 5.1 for a summary checklist for evaluating the test plan.

GENERAL GUIDELINES FOR ITEM WRITING

There are a number of general suggestions that apply to the writing of all item types. These provide a general framework for writing items that function as intended and that contribute to more valid and reliable results.

1. **Select the type of test item that measures the intended learning outcome most directly.** Use a supply-type item if supplying the answer is an important element of the task (e.g., writing). Use a selection-type item if appropriate (e.g., identification) or if both types are equally appropriate.
2. **Write the test item so that the performance it elicits matches the performance in the learning task.** The intended learning outcome specifies the learning task in performance terms and the test task should call forth the same performance.
3. **Write the test item so that the test task is clear and definite.** Keep the reading level low, use simple and direct language, and follow the rules for correct punctuation and grammar.
4. **Write the test item so that it is free from nonfunctional material.** Material not directly relevant to the problem being presented increases the reading load and may detract from the intent of the item. Use extraneous material only where its detection is part of the task (e.g., in math problems).
5. **Write the test item so that irrelevant factors do not prevent an informed student from responding correctly.** Avoid trick questions that might cause a knowledgeable student to focus on the wrong aspect of the task. Use clear, unambiguous statements that maximize the

performance to be measured and minimize all other influences. For example, word problems measuring mathematical reasoning should keep reading level and computational demands simple if an uncontaminated measure of reasoning ability is desired.

6. **Write the test item so that irrelevant clues do not enable the uninformed student to respond correctly.** Removing unwanted clues from test items requires alertness during item writing and reviewing the items after setting them aside for a while. The most common clues for each item type will be considered in the following chapters. It is also important to prevent the information given in one item from providing an answer to another item in the test.

7. **Write the test item so that the difficulty level matches the intent of the learning outcome, the age group to be tested, and the use to be made of the results.** When difficulty is being evaluated, check to be certain that it is relevant to the intended learning outcome and that the item is free from sources of irrelevant difficulty (e.g., obscure materials, overly fine discriminations).

8. **Write the test item so that there is no disagreement concerning the answer.** Typically, the answer should be one that experts would agree is the correct or best answer. Most problems arise here when students are to provide the best answer (best procedure, best explanation). This involves a matter of judgment and to be defensible the answer must be clearly best and identified as such by experts in the area. Where experts disagree, it may be desirable to ask what a particular authority would consider to be the best method, the best reason, and the like. When attributed to a source, the answer can be judged as correct or incorrect.

9. **Write the test items far enough in advance that they can be later reviewed and modified as needed.** A good time to write test items is shortly after the material has been taught, while the questions and context are still clearly in mind. In any event, reviewing and editing items after they have been set aside for a while can detect flaws that were inadvertently introduced during the original item writing.

10. **Write more test items than called for by the test plan.** This will enable you to discard weak or inappropriate items during item review and make it easier to match the final set of items to the test specifications.

ARRANGING THE ITEMS IN THE TEST

After the final selection of the items to be included in a test, a decision must be made concerning the best arrangement of items. This arrangement will vary with the type of test being prepared, but the following guidelines should be helpful.

1. **For instructional purposes, it is usually desirable to group together items that measure the same outcome.** Each group of items can then be identified by an appropriate heading (e.g., knowledge, understanding, application). The inclusion of the headings helps to identify the areas where students are having difficulty and to plan for remedial action.

2. **Where possible, all items of the same type should be grouped together.** This arrangement makes it possible to provide only one set of directions for each item type. It also simplifies the scoring and the analysis of the results.

3. **The items should be arranged in terms of increasing difficulty.** This arrangement has motivational effects on students and will prevent them from getting "bogged down" by difficult items early in the test.

Because most classroom tests include only a few item types, it is usually possible to honor all three of these guidelines. When this is not feasible, the item arrangement that best fits the nature of the test and use to be made of the results should be used.

PREPARING CLEAR DIRECTIONS

The directions for an achievement test should be simple and concise and yet contain information concerning each of the following: (1) purpose of the test, (2) time allowed to complete the test, (3) how to record the answers, and (4) whether to guess when in doubt about an answer. The following sample directions for a multiple-choice test cover these four points.

EXAMPLES

Directions: This is a test of what you have learned during the first five weeks of the course. The results of this test will be used to clarify any points of difficulty and thus help you complete the course successfully.

There are 60 multiple-choice items, and you have one hour to complete the test.

For each item, select the answer that *best* completes the statement, or answers the question, and circle the letter of that answer.

Since your score will be the number of items answered correctly, *be sure to answer every item.*

When two or more item types are included in the same test, it is usually desirable to provide general directions for the test as a whole and specific directions for each part. When this is done, the general directions should contain the information about purpose, time allowed, and what to do about guessing, and the specific directions should describe how to record the answers for that particular part. Also, some items, such as key-type exercises, require special directions for each item.

The use of separate answer sheets requires some elaboration of the instructions for recording the answers. If students are not familiar with the use of separate answer sheets, it might also be desirable to present a sample item with the correct answer properly marked.

Box 5.2 provides a checklist for evaluating the assembled text.

BOX 5.2   Checklist for Evaluating the Assembled Test

1. *Balance*   Do the items measure a representative sample of the learning tasks in the achievement domain?

2. *Relevance*   Do the test items present relevant tasks?

3. *Conciseness*   Are the test tasks stated in simple, clear language?

4. *Soundness*   Are the items of proper difficulty, free of defects, and do they have answers that are defensible?

5. *Independence*   Are the items free from overlapping, so that one item does not aid in answering another?

6. *Arrangement*   Are items measuring the same outcome grouped together?

                      Are items of the same type grouped together?

                      Are items in order of increasing difficulty?

7. *Numbering*   Are the items numbered in order throughout the test?

8. *Directions*   Are there directions for the whole test and each part?

                      Are the directions concise and at the proper reading level?

                      Do the directions include time limits and how to record answers?

                      Do the directions tell what to do about guessing?

9. *Spacing*   Does the spacing on the page contribute to ease of reading and responding?

10. *Typing*   Is the final copy free of typographical errors?

ADMINISTERING AND SCORING THE TEST

The administration of a carefully prepared informal achievement test is largely a matter of providing proper working conditions, keeping interruptions to a minimum, and arranging enough space between students to prevent cheating. The written directions should be clear enough to make the test self-administering, but in some situations it may be desirable to give the directions orally as well. With young students a blackboard illustration may also be useful. Above all, make certain that all the students know exactly what to do, and then provide them with the most favorable conditions in which to do it.

Scoring is facilitated if all answers are recorded on the left side of each test page. Under this arrangement, scoring is simply a matter of marking the correct answers on a copy of the test and placing it next to the column of answers on each student's paper. If a separate answer sheet is used, it is usually better to punch out the letters of the correct answers on a copy of the answer sheet and use this as a scoring stencil. The stencil is laid over each answer sheet and the correctly marked answers appear through the holes. Where no mark appears, a red line can be drawn across the hole. This indicates to the student the correct answer for each item missed. If machine scoring is to be used, simply scan the students' papers to make certain that only one answer was marked for each item.

ANALYZING THE EFFECTIVENESS OF TEST ITEMS

After a test has been administered, the items should be analyzed for their effectiveness. One method of evaluating the test is to review the test item-by-item when it is handed back to students for a discussion of the results. Significant comments made during the discussion can be recorded on a blank copy of the test. The flexibility of this procedure makes it possible to pursue comments about particular items, to ask students why they selected the response they did (both correct and incorrect selections), and to spend as much time on each item as seems warranted. This procedure may bring forth some unjustified criticisms of the test, but it will also help identify defective items in need of revision. The extra time used in discussing the test results will not be wasted because students will be obtaining a review of the course material covered by the test.

Simple Item-Analysis Procedure ← p. 90

The discussion of test results and review of the items can be much more effective if a simple tally of student responses is made on the master copy of the test. Recording the results of the one-third highest scoring students (H) and one-third lowest scoring students (L), like that in Figure 5.1, makes the results easily interpretable. The correct answer is circled and the numbers to the left of each alternative indicate how many students in each group selected that alternative.

The result in Figure 5.1 provides all the information we need to estimate the following types of item-analysis information.

1. The difficulty of the item (percentage of students answering the item correctly).
2. The discriminating power of the item (how well the item discriminates between high and low scorers).
3. The effectiveness of each alternative (all should be chosen and each one more frequently by the low scoring group).

By simply looking at the answer sheet in Figure 5.1, we can see that 8 students in the high-scoring group and 4 students in the low-scoring group selected the correct answer. Also, more students in the low-scoring group selected each wrong alternative than in the high-scoring group, indicating that the distracters seem to be distracting those students who haven't learned the meaning of the term.

To illustrate the procedure, suppose 30 students were administered a test, with the item in Figure 5.1 as the first item. Because we are using 10 students (top one-third) in the high-scoring group and 10 students (bottom one-third) in the low-scoring group, we can mentally calculate the usual indexes of difficulty and discriminating power by using the following simple steps.

UNIT TEST

Name _____   Date _____

Directions:

This test measures the knowledge, understandings, and applications you have acquired during the first four weeks.

There are 65 objective items, and you will have the full class period to complete the test.

Select the best answer for each item and circle the letter of that answer.

Your score will be the number of items answered correctly, so *be sure to answer every item.*

KNOWLEDGE OF TERMS

H	L	
1	3	1. An assessment instrument is properly classified as *objective* when
1	2	A. the instrument uses objective-type questions.
0	1	B. the responses called forth by the instrument are free of opinion.
8	4	C. those preparing the instrument used standard procedures of construction.

H L
1 3   1. An assessment instrument is properly classified as *objective* when
1 2   A. the instrument uses objective-type questions.
0 1   B. the responses called forth by the instrument are free of opinion.
                C. those preparing the instrument used standard procedures of
                    construction.
8 4   Ⓓ there is agreement among scorers concerning the correctness
                of the answers.

FIGURE 5.1   Test Copy with Item-Analysis Data to Left of Items (H = 1/3 Highest Scorers, L = 1/3 Lowest Scores).

1. Determine the percentage of high scorers and low scorers passing the item by adding a zero.

$$H = 8 \text{ out of } 10 = 80$$
$$L = 4 \text{ out of } 10 = 40$$

2. Obtain *item difficulty* by adding the percentage correct in the high and low groups and dividing by 2. Add a percent sign to the answer.

$$\frac{80 + 40}{2} = 60\%$$

3. Obtain *discriminating power* by subtracting the percentage correct in the low group from the percentage correct in the high group. Add a decimal point to the answer.

$$80 - 40 = .40$$

The description of the procedure makes it sound more complicated than it is, but making a few mental calculations like this will reveal its simplicity. Item difficulty typically uses the percent sign and, of course, can range from 0 to 100 percent. Our **difficulty index** is based on the high- and low-scoring groups only, but this provides a satisfactory approximation of item difficulty. The **discrimination index** typically uses the decimal point and thus ranges from 0 to 1.00.

H	L	
		1. An assessment instrument is properly classified as *objective* when
0	2	A. the instrument uses objective-type questions.
0	3	B. the responses called forth by the instrument are free of opinion.
0	3	C. those preparing the instrument used standard procedures of construction.
10	2	D. there is agreement among scorers concerning the correctness of the answers.

FIGURE 5.2   Expected Distribution of Highest Scorers and Lowest Scorers.

For purposes of comparison, it is advisable to determine the difficulty and discriminating indexes that would be expected if an item was free from defects. For example, an ideal item would be answered correctly by all of the students in the high-scoring group, and the answers among students in the low-scoring group would be relatively equally distributed across the alternatives. In our example, we would expect all 10 students in the high-scoring group to answer the item correctly and 2 (or 3) students in the low-scoring group to answer correctly if instruction related to this item was adequate and the item is free from defects. This distribution is illustrated in Figure 5.2. Thus, we would expect the item difficulty index to range between 60 and 65 percent, and the discriminating index to range between .7 and .8.

This simple method of analyzing the test results can be used as an aid in discussing the items when reviewing the test. Items that most students answer correctly can be skipped over or treated lightly, items missed by most students can be discussed in more detail, and defective items can be pointed out to students rather than defended as fair. Also, the frequency with which each incorrect answer is chosen may reveal common errors and misconceptions that can be corrected on the spot or serve as a basis for remedial work. Discussing the reasons students have selected the right or wrong answer for an item can sometimes be revealing. We assume that if they selected the correct answer they had learned the material. Not necessarily so, when using selection-type items (see Box 5.3 for common reasons for selecting alternatives). Having students discuss the reasons for their choices provides insights into student thinking that may contribute to both improved teaching and improved test construction skills.

Although the method of **item analysis** presented here is a crude one, it is probably satisfactory for most classroom tests. We are using it primarily as a basis for reviewing the items with students and for any insights the results might give us for improving test items in the future. A more detailed description of item analysis and cautions in interpreting item-analysis data can be found in Linn and Gronlund (2000).

Because of the small number of students involved in classroom testing, item-analysis information must be interpreted with great caution. If a test item is reused with a new group, the results may be quite different, due to changes in the instruction, the study habits of students, or some other factor. The tentative nature of the item-analysis data is not of great concern, however, when used to review tests with students for the purpose of improving learning.

BOX 5.3   Common Reasons for Selecting Multiple-Choice Alternatives

Bases for Correct Choice

1. Possesses required information or skill.
2. Uses partial information that favors answer.
3. Uses clues given in the item.
4. Uses information from other items in the test.
5. Makes a blind, lucky guess.

Bases for Incorrect Choice

1. Lacks the information or skill required by the item.
2. Uses partial information that favors a distracter.
3. Uses misinformation that favors a distracter.
4. Makes a blind, unlucky guess.
5. Marks wrong answer through carelessness.

Summary of Points

1. Preparing and using an achievement test includes specifying the instructional objectives in performance terms, preparing a table of specifications, constructing relevant test items, arranging the items in the test, preparing clear directions, reviewing and evaluating the assembled test, administering the test, and making an item analysis.
2. Test specifications typically consist of a twofold table of specifications that indicates the sample of performance tasks to be measured.
3. The types of test items used in a test should be determined by how directly they measure the intended learning outcomes and how effective they are as measuring instruments.
4. Each test item should provide a task that matches the student performance described in a specific learning outcome.
5. The functioning content of test items can be improved by eliminating irrelevant barriers and unintended clues during item writing.
6. The difficulty of a test item should match the difficulty of the learning task to be measured. Beware of irrelevant sources of difficulty (e.g., obscure material).
7. An achievement test should be short enough to permit all students to attempt all items during the testing time available.
8. A test should contain a sufficient number of test items for each type of interpretation to be made. Interpretations based on fewer than 10 items should be considered highly tentative.
9. Following a general set of guidelines during item writing will result in higher quality items that contribute to the validity and reliability of the test results.
10. Item arrangement within the test will vary with the type of test used. Where possible, items should be grouped by major learning outcome

(e.g., knowledge, understanding, application); similar items should be grouped together and should be arranged in order of increasing difficulty.

11. Test directions should clearly indicate the purpose of the test, the time allowed, how to record the answers, and to answer every item.
12. A correction for guessing should be used for speed tests only.
13. Review and evaluate the assembled test before using.
14. Administer the test under controlled conditions.
15. Item analysis provides a means of evaluating the items and is useful in reviewing the test with students.

References and Additional Reading

Carey, L. M. *Measuring and Evaluating School Learning*, 3rd ed. (Boston: Allyn and Bacon, 2001).

Gronlund, N. E., & Brookhart, S. M. *Gronlund's Writing Instructional Objectives*, 8th ed. (Upper Saddle River, NJ: Pearson/Merrill/Prentice Hall, 2009).

Linn, R. L., & Gronlund, N. E. *Measurement and Assessment in Teaching*, 8th ed. (Upper Saddle River, NJ: Merrill/Prentice Hall, 2000).

Oosterhoff, A. C. *Classroom Application of Educational Measurement*, 3rd ed. (Upper Saddle River, NJ: Merrill/ Prentice Hall, 2001).

Stiggins, R. J. *Student-Involved Classroom Assessment*, 3rd ed. (Upper Saddle River, NJ: Merrill/Prentice Hall, 2001).

Self-Assessment

MULTIPLE CHOICE

DIRECTIONS: Select the best answer for each item by circling the corresponding letter.

1. The purpose of a table of specifications is to
   (a) ensure that the test measures a sample of the learning outcomes
   (b) determine how difficult the test items should be
   (c) identify learning outcomes and content areas measured by the test
   (d) ensure that the test items obtain a spread of scores

2. Test items used to measure the lowest level of the cognitive taxonomy are
   (a) analysis
   (b) application
   (c) understand
   (d) remember

3. Identifies, names, defines, describes, lists, matches, selects, and outlines are verbs used for which level of the cognitive taxonomy?
   (a) Analysis
   (b) Application
   (c) Understand
   (d) Remember

4. Which of the following would indicate the lowest level of learning for a student?
   (a) Applies a principle
   (b) Gives a textbook definition of a principle

(c) Explains a principle in his own words
(d) States an example of the principle

5. The weight assigned to each topic area in a table of specifications should be determined by the
    (a) complexity of the topic area
    (b) instructional time devoted to the topic area
    (c) emphasis given in leading published tests
    (d) method used to evaluate the topic area

6. The ideal difficulty for an item in a standardized, norm-referenced multiple-choice test that has four alternatives with 15 in the high group and 15 in the low group would range between
    (a) 0 and 25 percent
    (b) 30 and 40 percent
    (c) 60 and 65 percent
    (d) 80 and 100 percent

SUPPLY-TYPE ITEMS

DIRECTIONS: Using the information provided below, answer the questions that follow. Place your answers on the lines provided.

A test with 100 multiple-choice items, each with 4 alternatives, was administered to 28 students. The test papers have been arranged in order from the highest to lowest score and the 10 highest and 10 lowest scored papers have been selected to perform an item analysis for each item. Below is the number of students in the high and low groups who selected each alternative for item 1.

HIGH	LOW	ALTERNATIVES
2	1	A
7	4	B (correct alternative)
0	3	C
1	2	D

7. What is the index of difficulty for item 1? _____

8. What is the discriminating power for item 1? _____

9. A five-item multiple-choice pretest was given to a group of 35 students before instruction. The same test is given to the students after instruction. The students must answer all the items correctly to pass. Five students answered item 1 correctly of the pretest, while 31 students answered the item correctly after instruction.

What is the sensitivity to instructional effects for item 1? _____

Restricted-Response Essay

10. The authors of your textbook discuss the procedure for conducting a simple item analysis. List and describe each step in the procedure. Confine your answer to one page.

WRITING SELECTION ITEMS
Multiple Choice

Studying this chapter should enable you to

1. Describe the characteristics of multiple-choice items.
2. Describe the strengths and limitations of multiple-choice items.
3. Distinguish between well-stated and poorly stated multiple-choice items.
4. Identify and correct faults in poorly stated multiple-choice items.
5. Match multiple-choice items to intended learning outcomes.
6. Construct multiple-choice items that are well stated, relevant to important learning outcomes, and free of defects.

Multiple-choice items are the most widely used and highly regarded of the selection-type items. They can be designed to measure a variety of learning outcomes, from simple to complex, and can provide the highest quality items. Because they play such an important role in achievement testing, they will be treated in this chapter in considerable detail. Other selection-type items (true-false, matching, and interpretive exercise) will be described in the following chapter.

Answers *Question*

NATURE OF MULTIPLE-CHOICE ITEMS

The multiple-choice item consists of a *stem,* which presents a problem situation, and several *alternatives* (*options* or *choices*), which provide possible solutions to the problem. The stem may be a question or an incomplete statement. The alternatives include the correct answer and several plausible wrong answers called *distracters.* The function of the latter is to distract those students who are uncertain of the answer.

The following items illustrate the question form and the incomplete-statement form of a multiple-choice item.

→ *p. 85*

EXAMPLE

Which one of the following item types is an example of a supply-type test item?
a.   Multiple-choice item.
b.   True-false item.
c.   Matching item.
*d.   Short-answer item.

An example of a supply-type test item is the
a.   multiple-choice item.
b.   true-false item.
c.   matching item.
*d.   short-answer item.

Although stated differently, both stems pose the same problem. Note, however, that the incomplete statement is more concise. This is typically the case. The question form is easier to write and forces the test maker to pose a clear problem but tends to result in a longer stem. An effective procedure for the beginner is to start with a question and shift to the incomplete statement whenever greater conciseness can be obtained.

The alternatives in the preceding examples contain only one correct answer, and the distracters are clearly incorrect. Another type of multiple-choice item is the *best-answer* form in which the alternatives are all partially correct but one is clearly better than the others. This type is used for more complex achievement, as when the student must select the best reason for an action, the best method for doing something, or the best application of a principle. Thus, whether the correct-answer or best-answer form is used depends on the learning outcomes to be measured.

EXAMPLE

Which item is *best* for measuring computational skill?
a.   Multiple-choice item.
b.   True-false item.
c.   Matching item.
*d.   Short-answer item.

The examples given illustrate the use of four alternatives. Multiple-choice items typically include three, four, or five choices. The larger number will, of course, reduce the student's chances of obtaining the correct answer by guessing. Theoretically, with five alternatives there is only one chance in five of guessing the answer, whereas with four alternatives there is one chance in four. It is frequently difficult to obtain five plausible choices, however, and items are not improved by adding obviously wrong answers. See Box 6.1 for strengths and limitations of multiple-choice items.

BOX 6.1   Multiple-Choice Items

Strengths

1. Learning outcomes from simple to complex can be measured.
2. Highly structured and clear tasks are provided.
3. A broad sample of achievement can be measured.
4. Incorrect alternatives provide diagnostic information.
5. Scores are less influenced by guessing than true-false items.
6. Scoring is easy, objective, and reliable.

Limitations

1. Constructing good items is time consuming.
2. It is frequently difficult to find plausible distracters.
3. This item is ineffective for measuring some types of problem solving and the ability to organize and express ideas.
4. Score can be influenced by reading ability.

RULES FOR WRITING MULTIPLE-CHOICE ITEMS

An effective multiple-choice item presents students with a task that is both important and clearly understood, and one that can be answered correctly by anyone who has achieved the intended learning outcome. Nothing in the content or structure of the item should prevent an informed student from responding correctly. Similarly, nothing in the content or structure of the item should enable an uninformed student to select the correct answer. The following rules for item writing are intended as guides for the preparation of multiple-choice items that function as intended.

1. Design each item to measure an important learning outcome. The problem situation around which an item is to be built should be important and should be related to the intended learning outcome to be measured. When writing the item, focus on the functioning content of the item and resist the temptation to include irrelevant material or more obscure and less significant content to increase item difficulty. Remember that the purpose of each item is to call forth the type of performance that will help determine the extent to which the intended learning outcomes have been achieved.

Items designed to measure complex achievement must contain some novelty. For example, where a memory item might require the identification of a textbook definition of a term, an understanding item may require the identification of a modified form of it, and an application item may require the identification of an example of its proper use. Both the understanding and application items would function as intended, however, only if the material was new to the students. Thus, items measuring complex achievement should require students to demonstrate that they have grasped the meaning of the material and can use it in situations that are new to them.

   2. Present a single, clearly formulated problem in the stem of the item. The task set forth in the stem of the item should be so clear that a student can understand it without reading the alternatives. In fact, a good check on the clarity and completeness of a multiple-choice stem is to cover the alternatives and determine whether it could be answered without the choices. Try this on the two sample items that follow.

EXAMPLE

Poor: A table of specifications
   a.   indicates how a test will be used to improve learning.
   *b.   provides a more balanced sampling of content.
   c.   arranges the instructional objectives in order of their importance.
   d.   specifies the method of scoring to be used on a test.

Better: What is the main advantage of using a table of specifications when preparing an achievement test?
   a.   It reduces the amount of time required.
   *b.   It improves the sampling of content.
   c.   It makes the construction of test items easier.
   d.   It increases the objectivity of the test.

   The first of these examples is no more than a collection of true-false statements with a common stem. The problem presented in the stem of the improved version is clear enough to serve as a supply-type short-answer item. The alternatives simply provide a series of possible answers from which to choose.
   Note also in the second version that a *single* problem is presented in the stem. Including more than one problem usually adds to the complexity of the wording and reduces the diagnostic value of the item. When students *fail* such an item, there is no way to determine which of the problems prevented them from responding correctly.
   3. State the stem of the item in simple, clear language. The problem in the stem of a multiple-choice item should be stated as precisely as possible and should be free of unnecessarily complex wording and sentence structure. Anyone who possesses the knowledge measured by a test item should be able to select the correct answer. Poorly stated item stems frequently introduce sufficient ambiguity to prevent a knowledgeable student from responding correctly. Also, complex sentence structure may make the item a measure more of reading comprehension than of the intended outcome. The first of the two examples that follow is an extreme instance of this problem.

EXAMPLE

Poor: The paucity of plausible, but incorrect, statements that can be related to a central idea poses a problem when constructing which one of the following types of test items?
a.   Short answer.
b.   True-false.
*c.   Multiple choice.
d.   Essay.

Better: The lack of plausible, but incorrect, alternatives will cause the greatest difficulty when constructing
a.   short-answer items.
b.   true-false items.
*c.   multiple-choice items.
d.   essay items.

Another common fault in stating multiple-choice items is to load the stem with irrelevant and, thus, nonfunctioning material. This is probably caused by the instructor's desire to continue to teach the students—even while testing them. The following example illustrates the use of an item stem as "another chance to inform students."

EXAMPLE

Poor: Testing can contribute to the instructional program of the school in many important ways. However, the main function of testing in teaching is:

Better: The main function of testing in teaching is:

The first version increases reading time and makes no contribution to the measurement of the specific outcome. Time spent in reading such irrelevant material could be spent more profitably in thinking about the problem presented. But if the purpose of an item is to measure a student's ability to distinguish between relevant and irrelevant material, this rule must, of course, be disregarded.

   4. Put as much of the wording as possible in the stem of the item. Avoid repeating the same material in each of the alternatives. By moving all of the common content to the stem, it is usually possible to clarify the problem further and to reduce the time the student needs to read the alternatives. Note the improvement in the following item when this rule is followed.

EXAMPLE

Poor: In *objective* testing, the term *objective*
a.   refers to the method of identifying the learning outcomes.
b.   refers to the method of selecting the test content.
c.   refers to the method of presenting the problem.
*d.   refers to the method of scoring the answers.

Better: In *objective* testing, the term *objective* refers to the method of
a.   identifying the learning outcomes.
b.   selecting the test content.
c.   presenting the problem.
*d.   scoring the answers.

In many cases the problem is not simply to move the common words to the stem but to reword the entire item. The following examples illustrate how an item can be improved by revising the stem and shortening the alternatives.

EXAMPLE

Poor: Instructional objectives are most apt to be useful for test-construction purposes when they are stated in such a way that they show
a.   the course content to be covered during the instructional period.
*b.   the kinds of performance students should demonstrate upon reaching the goal.
c.   the things the teacher will do to obtain maximum student learning.
d.   the types of learning activities to be participated in during the course.

Better: Instructional objectives are most useful for test-construction purposes when they are stated in terms of
a.   course content.
*b.   student performance.
c.   teacher behavior.
d.   learning activities.

It is, of course, impossible to streamline all items in this manner, but economy of wording and clarity of expression are important goals to strive for in test construction. Items function better when slim and trim.

   5. State the stem of the item in positive form, wherever possible. A positively phrased test item tends to measure more important learning outcomes than a negatively stated item. This is because knowing such things as the *best* method or the *most relevant* argument typically has greater educational significance than knowing the *poorest* method or the *least relevant* argument.

The use of negatively stated items in stems results all too frequently from the ease with which such items can be constructed rather than from the importance of the learning outcomes measured. The test maker who becomes frustrated by the inability to think of a sufficient number of plausible distracters for an item, as in the first following example, suddenly realizes how simple it would be to construct the second version.

EXAMPLE

Item one: Which one of the following is a category in the revised taxonomy of the cognitive domain?
*a.   Understand.
 b.   *(distracter needed)*
 c.   *(distracter needed)*
 d.   *(distracter needed)*

Item two: Which one of the following is *not* a category in the revised taxonomy of the cognitive domain?
 a.   Understand.
 b.   Apply.
 c.   Analyze.
*d.   *(answer needed)*

Note in the second version that the categories of the taxonomy serve as distracters and that all that is needed to complete the item is a correct answer. This could be any term that appears plausible but is *not* one of the categories listed in the taxonomy. Although such items are easily constructed, they are apt to have a low level of difficulty and are likely to measure relatively unimportant learning outcomes. Being able to identify answers that do *not* apply provides no assurance that the student possesses the desired knowledge.

This solution to the lack of sufficient distracters is most likely to occur when the test maker is committed to the use of multiple-choice items only. A more desirable procedure for measuring the "ability to recognize the categories

---

EXAMPLE

Directions: Indicate which of the following are categories in the taxonomy of the cognitive domain by circling Y for *yes* and N for *no.*

*Y N	Understand
Y N*	Critical Thinking
Y N*	Reasoning
*Y N	Create

---

in the taxonomy of the cognitive domain" is to switch to a modified true-false form, as in the following example.

In responding to this item, the student must make a separate judgment for each statement—the statement either is or is not one of the categories. Thus, the item calls for the type of performance stated in the learning outcome, yet it avoids the problems of an insufficient number of distracters and of negative phrasing.

6. Emphasize negative wording whenever it is used in the stem of an item. In some instances the use of negative wording is basic to the measurement of an important learning outcome. Knowing that you should *not* cross the street against a red light or should *not* mix certain chemicals, for example, is so important that these precepts might be directly taught and directly tested. Any potentially dangerous situation may require a negative emphasis. There are also, of course, less dire circumstances where negative phrasing is useful. Almost any set of rules or procedures places some emphasis on practices to be avoided.

When negative wording is used in the stem of an item, it should be emphasized by being underlined or capitalized and by being placed near the end of the statement.

EXAMPLE

Poor: Which one of the following is not a desirable practice when preparing multiple-choice items?
  a.   Stating the stem in positive form.
  b.   Using a stem that could function as a short-answer item.
  c.   Underlining certain words in the stem for emphasis.
*d.   Shortening the stem by lengthening the alternatives.

Better: All of the following are desirable practices when preparing multiple-choice items EXCEPT
  a.   stating the stem in positive form.
  b.   using a stem that could function as a short-answer item.
  c.   underlining certain words in the stem for emphasis.
*d.   shortening the stem by lengthening the alternatives.

The improved version of this item ensures that the item's negative aspect will not be overlooked, and it furnishes the student with the proper mindset just before reading the alternatives.

7. Make certain that the intended answer is correct or clearly best. When the correct-answer form of a multiple-choice item is used, there should be only one correct answer and it should be unquestionably correct. With the best-answer form, the intended answer should be one that competent authorities would agree is clearly the best. In the latter case it may also be necessary to include "of the following" in the stem of the item to allow for equally satisfactory answers that have not been included in the item.

EXAMPLE

Poor: What is the best method of selecting course content for test items?

Better: Which one of the following is the best method of selecting course content for test items?

The proper phrasing of the stem of an item can also help avoid equivocal answers when the correct-answer form is used. In fact, an inadequately stated problem frequently makes the intended answer only partially correct or makes more than one alternative suitable.

EXAMPLE

Poor: What is the purpose of classroom testing?

Better: One purpose of classroom testing is

(or)

The main purpose of classroom testing is

It is, of course, also necessary to check each of the distracters in the item to make certain that none of them could be defended as the correct answer. This will not only improve the quality of the item but also prevent a disruptive argument during the discussion of the test results.

8. Make all alternatives grammatically consistent with the stem of the item and parallel in form. The correct answer is usually carefully phrased so that it is grammatically consistent with the stem. Where the test maker is apt to slip is in stating the distracters. Unless care is taken to check them against the wording in the stem and in the correct answer, they may be inconsistent in tense, article, or grammatical form. This, of course, could provide a clue to the correct answer, or at least make some of the distracters ineffective.

A general step that can be taken to prevent grammatical inconsistency is to avoid using the articles "a" or "an" at the end of the stem of the item.

EXAMPLE

Poor: The recall of factual information can be measured best with a
a.   matching item.
b.   multiple-choice item.
*c.   short-answer item.
d.   essay question.

Better: The recall of factual information can be measured best with
a.   matching items.
b.   multiple-choice items.
*c.   short-answer items.
d.   essay questions.

nouns

TOURO COLLEGE LIBRARY

The indefinite article "a" in the first version makes the last distracter obviously wrong. By simply changing the alternatives from singular to plural, it is possible to omit the article. In other cases, it may be necessary to add an article ("a," "an," or as appropriate) to each alternative or to rephrase the entire item.

Stating all of the alternatives in parallel form also tends to prevent unnecessary clues from being given to the students. When the grammatical structure of one alternative differs from that of the others, some students may more readily detect that alternative as a correct or an incorrect response.

EXAMPLE

Poor: Why should negative terms be avoided in the stem of a multiple-choice item?
*a.   They may be overlooked.
b.   The stem tends to be longer.
c.   The construction of alternatives is more difficult.
d.   The scoring is more difficult.

Better: Why should negative terms be avoided in the stem of a multiple-choice item?
*a.   They may be overlooked.
b.   They tend to increase the length of the stem.
c.   They make the construction of alternatives more difficult.
d.   They may increase the difficulty of the scoring.

In the first version some students who lack the knowledge called for are apt to select the correct answer because of the way it is stated. The parallel grammatical structure in the second version removes this clue.

9. Avoid verbal clues that might enable students to select the correct answer or to eliminate an incorrect alternative. One of the most common sources of extraneous clues in multiple-choice items is the wording of the item. Some such clues are rather obvious and are easily avoided. Others require the constant attention of the test maker to prevent them from slipping in unnoticed. Let's review some of the verbal clues commonly found in multiple-choice items.

A. *Similarity of wording in both the stem and the correct answer* is one of the most obvious clues. Key words in the stem may unintentionally be repeated verbatim in the correct answer, a synonym may be used, or the words may simply sound or look alike.

EXAMPLE

Poor: Which one of the following would you consult first to locate research articles on achievement testing?
a.   *Journal of Educational Psychology*
b.   *Journal of Educational Measurement*

    c.   *Journal of Consulting Psychology*
 *d.   *Review of Educational Research*

The word "research" in both the stem and the correct answer is apt to provide a clue to the correct answer to the uninformed but testwise student. Such obvious clues might better be used in both the stem and an *incorrect* answer, in order to lead the uninformed *away* from the correct answer.

    B. *Stating the correct answer in textbook language or stereotyped phraseology* may cause students to select it because it looks better than the other alternatives, or because they vaguely recall having seen it before.

EXAMPLE

    Poor: Learning outcomes are most useful in preparing tests when they are
 *a.   clearly stated in performance terms.
   b.   developed cooperatively by teachers and students.
   c.   prepared after the instruction has ended.
   d.   stated in general terms.

The pat phrasing of the correct answer is likely to give it away. Even the most poorly prepared student is apt to recognize the often repeated phrase "clearly stated in performance terms," without having the foggiest notion of what it means.

    C. *Stating the correct answer in greater detail* may provide a clue. Also, when the answer is qualified by modifiers that are typically associated with true statements (for example, "sometimes," "may," "usually"), it is more likely to be chosen.

EXAMPLE

    Poor: Lack of attention to learning outcomes during test preparation
   a.   will lower the technical quality of the items.
   b.   will make the construction of test items more difficult.
   c.   will result in the greater use of essay questions.
 *d.   may result in a test that is less relevant to the instructional program.

The term "may" is rather obvious in this example, but this type of error is common and appears frequently in a subtler form.

    D. *Including absolute terms in the distracters* enables students to eliminate them as possible answers because such terms ("always," "never," "all," "none," "only,") are commonly associated with false statements. This makes the correct answer obvious, or at least increases the chances that the students who do not know the answer will guess it.

EXAMPLE

Poor: Achievement tests help students improve their learning by
a.   encouraging them all to study hard.
*b.   informing them of their progress.
c.   giving them all a feeling of success.
d.   preventing any of them from neglecting their assignments.

Such absolutes tend to be used by the inexperienced test maker to ensure that the incorrect alternatives are clearly wrong. Unfortunately, they are easily recognized by the student as unlikely answers, making them ineffective as distracters.

    E. *Including two responses that are all inclusive* makes it possible to eliminate the other alternatives, since one of the two must obviously be the correct answer.

EXAMPLE

Poor: Which one of the following types of test items measures learning outcomes at the recall level?
*a.   Supply-type items.
b.   Selection-type items.
c.   Matching items.
d.   Multiple-choice items.

Since the first two alternatives include the only two major types of test items, even poorly prepared students are likely to limit their choices to these two. This, of course, gives them a fifty-fifty chance of guessing the correct answer.

    F. *Including two responses that have the same meaning* makes it possible to eliminate them as potential answers. If two alternatives have the same meaning and only one answer is to be selected, it is fairly obvious that both alternatives must be incorrect.

EXAMPLE

Poor: Which one of the following is the most important characteristic of achievement-test results?
a.   Consistency.
b.   Reliability.
*c.   Relevance.
d.   Objectivity.

In this item both "consistency" and "reliability" can be eliminated because they mean essentially the same thing.

Extraneous clues to the correct answer must be excluded from test items if the items are to function as intended. It is frequently good practice, however, to use such clues to lead the uninformed away from the correct answer. If not overdone, this can contribute to the plausibility of the incorrect alternatives.

10. Make the distracters plausible and attractive to the uninformed. The distracters in a multiple-choice item should be so appealing to the students who lack the knowledge called for by the item that they select one of the distracters in preference to the correct answer. This is the ideal, of course, but one toward which the test maker must work continually. The art of constructing good multiple-choice items depends heavily on the development of effective distracters.

You can do a number of things to increase the plausibility and attractiveness of distracters:

A. Use the common misconceptions or errors of students as distracters.
B. State the alternatives in the language of the student.
C. Use "good-sounding" words ("accurate," "important,") in the distracters as well as in the correct answer.
D. Make the distracters similar to the correct answer in both length and complexity of wording.
E. Use extraneous clues in the distracters, such as stereotyped phrasing, scientific-sounding answers, and verbal associations with the stem of the item. But don't overuse these clues to the point where they become ineffective.
F. Make the alternatives homogeneous, but in doing so beware of fine discriminations that are educationally insignificant.

The greater plausibility resulting from the use of more homogenous alternatives can be seen in the improved version of the following item.

EXAMPLE

Poor: Obtaining a dependable ranking of students is of major concern when using
*a.   norm-referenced summative tests.
b.   behavior descriptions.
c.   checklists.
d.   questionnaires.

Better: Obtaining a dependable ranking of students is of major concern when using
*a.   norm-referenced summative tests.
b.   teacher-made diagnostic tests.
c.   mastery achievement tests.
d.   criterion-referenced formative tests.

The improved version not only increases the plausibility of the distracters but it also calls for a type of discrimination that is more educationally significant.

11. Vary the relative length of the correct answer to eliminate length as a clue. There is a tendency for the correct answer to be longer than the alternatives because of the need to qualify statements to make them unequivocally correct. This, of course, provides a clue to the testwise student. Learning this fact, the inexperienced test maker frequently makes a special effort to avoid ever having the correct answer longer than the other alternatives. This, of course, also provides a clue, and the alert student soon learns to dismiss the longest alternative as a possible answer.

The relative length of the correct answer can be removed as a clue by varying it in such a manner that no apparent pattern is provided. That is, it should sometimes be longer, sometimes shorter, and sometimes of equal length—but never consistently or predominantly of one relative length. In some cases it is more desirable to make the alternatives approximately equal length by adjusting the distracters rather than the correct answer.

EXAMPLE

Poor: One advantage of multiple-choice items over essay questions is that they
   a.   measure more complex outcomes.
   b.   depend more on recall.
   c.   require less time to score.
*d.   provide for a more extensive sampling of course content.

Better: One advantage of multiple-choice items over essay questions is that they
   a.   provide for the measurement of more complex learning outcomes.
   b.   place greater emphasis on the recall of factual information.
   c.   require less time for test preparation and scoring.
*d.   provide for a more extensive sampling of course content.

Lengthening the distracters, as was done in the improved version, removes length as a clue and increases the plausibility of the distracters, which are now more similar to the correct answer in complexity of wording.

12. Avoid using the alternative "all of the above," and use "none of the above" with extreme caution. When test makers are having difficulty in locating a sufficient number of distracters, they frequently resort to the use of "all of the above" or "none of the above" as the final option. These special alternatives are seldom used appropriately and almost always render the item less effective than it would be without them.

The inclusion of "all of the above" as an option makes it possible to answer the item on the basis of partial information. Since students are to select only one answer, they can detect "all of the above" as the correct choice simply by noting that two of the alternatives are correct. They can also detect it as a wrong answer by recognizing that at least one of the alternatives is incorrect; of course, their chance of guessing the correct answer from the remaining choices then increases proportionately. Another difficulty with this option is that some students, recognizing that the first choice is correct, will select it without reading the remaining alternatives.

Obviously, the use of "none of the above" is not possible with the best-answer type of multiple-choice item, since the alternatives vary in appropriateness and the criterion of absolute correctness is not applicable. When used as the right answer in a correct-answer type of item, this option may be measuring nothing more than the ability to detect incorrect answers. Recognizing that certain answers are wrong is no guarantee that the student knows what is correct. For example, a student may be able to answer the following item correctly without being able to name the categories in the taxonomy.

EXAMPLE

Poor: Which of the following is a category in the revised taxonomy of the cognitive domain?
  a. Critical Thinking.
  b. Scientific Thinking.
  c. Reasoning Ability.
  *d. None of the above.

All students need to know to answer this item correctly is that the taxonomy categories are new and different from those that they have commonly associated with intellectual skills. Items such as this provide rather poor evidence for judging a student's achievement.

The alternative "none of the above" is probably used more widely with computational problems that are presented in multiple-choice form. The publishers of standardized achievement tests have resorted to multiple-choice items for such problems in order to make machine scoring possible, and they have resorted to the alternative "none of the above" in order to reduce the likelihood of the student estimating the answer without performing the entire computation. Although this use of "none of the above" may be defensible, there is seldom a need to use multiple-choice items for computational problems in classroom tests. The supply-type item that requires the student to solve the problems and record the answers provides the most direct and useful measure of computational skill. This is another case in which it is desirable to switch from multiple-choice items to another item type in order to obtain more effective measurement.

13. Vary the position of the correct answer in a random manner. The correct answer should appear in each alternative position about the same number of times, but its placement should not follow a pattern that may be apparent to the person taking the test. Students who detect that the correct answer never appears in the same position more than twice in a row, or that A is the correct answer on every fourth item, are likely to obtain a higher score than their knowledge would warrant. Such clues can be avoided by random placement of the correct answer.

The easiest way to randomly assign the position of the correct answer in a multiple-choice item is to develop a code with the aid of a book: simply open any book at a random place, look at the right-hand page, and let the last digit of the page number determine the placement of the correct answer. Since the right-hand page always ends in an odd number, the code might be as follows: the digit 1 indicates that the correct answer will be placed in position A, 3 = B, 5 = C, 7 = D, and 9 = E.

Sufficient variation without a discernible pattern might also be obtained by simply placing the responses in alphabetical order, based on the first letter in each, and letting the correct answer fall where it will.

When the alternative responses are numbers, they should always be listed in order of size, preferably in ascending order. This will eliminate the possibility of a clue, such as the correct answer being the only one that is not in numerical order.

14. Control the difficulty of the item either by varying the problem in the stem or by changing the alternatives. It is usually preferable to increase item difficulty by increasing the level of knowledge called for by making the problem more complex. However, it is also possible to increase difficulty by making the alternatives more homogeneous. When this is done, care must be taken that the finer discriminations called for are educationally significant and are in harmony with the learning outcomes to be measured.

15. Make certain each item is independent of the other items in the test. Occasionally information given in the stem of one item will help the students answer another item. This can be remedied easily by a careful review of the items before they are assembled into a test.

A different type of problem occurs when the correct answer to an item depends on knowing the correct answer to the item preceding it. The student who is unable to answer the first item, of course, has no basis for responding to the second. Such chains of interlocking items should be avoided. Each item should be an independently scorable unit.

16. Use an efficient item format. The alternatives should be listed on separate lines, under one another, like the examples in this chapter. This makes the alternatives easy to read and compare. It also contributes to ease of scoring since the letters of the alternatives all appear on the left side of the paper. A copy of the test can be used as a scoring stencil: Simply circle the letters of the correct answers on the copy, then place the copy next to the student's paper so that the columns of letters correspond.

The use of letters in front of the alternatives is preferable to the use of numbers, since numerical answers in numbered items may be confusing to the students.

17. Follow the normal rules of grammar. If the stem is in question form, begin each alternative with a capital letter and end with a period or other appropriate punctuation mark. Omit the period with numerical answers, however, to avoid confusion with decimal points. When the stem is an incomplete statement, start each alternative with a lowercase letter and end with whatever terminal punctuation mark is appropriate.

18. Break (or bend) any of these rules if it will improve the effectiveness of the item. These rules for constructing multiple-choice items are stated rather dogmatically as an aid to the beginner. As experience in item writing is obtained, situations are likely to occur where ignoring or modifying a rule may be desirable. In a problem-solving item, for example, it may be useful to include extraneous information in the stem to see if students can select what is needed to solve the problem. Until sufficient experience in item writing is gained, however, following the rules in this chapter will yield test items of fairly good quality. See Box 6.2 for a summary checklist.

BOX 6.2 Checklist for Evaluating Multiple-Choice Items

1. Is this type of item appropriate for measuring the intended learning outcome?
2. Does the item task match the learning task to be measured?
3. Does the stem of the item present a single, clearly formulated problem?
4. Is the stem stated in simple, clear language?
5. Is the stem worded so that there is no repetition of material in the alternatives?
6. Is the stem stated in positive form wherever possible?
7. If negative wording is used in the stem, is it emphasized (by underlining or caps)?
8. Is the intended answer correct or clearly best?
9. Are all alternatives grammatically consistent with the stem and parallel in form?
10. Are the alternatives free from verbal clues to the correct answer?
11. Are the distracters plausible and attractive to the uninformed?
12. To eliminate length as a clue, is the relative length of the correct answer varied?
13. Has the alternative "all of the above" been avoided and "none of the above" used only when appropriate?
14. Is the position of the correct answer varied so that there is no detectable pattern?
15. Does the item format and grammar usage provide for efficient test taking?

Summary of Points

1. The multiple-choice item is the most highly regarded and useful selection-type item.
2. The multiple-choice item consists of a stem and a set of alternative answers (options or choices).
3. The multiple-choice item can be designed to measure various intended learning outcomes, ranging from simple to complex.
4. Items designed to measure achievement beyond the knowledge level must contain some novelty.
5. The stem of a multiple-choice item should present a single, clearly formulated problem that is related to an important learning outcome.
6. The intended answer should be correct or clearly best, as agreed upon by authorities.

7. The distracters (incorrect alternatives) should be plausible enough to lead the uninformed away from the correct answer.

8. The items should be written in simple, clear language that is free of non-functioning content.

9. The items should be free of irrelevant sources of difficulty (e.g., ambiguity) that might prevent an informed examinee from answering correctly.

10. The items should be free of irrelevant clues (e.g., verbal associations) that might enable an uninformed examinee to answer correctly.

11. The item format should provide for efficient responding and follow the normal rules of grammar.

12. The rules of item writing provide a framework for preparing effective multiple-choice items, but experience in item writing may result in modifications to fit particular situations.

References and Additional Reading

Carey, L. M. *Measuring and Evaluating School Learning*, 3rd ed. (Boston: Allyn and Bacon, 2001).

Haladyna, T. M. *Writing Test Items to Evaluate Higher Order Thinking* (Boston: Allyn and Bacon, 1997).

Linn, R. L., & Gronlund, N. E. *Measurement and Assessment in Teaching*, 8th ed. (Upper Saddle River, NJ: Merrill/Prentice Hall, 2000).

Oosterhoff, A. C. *Classroom Applications of Educational Measurement*, 3rd ed. (Upper Saddle River, NJ: Merrill/Prentice Hall, 2001).

Taylor, C. S., & Nolen, S. B. *Classroom Assessment: Supporting Teaching and Learning in Real Classrooms* (Upper Saddle River, NJ: Prentice Hall, Pearson, 2005).

Self-Assessment

MULTIPLE CHOICE

DIRECTIONS: Select the best answer for each item by circling the corresponding letter.

1. Follow all of the following for constructing multiple-choice items EXCEPT
   (a) design each item to measure an important learning outcome.
   (b) put as little wording as possible in the stem of the item.
   (c) state the stem of the item in positive form whenever possible.
   (d) ensure that each item is independent of other items in the test.

2. The lack of plausible, but incorrect, alternatives will cause the greatest difficulty when constructing
   (a) listing items.
   (b) multiple-choice items.
   (c) short-answer items.
   (d) true-false items.

3. Multiple-choice items designed to measure complex achievement contain
   (a) obscure content to increase difficulty.
   (b) new or novel material.

    (c) alternatives at the evaluate level.

    (d) different plausible distractors.

4. Increasing the number of alternatives in the items of a test produces the same effect as

    (a) confusing the answer.

    (b) giving the correct clue.

    (c) ensuring the objectives are tested.

    (d) lengthening the test.

TRUE-FALSE

DIRECTIONS: Read each statement and record as true or false on the lines provided.

5. _____ It is a good strategy to include answers to earlier items that help students answer subsequent items.

6. _____ Lack of plausible, but incorrect, alternatives should cause the test author to consider changing the test item from a multiple-choice to a true-false item.

7. _____ A limitation of multiple-choice items is that they can only measure simple learning outcomes.

8. _____ Scores from multiple-choice items are influenced more by guessing than true-false items.

9. _____ To increase the difficulty of multiple-choice items, it is a good strategy to state the stem in negative form.

RESTRICTED-RESPONSE ESSAY

10. The authors of your textbook discuss the strengths and limitations of multiple-choice items. Describe each strength and limitation. Confine your answer to one page.

7 WRITING SELECTION ITEMS
True-False, Matching, and Interpretive Exercise

Studying this chapter should enable you to

1. Describe the characteristics of each item type.
2. Describe the strengths and limitations of each item type.
3. Distinguish between well-stated and poorly stated items of each type.
4. Identify and correct faults in poorly stated items of each type.
5. Match each item type to intended learning outcomes.
6. Construct items of each type that are well-stated, relevant to important learning outcomes, and free of defects.

The multiple-choice item provides the most generally useful format for measuring achievement at various levels of learning. Thus, when selection-type items are to be used, an effective procedure is to start each item as a multiple-choice item and switch to another item type only when the learning outcome and content make it desirable to do so. For example, (1) when there are only two possible alternatives, a shift can be made to a true-false item; (2) when there are a number of similar factors to be related, a shift can be made to a matching item; and (3) when the items are to measure analysis, interpretation, and other complex outcomes, a shift can be made to the interpretive exercise. This procedure makes it possible to use the special strengths of the multiple-choice item and to use the other selection-type items more appropriately.

TRUE-FALSE ITEMS

True-false items are typically used to measure the ability to identify whether statements of fact are correct. The basic format is simply a declarative statement that the student must judge as true or false. There are modifications of this basic form in which the student must respond "yes" or "no," "agree" or "disagree," "right" or "wrong," "fact" or "opinion," and the like. Such variations are usually given the more general name of *alternative-response* items. In any event, this item type is characterized by the fact that only two responses are possible.

EXAMPLE

T   *F   True-false items are classified as a supply-type item.

In some cases the student is asked to judge each statement as true or false, and then to change the false statements so that they are true. When this is done, a portion of each statement is underlined to indicate the part that can be changed. In the example given, for instance, the words "supply-type" would be underlined. The key parts of true statements, of course, must also be underlined.

Another variation is the cluster-type true-false format. In this case, a series of items is based on a common stem.

EXAMPLE

Which of the following terms indicate observable student performance? Circle Y for yes and N for no.

*Y	N	1. Explains
*Y	N	2. Identifies
Y	*N	3. Learns
*Y	N	4. Predicts
Y	*N	5. Realizes

This item format is especially useful for replacing multiple-choice items that have more than one correct answer. Such items are impossible to score satisfactorily. This is avoided with the cluster-type item because it makes each alternative a separate scoring unit of one point. In our example, the student must record whether each term does or does not indicate observable student performance. Thus, this set of items provides an even better measure of the "ability to distinguish between performance and nonperformance terms" than would the single answer multiple-choice item. This is a good illustration of the procedure discussed earlier—that is, starting with multiple-choice items and switching to other item types when more effective measurement will result.

Despite the limitations of the true-false item, there are situations where it should be used. Whenever there are only two possible responses, the true-false item, or some adaptation of it, is likely to provide the most effective measure. Situations of this type include a simple "yes" or "no" response in classifying objects, determining whether a rule does or does not apply, distinguishing fact from opinion, and indicating whether arguments are relevant or irrelevant. As we indicated earlier, the best procedure is to use the true-false, or alternative-response, item only when this item type is more appropriate than the multiple-choice form. See Box 7.1 for a summary of strengths and limitations.

BOX 7.1   True-False Items

Strengths

1. The item is useful for outcomes where there are only two possible alternatives (e.g., fact or opinion, valid or invalid).
2. Less demand is placed on reading ability than in multiple-choice items.
3. A relatively large number of items can be answered in a typical testing period.
4. Complex outcomes can be measured when used with interpretive exercises.
5. Scoring is easy, objective, and reliable.

Limitations

1. It is difficult to write items beyond the knowledge level that are free from ambiguity.
2. Making an item false provides no evidence that the student knows what is correct.
3. No diagnostic information is provided by the incorrect answers.
4. Scores are more influenced by guessing than with any other item type.

Rules for Writing True-False Items

The purpose of a true-false item, as with all item types, is to distinguish between those who have and those who have not achieved the intended learning outcome. Achievers should be able to select the correct alternative without difficulty, while nonachievers should find the incorrect alternative at least as attractive as the correct one. The rules for writing true-false items are directed toward this end.

1. Include only one central idea in each statement. The main point of the item should be in a prominent position in the statement. The true-false decision should not depend on some subordinate point or trivial detail. The use of several ideas in each statement should generally be avoided because these tend to be confusing, and the answer is more apt to be influenced by reading ability than the intended outcome.

EXAMPLE

Poor: T   *F   The true-false item is also called an alternative-response item.

Better: *T   F   The true-false item, which is favored by test experts, is also called an alternative-response item.

The "poor" example must be marked false because test experts do not favor the true-false item. Such subordinate points are easily overlooked when reading the item. If the point is important, it should be included as the main idea in a separate item.

2. Keep the statement short and use simple vocabulary and sentence structure. A short, simple statement will increase the likelihood that the point of the item is clear. All students should be able to grasp what the statement is saying. Passing or failing the item should depend solely on whether a student has achieved the necessary knowledge.

EXAMPLE

Poor.	*T	F	The true-false item is more subject to guessing but it should be used in place of a multiple-choice item, if well constructed, when there is a dearth of distracters that are plausible.
Better.	*T	F	The true-false item should be used in place of a multiple-choice item when only two alternatives are possible.

Long, involved statements like the "poor" version tend to contaminate the achievement measure with a measure of reading comprehension. A basic rule of item writing is to focus on the intended function of the item and remove all irrelevant influences.

3. Word the statement so precisely that it can unequivocally be judged true or false. True statements should be true under all circumstances and yet free of qualifiers ("may," "possible," and so on), which might provide clues. This requires the use of precise words and the avoidance of such vague terms as "seldom," "frequently," and "often." The same care, of course, must also be given to false statements so that their falsity is not too readily apparent from differences in wording. At first glance, this seems like a simple rule to follow but it causes frequent problems.

EXAMPLE

Poor:	T	*F	Lengthening a test will increase its reliability.
Better:	*T	F	Lengthening a test by adding items like those in the test will increase its reliability.

The "poor" version of this item must be marked false because it is not true under all conditions. For example, if items are added to the test that all students fail, reliability would not be changed. However, the "poor" version would not be a good item to use in a test because it requires students to mark a very important principle of measurement false. We could say "usually will increase," but the qualifier would encourage those who are uninformed to mark it true and they would receive an unearned point. The "better" version has no such "giveaway" to the answer. In fact, an uninformed student might think that adding similar items to a test of low reliability could not possibly increase reliability—but it does. This example illustrates the great care needed in phrasing statements so that they are unequivocally true but do not contain "giveaways" to the answer.

4. Use negative statements sparingly and avoid double negatives. The "no" and/or "not" in negative statements are frequently over-looked and they are read as positive statements. Thus, negative statements should be used only when the learning outcome requires it (e.g., in avoiding a harmful practice), and then the negative words should be emphasized by underlining or by use of capital letters. Statements including double negatives tend to be so confusing that they should be restated in positive form.

EXAMPLE

Poor: *T   F   Correction-for-guessing is not a practice that should never be used in testing.

Better.   *T   F   Correction-for-guessing is a practice that should sometimes be used in testing.

The double negatives in the "poor" version introduce sufficient ambiguity to cause the item to be a measure of reading comprehension. The "better" version clearly states the same idea in positive form.

5. Statements of opinion should be attributed to some source unless used to distinguish facts from opinion. A statement of opinion is not true or false by itself, and it is poor instructional practice to have students respond to it as if it were a factual statement. Obviously, the only way students could mark such an item correctly would be to agree with the opinion of the item writer. It is much more defensible to attribute the item to some source, such as an individual or organization. It then becomes a measure of how well the student knows the beliefs or values of that individual or organization.

EXAMPLE

Poor.   T   F   Testing should play a major role in the teaching–learning process.

Better.   *T   F   Gronlund believes that testing should play a major role in the teaching–learning process.

In some cases, it is useful to use a series of opinion statements that pertain to the same individual or organization. This permits a more comprehensive measure of how well the student understands a belief or value system.

EXAMPLE

Would the author of your textbook agree or disagree with the following statements? Circle A for agree, D for disagree.

*A   D   1. The first step in achievement testing is to state the intended learning outcomes in performance terms.

A   *D   2. True-false tests are superior to multiple-choice tests for measuring achievement.

Using about 10 items like those listed here would provide a fairly good indication of the students' grasp of the author's point of view. Items like this are useful for measuring how well students understand a textbook without requiring them to agree with the opinions expressed. It is desirable, of course, to select opinion statements that are shared by many experts in the area.

Another valuable use of opinion statements is to ask students to distinguish between statements of fact and statements of opinion. This is an important outcome in its own right and is a basic part of critical thinking.

EXAMPLE

Read each of the following statements and circle F if it is a *fact* and circle O if it is an *opinion*.

*F	O	1. The true-false item is a selection-type item.
F	*O	2. The true-false item is difficult to construct.
F	*O	3. The true-false item encourages student guessing.
*F	O	4. The true-false item can be scored objectively.

In addition to illustrating the use of opinion statements in test items, the last two examples illustrate variations from the typical true-false format. These are more logically called *alternative-response* items.

6. When cause-effect relationships are being measured, use only true propositions. The true-false item can be used to measure the "ability to identify cause-effect relationships," and this is an important aspect of understanding. When used for this purpose, both propositions should be true and only the relationship judged true or false.

EXAMPLE

Poor:	T	*F	True-false items are classified as objective items *because* students must supply the answer.
Better:	T	*F	True-false items are classified as objective items *because* there are only two possible answers.

The "poor" version is false because of the second part of the statement. With true-false items, students must *select* the answer rather than *supply* it. However, some students may mark this item false because they think the first part of the statement is incorrect. Thus, they receive one point because they *do not know* that true-false items are classified as objective items. Obviously, an item does not function as intended if misinformation can result in the correct answer. The problem with the "poor" version is that all three elements are permitted to vary (part one, part two, and the relationship between them) and it is impossible to tell what part the student is responding to when the item is marked false. In the "better" version both parts of the statement are true and the students must simply decide if the second part explains why the first part is true. In this case it does not, so it is marked false. Typically, a series of items like this is preceded by directions that make clear that only the relationship between the two parts of each statement is to be judged true or false.

7. Avoid extraneous clues to the answer. There are a number of *specific determiners* that provide verbal clues to the truth or falsity of an item. Statements that include such absolutes as "always," "never," "all," "none," and "only" tend to be false; statements with qualifiers such as "usually," "may," and "sometimes" tend to be true. Either these verbal clues must be eliminated from the statements, or their use must be balanced between true items and false items.

EXAMPLE

Poor.   T   *F   A statement of opinion should never be used in a true-false item.

Poor.   *T   F   A statement of opinion may be used in a true-false item.

Better.   *T   F   A statement of opinion, by itself, cannot be marked true or false.

The length and complexity of the statement might also provide a clue. True statements tend to be longer and more complex than false ones because of their need for qualifiers. Thus, a special effort should be made to equalize true and false statements in these respects.

A tendency to use a disproportionate number of true statements, or false statements, might also be detected and used as a clue. Having approximately, but not exactly, an equal number of each seems to be the best solution. When assembling the test, it is, of course, also necessary to avoid placing the correct answers in some discernible pattern (for instance, T, F, T, F). Random placement will eliminate this possible clue.

8. Base items on introductory material to measure more complex learning outcomes. True-false or alternative-response items are frequently used in interpreting written materials, tables, graphs, maps, or pictures. The use of introductory material makes it possible to measure various types of complex learning outcomes. These item types will be illustrated in the section on interpretive exercises later in this chapter. See Box 7.2 for summary checklist for evaluation of true-false items.

MATCHING ITEMS

The matching item is simply a variation of the multiple-choice form. A good practice is to switch to the matching format only when it becomes apparent that the same alternatives are being repeated in several multiple-choice items. See Box 7.3 for the strengths and limitations of matching items.

BOX 7.2   Checklist for Evaluating True-False Items

1. Is this type of item appropriate for measuring the intended learning outcome?
2. Does the item task match the learning task to be measured?
3. Does each statement contain one central idea?
4. Can each statement be unequivocally judged true or false?
5. Are the statements brief and stated in simple, clear language?
6. Are negative statements used sparingly and double negatives avoided?
7. Are statements of opinion attributed to some source?
8. Are the statements free of clues to the answer (e.g., verbal clues, length)?
9. Is there approximately an even number of true and false statements?
10. When arranged in the test, are the true and false items put in random order?

BOX 7.3   Matching Items

Strengths

1. A compact and efficient form is provided where the same set of responses fit a series of item stems (i.e., premises).
2. Reading and response time is short.
3. This item type is easily constructed if converted from multiple-choice items having a common set of alternatives.
4. Scoring is easy, objective, and reliable.

Limitations

1. This item type is largely restricted to simple knowledge outcomes based on association.
2. It is difficult to construct items that contain a sufficient number of homogeneous responses.
3. Susceptibility to irrelevant clues is greater than in other item types.

EXAMPLE

Which test item is *least* useful for educational diagnosis?

    a.   Multiple-choice item.

  *b.   True-false item.

    c.   Short-answer item.

Which test item measures the greatest variety of learning outcomes?

  *a.   Multiple-choice item.

    b.   True-false item.

    c.   Short-answer item.

Which test item is difficult to score objectively?

   a.   Multiple-choice item.
   b.   True-false item.
  *c.   Short-answer item.

Which test item provides the highest score by guessing?

   a.   Multiple-choice item.
  *b.   True-false item.
   c.   Short-answer item.

By switching to a matching format, we can eliminate the repetition of the alternative answers and present the same items in a more compact form. The matching format consists of a series of stems, called *premises,* and a series of alternative answers, called *responses.* These are arranged in columns with directions that set the rules for matching. The following example illustrates how our multiple-choice items can be converted to matching form.

EXAMPLE

Directions: Column A contains a list of characteristics of test items. On the line to the left of each statement, write the letter of the test item in Column B that best fits the statement. Each response in Column B may be used once, more than once, or not at all.

Column A	*Column B*
(B) 1. Is least useful for educational diagnosis.	A. Multiple-choice item.
(A) 2. Measures greatest variety of learning outcomes.	B. True-false item.
(C) 3. Is most difficult to score objectively.	C. Short-answer item.
(B) 4. Provides the highest score by guessing.	

The conversion to matching item illustrated here is probably the most defensible use of this item type. All too frequently, matching items consist of a disparate collection of premises, each of which has only one or two plausible answers. This can be avoided by starting with multiple-choice items and switching to the matching format only when it provides a more compact and efficient means of measuring the same achievement. In our example, we could have also expanded the item by adding other similar premises and responses.

Rules for Writing Matching Items

A good matching item should function the same as a series of multiple-choice items. As each premise is considered, all of the responses should serve as plausible alternatives. The rules for item writing are directed toward this end.

1. Include only homogeneous material in each matching item. In our earlier example of a matching item, we included *only* types of test items and their characteristics. Similarly, an item might include *only* authors and their works, inventors and their inventions, scientists and their discoveries, or historical events and their dates. This homogeneity is necessary if all responses are to serve as plausible alternatives (see earlier example).

2. Keep the lists of items short and place the brief responses on the right. A short list of items (say fewer than 10) will save reading time, make it easier for the student to locate the answer, and increase the likelihood that the responses will be homogeneous and plausible. Placing the brief responses on the right also saves reading time.

3. Use a larger, or smaller, number of responses than premises, and permit the responses to be used more than once. Both an uneven match and the possibility of using each response more than once reduce the guessing factor. As we noted earlier, proper use of the matching form requires that *all responses be plausible alternatives for each premise*. This, of course, dictates that each response be eligible for use more than once.

4. Place the responses in alphabetical or numerical order. This will make selection of the responses easier and avoid possible clues due to placement.

5. Specify in the directions the basis for matching and indicate that each response may be used once, more than once, or not at all. This will clarify the task for all students and prevent any misunderstanding. Take care, however, not to make the directions too long and involved. The previous example illustrates adequate detail for directions.

6. Put all of the matching item on the same page. This will prevent the distraction of flipping pages back and forth and prevent students from overlooking responses on another page. See Box 7.4 for a summary checklist for evaluating matching items.

THE INTERPRETIVE EXERCISE

Complex learning outcomes can frequently be more effectively measured by basing a series of test items on a common selection of introductory material.

BOX 7.4   Checklist for Evaluating Matching Items

1. Is this type of item appropriate for measuring the intended learning outcome?
2. Does the item task match the learning task to be measured?
3. Does each matching item contain only homogeneous material?
4. Are the lists of items short with the brief responses on the right?
5. Is an uneven match provided by making the list of responses longer or shorter than the list of premises?
6. Are the responses in alphabetical or numerical order?
7. Do the directions clearly state the basis for matching and that each response can be used once, more than once, or not at all?
8. Does the complete matching item appear on the same page?

This may be a paragraph, a table, a chart, a graph, a map, or a picture. The test items that follow the introductory material may be designed to call forth any type of intellectual ability or skill that can be measured objectively. This type of exercise is commonly called an *interpretive exercise,* and both multiple-choice items and alternative-response items are widely used to measure interpretation of the introductory material.

The following example illustrates the use of multiple-choice items. Note that this item type makes it possible to measure a variety of learning outcomes with the same selection of introductory material. In this particular case, item 1 measures the *ability to recognize unstated assumptions,* item 2 the *ability to identify the meaning of a term,* and item 3 the *ability to identify relationships.*

EXAMPLE

Directions: Read the following comments a teacher made about testing. Then answer the questions that follow by circling the letter of the best answer.

"Students go to school to learn, not to take tests. In addition, tests cannot be used to indicate a student's absolute level of learning. All tests can do is rank students in order of achievement, and this relative ranking is influenced by guessing, bluffing, and the subjective opinions of the teacher doing the scoring. The teaching–learning process would benefit if we did away with tests and depended on student self-evaluation."

1. Which one of the following unstated assumptions is this teacher making?
    a. Students go to school to learn.
    b. Teachers use essay tests primarily.
    *c. Tests make no contribution to learning.
    d. Tests do not indicate a student's absolute level of learning.

2. Which one of the following types of tests is this teacher primarily talking about?
    a. Diagnostic test.
    b. Formative test.
    c. Pretest.
    *d. Summative test.

3. Which one of the following propositions is most essential to the final conclusion?
    *a. Effective self-evaluation does not require the use of tests.
    b. Tests place students in rank order only.
    c. Tests scores are influenced by factors other than achievement.
    d. Students do not go to school to take tests.

The next example uses a modified version of the alternative-response form. This is frequently called a *key-type* item because a common set of alternatives is used in responding to each question. Note that the key-type item is devoted entirely to the measurement of one learning outcome. In this example the item measures the *ability to recognize warranted and unwarranted inferences.*

EXAMPLE

Directions: Paragraph A contains a description of the testing practices of Mr. Smith, a high school teacher. Read the description and each of the statements that follow it. Mark each statement to indicate the type of INFERENCE that can be drawn about it from the material in the paragraph. Place the appropriate letter in front of each statement using the following KEY:

> T—if the statement may be INFERRED as TRUE.
>
> F—if the statement may be INFERRED as UNTRUE.
>
> N—if NO INFERENCE may be drawn about it from the paragraph.

Paragraph A

Approximately one week before a test is to be given, Mr. Smith carefully goes through the textbook and constructs multiple-choice items based on the material in the book. He always uses the exact wording of the textbook for the correct answer so that there will be no question concerning its correctness. He is careful to include some test items from each chapter. After the test is given, he lists the scores from high to low on the blackboard and tells each student his or her score. He does not return the test papers to the students, but he offers to answer any questions they might have about the test. He puts the items from each test into a test file, which he is building for future use.

Statements on Paragraph A

(T) **1.** Mr. Smith's tests measure a limited range of learning outcomes.
(F) **2.** Some of Mr. Smith's test items measure at the understanding level.
(N) **3.** Mr. Smith's tests measure a balanced sample of subject matter.
(N) **4.** Mr. Smith uses the type of test item that is best for his purpose.
(T) **5.** Students can determine where they rank in the distribution of scores on Mr. Smith's tests.
(F) **6.** Mr. Smith's testing practices are likely to motivate students to overcome their weaknesses.

Key-type items are fairly easy to develop and can be directly related to specific learning outcomes. The key categories can, of course, be reused by simply changing the introductory material and the statements. Thus, they provide a standard framework for test preparation. Other common key categories include the following: (1) The argument is relevant, irrelevant, or neither; (2) the statement is supported by the evidence, refuted by the evidence, or neither; (3) the assumption is necessary or unnecessary; and (4) the conclusion is valid, invalid, or its validity cannot be determined. Although such standard key

BOX 7.5   Interpretive Exercises

Strengths

1. An efficient means of measuring the interpretation of printed information in various forms (e.g., written, charts, graphs, maps, pictures) is provided.
2. More meaningful complex learning outcomes can be measured than with the single-item format.
3. The use of introductory material provides a common basis for responding.
4. Scoring is easy, objective, and reliable.

Limitations

1. It is difficult to construct effective items.
2. Written material is highly dependent on reading skill.
3. This item type is highly subject to extraneous clues.
4. It is ineffective in measuring the ability to originate, organize, and express ideas.

categories should not be applied in a perfunctory manner, they can provide guidelines to simplify the construction of the interpretive exercise. See Box 7.5 for strengths and limitations.

Rules for Constructing Interpretive Exercises

The effectiveness of interpretive exercises, such as those illustrated earlier, depends on the care with which the introductory material is selected and the skill with which the dependent items are prepared. The following rules provide guidelines for preparing high-quality exercises of this type.

1. Select introductory material that is relevant to the learning outcomes to be measured. The introductory material may take many forms: written material, table, chart, graph, map, picture, or cartoon. In some cases the interpretation of the introductory material is an important learning outcome in its own right, as in the "interpretation of a weather map" or "the interpretation of a line graph." Here the nature of the introductory material is clearly prescribed by the intended outcome. In other cases, however, the introductory material simply provides the means for measuring other important outcomes. The "ability to distinguish between valid and invalid conclusions," for example, may be measured with different types of introductory material. In this instance we should select the type of material that provides the most direct measure of the learning outcome, is familiar to the examinees, and places the least demand on reading ability. For young children this means pictorial materials should typically be favored.

2. Select introductory material that is new to the examinees. Although the form of the material should be familiar to the examinees, the specific content used in an exercise should be new to them. Thus, if they are asked to identify relationships shown in a graph, the type of graph should be familiar but the specific data in the graph must be new. If the data were the same as that presented in the classroom or described in the textbook, the exercise would measure nothing more than the simple recall of information. To measure complex outcomes, some novelty is necessary. How much depends on the specific nature of the intended outcome.

In some cases it is possible to locate introductory material that is new to the examinees by reviewing sources that are not readily available to them. Then it is simply a matter of adapting the material for testing purposes. In other cases it is necessary to prepare completely new material (i.e., write a paragraph, construct a graph, make a map, or draw a picture). In either case further revision will probably be needed when the dependent test items are being prepared. The process is essentially a circular one, with the writing of items requiring some changes in the introductory material and changes there providing ideas for new items. In carrying out this process of adapting and revising the material, be careful not to introduce so much novelty that the exercise no longer provides a valid measure of the intended learning outcome.

3. Keep the introductory material brief and readable. It is inefficient for both the test maker and the test taker to use extended introductory material and only one or two test items. If the introductory material is in written form, excessively long selections will also create problems for individuals with inadequate reading skills. Ideally, it should be a brief, concise selection that contains enough ideas for several relevant test items. Material of this type can frequently be obtained from summaries, digests, and other condensed forms of written material. In some cases pictures or diagrams may provide the most concise summary of the material. As noted earlier, we should always favor the type of material that places the least demand on reading ability.

4. Construct test items that call forth the type of performance specified in the learning outcome. To adequately measure the intended interpretation of the introductory material requires careful phrasing of the questions and special attention to two important cautions. First, *the answer to an item should not be given directly in the material* since some mental process beyond "recognition of a stated fact" is required in measures of intellectual skills. Second, *it should not be possible to answer the question without the introductory material*. If an item can be answered on the basis of general knowledge, it is not measuring the ability to interpret the material in the exercise. A good check on this type of error is to cover the introductory material and attempt to answer the questions without it.

5. Follow the rules of effective item writing that pertain to the type of objective item used. All of the rules for constructing the various types of objective test items discussed in the last two chapters are applicable to the construction of items used in interpretive exercises. Even greater care must be taken to avoid extraneous clues, however, since items in interpretive exercises seem especially prone to such clues, and they tend to be more difficult to detect in these items. If the introductory material includes illustrations, for example, special attention should be directed to such things as the size, shape, and position of objects as possible extraneous clues. These are frequently overlooked by the test maker who is concentrating on the intricacies of the mental response required, but not by the unprepared student who is frantically searching for any solution to the problem.

BOX 7.6   Checklist for Evaluating Interpretive Exercises

1. Is this type of exercise appropriate for measuring the intended learning outcome?
2. Is the introductory material relevant to the learning outcomes?
3. Is the introductory material familiar but new to the examinees?
4. Is the introductory material brief and at the appropriate reading level?
5. Do the test items call forth the performance specified in the learning outcomes?
6. Do the test items call for interpretation (rather than recognition or recall)?
7. Do the test items meet the criteria of effective item writing that apply to the item type used?
8. Is the interpretive exercise free of extraneous clues?

The greatest help in constructing interpretive exercises is to review a wide range of sample exercises that use different types of introductory material and different forms of dependent test items. For locating illustrative exercises, see the list of references at the end of the chapter. See Box 7.6 for a summary checklist for evaluating interpretive exercises.

Summary of Points

1. A good practice is to start with multiple-choice items and switch to other selection-type items when more appropriate.
2. The true-false or alternative-response item is appropriate when there are only two possible alternatives.
3. The true-false item is used primarily to measure knowledge of specific facts, although there are some notable exceptions.
4. Each true-false statement should contain only one central idea, be concisely stated, be free of clues and irrelevant sources of difficulty, and have an answer on which experts would agree.
5. Modifications of the true-false item are especially useful for measuring the ability to "distinguish between fact and opinion" and "identify cause-effect relationships."
6. Modifications of the true-false item can be used in interpretive exercises to measure various types of complex learning outcomes.
7. The matching item is a variation of the multiple-choice form and is appropriate when it provides a more compact and efficient means of measuring the same achievement.
8. The matching item consists of a list of *premises* and a list of the *responses* to be related to the premises.
9. A good matching item is based on homogeneous material, contains a brief list of premises and an uneven number of responses (more or less) that can be used more than once, and has the brief responses in the right-hand column.

10. The directions for a matching item should indicate the basis for matching and that each response can be used once, more than once, or not at all.
11. The interpretive exercise consists of a series of selection-type items based on some type of introductory material (e.g., paragraph, table, chart, graph, map, or picture).
12. The interpretive exercise uses both multiple-choice and alternative-response items to measure a variety of complex learning outcomes.
13. The introductory material used in an interpretive exercise must be relevant to the outcomes to be measured, new to examinees, at the proper reading level, and as brief as possible.
14. The test items used in an interpretive exercise should call for the intended type of interpretation, and the answers to the items should be dependent on the introductory material.
15. The test items used in an interpretive exercise should be in harmony with the rules for constructing that item type.

References and Additional Reading

Carey, L. M. *Measuring and Evaluating School Learning*, 3rd ed. (Boston: Allyn and Bacon, 2001).
Linn, R. L., & Gronlund, N. E. *Measurement and Assessment in Teaching*, 8th ed. (Upper Saddle River, NJ: Merrill/Prentice Hall, 2000).
Mehrens, W. A., & Lehmann, I. J. *Measurement and Evaluation in Education and Psychology*, 4th ed. (New York: Holt, Rinehart and Winston, 1991).
Oosterhoff, A. C. *Developing and Using Classroom Assessments*, 2nd ed. (Upper Saddle River, NJ: Prentice Hall, 1999).
Taylor, C. S., & Nolen, S. B. *Classroom Assessment: Supporting Teaching and Learning in Real Classrooms* (Upper Saddle River, NJ: Prentice Hall, Pearson, 2005).

Self-Assessment

MULTIPLE CHOICE

DIRECTIONS: Select the best answer for each item by circling the corresponding letter.

1. Which of the following is the best-stated true-false item?
   (a) A barometer may be helpful in predicting weather
   (b) A rising barometer forecasts fair weather
   (c) All barometers give precise measures of air pressure
   (d) The barometer is the most useful weather instrument

2. The matching item consists of
   (a) stems and distracters
   (b) premises and responses
   (c) stems and responses
   (d) premises and distracters

3. Asking students to judge each statement as true or false, and then to change the false statements so they are true increases the item's level of
   (a) validity
   (b) reliability
   (c) plausibility
   (d) difficulty

4. A series of selection-type test items based on introductory material such as a graph is an example of
   (a) a restricted-response essay
   (b) an interpretive exercise
   (c) an extended-response essay
   (d) a student portfolio

TRUE-FALSE

DIRECTIONS: Read each statement and record as true or false on the lines provided.

5. _____ A statement of opinion, by itself, cannot be marked true or false.

6. _____ In writing true-false items, one useful rule is to include absolute terms like "always" or "never."

7. _____ Scores from true-false items are more likely to be influenced by student guessing than matching items.

8. _____ A limitation of the interpretive exercise is that scoring is highly subjective.

9. _____ A true-false item with the correct answer being "false" provides evidence that the student knows the correct answer.

Restricted-Response Essay

10. The authors of your textbook discuss the strengths and limitations of true-false items. Describe each strength and limitation. Confine your answer to one page.

8 WRITING SUPPLY ITEMS
Short Answer and Essay

Studying this chapter should enable you to

1. Describe the strengths and limitations of short-answer items.
2. Distinguish between well-stated and poorly stated short-answer items.
3. Identify and correct faults in poorly stated short-answer items.
4. Match short-answer items to intended learning outcomes.
5. Construct short-answer items that are well stated, relevant to important learning outcomes, and free of defects.
6. Describe the strengths and limitations of essay questions.
7. Distinguish between restricted-response and extended-response essay questions.
8. Describe the strengths and limitations of essay questions.
9. Write essay questions that present a clear task, are relevant to important learning outcomes, and provide guidelines for scoring.
10. Score essay answers more effectively.

As noted in the last two chapters, selection-type items can be designed to measure a variety of learning outcomes, ranging from simple to complex. They tend to be favored in achievement tests because they provide (1) greater control of the type of response students can make, (2) broader sampling of achievement, and (3) quicker and more objective scoring. Despite these advantages, supply-type items can also play an important role in measuring achievement.

Supply-type items require students to produce the answer. This may be a single-word or a several-page response. Although the length of the response ranges along a continuum, supply-type items are typically divided into (1) short-answer items, (2) restricted-response essay, and (3) extended-response essay (see Figure 8.1).

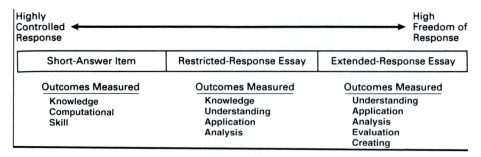

FIGURE 8.1 Supply-Type Items Arranged Along a "Control of Response" Continuum and a List of Learning Outcomes Typically Measured by Each Item Type

SHORT-ANSWER ITEMS

The short-answer (or completion) item requires the examinee to supply the appropriate words, numbers, or symbols to answer a question or complete a statement.

EXAMPLES

What are the incorrect responses in a multiple-choice item called? *(distracters)*

The incorrect responses in a multiple-choice item are called *(distracters)*.

This item type also includes computational problems and any other simple item form that requires supplying the answer rather than selecting it. Except for its use in computational problems, the short-answer item is used primarily to measure simple recall of knowledge.

The short-answer item appears to be easy to write and use, but there are two major problems in constructing short-answer items. First, it is extremely difficult to phrase the question or incomplete statement so that only one answer is correct. In the example we have noted, for instance, a student might respond with any one of a number of answers that could be defended as appropriate. The student might write "incorrect alternatives," "wrong answers," "inappropriate options," "decoys," "foils," or some other equally descriptive response. Second, there is the problem of spelling. If credit is given only when the answer is spelled correctly, the poor spellers will be prevented from showing their true level of achievement, and the test scores will become an uninterpretable mixture of knowledge and spelling skill. On the other hand, if attempts are made to ignore spelling during the scoring process, there is still the problem of deciding whether a badly spelled word represents the intended answer. This, of course, introduces an element of subjectivity that tends to make the scores less dependable as measures of achievement. See Box 8.1 for strengths and limitations.

Due to these weaknesses, the short-answer item should be reserved for those special situations where supplying the answer is a necessary part of the

BOX 8.1   Short-Answer Items

Strengths

1. It is easy to write test items.
2. Guessing is less likely than in selection-type items.
3. This item type is well suited to computational problems and other learning outcomes where supplying the answer is important.
4. A broad range of knowledge outcomes can be measured.

Limitations

1. It is difficult to phrase statements so that only one answer is correct.
2. Scoring is contaminated by spelling ability when responses are *non*verbal.
3. Scoring is tedious and time consuming.
4. This item type is not very adaptable to measuring complex learning outcomes.

---

learning outcome to be measured—for example, where the intent is to have students *recall* the information, where computational problems are used, or where a selection-type item would make the answer obvious. In these situations, the use of the short-answer item can be defended despite its shortcomings.

Rules for Writing Short-Answer Items

1. State the item so that only a single, brief answer is possible. This requires great skill in phrasing and the use of precise terms. What appears to be a simple, clear question to the test maker can frequently be answered in many different ways, as we noted with the previous sample item. It helps to review the item with this rule in mind and revise as needed.

2. Start with a direct question and switch to an incomplete statement only when greater conciseness is possible by doing so. The use of a direct question increases the likelihood that the problem will be stated clearly and that only one answer will be appropriate. Also, incomplete statements tend to be less ambiguous when they are based on problems that were first stated in question form.

EXAMPLE

What is another name for true-false items? *(alternative-response items)*

True-false items are also called *(alternative-response items)*.

In some cases, it is best to leave it in question form. This may make the item clearer, especially to younger students.

3. It is best to leave only one blank, and it should relate to the main point of the statement. Leaving several blanks to be filled in is often confusing, and the answer to one blank may depend on the answer in another.

EXAMPLE

> *Poor:*   In terms of type of response, the *(matching)* item is most like the *(multiple-choice)* item.
>
> *Better:*   In terms of type of responses, which item is most like the matching item? *(multiple choice)*.

In the "poor" version, a number of different responses would have to be given credit, such as "short answer" and "essay," and "true-false" and "multiple choice." Obviously, the item would not function as originally intended.

It is also important to avoid asking students to respond to unimportant or minor aspects of a statement. Focus on the main idea of the item and leave a blank only for the key response.

4. Place the blanks at the end of the statement. This permits the student to read the complete problem before coming to the blank to be filled. With this procedure, confusion and rereading of the item is avoided, and scoring is simplified. Constructing incomplete statements with blanks at the end is more easily accomplished when the item is first stated as a direct question, as suggested earlier. In some cases, it may be a matter of rewording the item and changing the response to be made.

EXAMPLE

> *Poor:*   *(Reliability)* is likely to increase when a test is lengthened.
>
> *Better:*   When a test is lengthened, reliability is likely to *(increase)*.

With this particular item, the "better" version also provides a more clearly focused item. The "poor" version could be answered by "validity," "time for testing," "fatigue," and other unintended but clearly correct responses. This again illustrates the great care needed in phrasing short-answer items.

5. Avoid extraneous clues to the answer. One of the most common clues in short-answer items is the length of the blank. If a long blank is used for a long word and a short blank for a short word, this is obviously a clue. Thus, all blanks should be uniform in length. Another common clue is the use of the indefinite article "a" or "an" just before the blank. It sometimes gives away the answer, or at least rules out some possible incorrect answers.

EXAMPLE

> *Poor:*   The supply-type item used to measure the ability to organize and integrate material is called an *(essay item)*.
>
> *Better:*   Supply-type items used to measure the ability to organize and integrate material are called *(essay items)*.

1(646) 705-6791

The "poor" version rules out "short-answer item," the only other supply-type item, because it does not follow the article "an." One solution is to include both articles, using a(an). Another solution is to eliminate the article by switching to plural, as shown in the "better" version.

6. For numerical answers, indicate the degree of precision expected and the units in which they are to be expressed. Indicating the degree of precision (e.g., to the nearest whole number) will clarify the task for students and prevent them from spending more time on an item than is required. Indicating the units in which to express the answer will aid scoring by providing a more uniform set of responses (e.g., minutes rather than fractions of an hour). When the learning outcome requires knowing the type of unit in common use and the degree of precision expected, this rule must then be disregarded. See Box 8.2 for a summary checklist.

ESSAY QUESTIONS

The most notable characteristic of the essay question is the freedom of response it provides. As with the short-answer item, students must produce their own answers. With the essay question, however, they are free to decide how to approach the problem, what factual information to use, how to organize the answer, and what degree of emphasis to give each aspect of the response. Thus, the essay question is especially useful for measuring the ability to organize, integrate, and express ideas. These are the types of performance for which selection-type items and short-answer items are so inadequate.

In deciding when and how to use essay questions, it may be desirable to compare their relative merits with those of selection-type items, as shown in Table 8.1. As can be seen in the table, both item types are efficient for certain purposes and inefficient for others. It is also apparent that the two types tend to complement each other in terms of the types of learning outcomes measured and the effect they are most likely to have on learning. Thus, it is not a matter of using either selection-type items or essay questions, but rather when should each be used. Tests may frequently require both types in order to obtain adequate coverage of the intended learning outcomes.

BOX 8.2 Checklist for Evaluating Short-Answer Items

1. Is this type of item appropriate for measuring the intended learning outcome?
2. Does the item task match the learning task to be measured?
3. Does the item call for a single, brief answer?
4. Has the item been written as a direct question or a well-stated incomplete sentence?
5. Does the desired response relate to the main point of the item?
6. Is the blank placed at the end of the statement?
7. Have clues to the answer been avoided (e.g., "a" or "an," length of the blank)?
8. Are the units and degree of precision indicated for numerical answers?

TABLE 8.1 Summary Comparison of Selection-Type Items and Essay

	Selection-Type Items	Essay Questions
Learning Outcomes Measured	Good for measuring the recall of knowledge, understanding, and application levels of learning; inadequate for organizing and expressing ideas.	Inefficient for measuring the recall of knowledge; best for ability to organize, integrate, and express ideas.
Sampling of Content	The use of a large number of items results in broad coverage, which makes representative sampling of content feasible.	The use of a small number of items limits coverage, which makes representative sampling of content infeasible.
Preparation of Items	Preparation of good items is difficult and time consuming.	Preparation of good items is difficult but easier than selection-type items.
Scoring	Objective, simple, and highly reliable.	Subjective, difficult, and less reliable.
Factors Distorting Scores	Reading ability and guessing.	Writing ability and bluffing.
Probable Effect on Learning	Encourages students to remember, interpret, and use the ideas of others.	Encourages students to organize, integrate, and express their own ideas.

Types of Essay Questions

The freedom of response permitted by essay questions varies considerably. Students may be required to give a brief and precise response, or they may be given great freedom in determining the form and scope of their answers. Questions of the first type are commonly called *restricted-response questions* and those of the second type are called *extended-response questions*. This is an arbitrary but convenient pair of categories for classifying essay questions.

RESTRICTED-RESPONSE QUESTIONS.   The restricted-response question places strict limits on the answer to be given. The boundaries of the subject matter to be considered are usually narrowly defined by the problem, and the specific form of the answer is also commonly indicated (by words such as "list," "define," and "give reasons"). In some cases the response is limited further by the use of introductory material or by the use of special directions.

EXAMPLE

Describe the relative merits of selection-type test items and essay questions for measuring learning outcomes at the understanding level. Confine your answer to one page.

EXAMPLE

Mr. Rogers, a ninth-grade science teacher, wants to measure his students' "ability to interpret scientific data" with a paper-and-pencil test.

1. Describe the steps that Mr. Rogers should follow.
2. Give reasons to justify each step.

Restricting the form and scope of the answers to essay questions has both advantages and disadvantages. Such questions can be prepared more easily, related more directly to specific learning outcomes, and scored more easily. On the other hand, they provide little opportunity for the students to demonstrate their abilities to organize, to integrate, and to develop essentially new patterns of response. The imposed limitations make restricted-response items especially useful for measuring learning outcomes at the understanding, application, and analysis levels of learning. They are of relatively little value for measuring outcomes at the evaluating and creating levels. At these levels the extended-response question provides the more appropriate measure.

EXTENDED-RESPONSE QUESTIONS.   The extended-response question gives students almost unlimited freedom to determine the form and scope of their responses. Although in some instances rather rigid practical limits may be imposed, such as time limits or page limits, restrictions on the material to be included in the answer and on the form of response are held to a minimum. Students must be given sufficient freedom to demonstrate skills of evaluating and creating, and just enough control to ensure that the intended intellectual skills and abilities will be called forth by the question. Thus, the amount of structure will vary from item to item depending on the learning outcomes being measured, but the stress will always be on providing as much freedom as the situation permits.

EXAMPLE

Evaluation Outcome: (The student is given a complete achievement test that includes errors or flaws in the directions, in the test items, and in the arrangement of the items.) Write a critical evaluation of this test using as evaluative criteria the rules and standards for test construction described in your textbook. Include a detailed analysis of the test's strengths and weaknesses and an evaluation of its overall quality and probable effectiveness.

The extended-response question provides for the creative integration of ideas, the overall evaluation of materials, and a broad approach to problem solving. These are all important learning outcomes and ones that cannot be measured by other types of test items. The biggest problem, of course, is to evaluate the answers with sufficient reliability to provide a useful measure of learning.

BOX 8.3   Essay Questions

Strengths

1. The highest level learning outcomes (analyzing, evaluating, creating) can be measured.
2. Preparation time is less than that for selection-type items.
3. The integration and application of ideas is emphasized.

Limitations

1. There is an inadequate sampling of achievement due to time needed for answering each question.
2. It is difficult to relate to intended learning outcomes because of freedom to select, organize, and express ideas.
3. Scores are raised by writing skill and bluffing and lowered by poor handwriting, misspelling, and grammatical errors.
4. Scoring is time consuming and subjective, and it tends to be unreliable.

This is a difficult and time-consuming task, but the importance of the outcomes would seem to justify the additional care and effort required (see Box 8.3).

Rules for Writing Essay Questions

The construction of clear, unambiguous essay questions that call forth the desired responses is a much more difficult task than is commonly presumed. The following rules will not make the task any easier, but their application will result in essay items of higher quality.

1. Use essay questions to measure complex learning outcomes only. Most recall of knowledge outcomes profit little from being measured by essay questions. These outcomes can usually be measured more effectively by objective items that lack the sampling and scoring problems that essay questions introduce. There may be a few exceptions, as when supplying the answer is a basic part of the learning outcome, but for most, recall of knowledge outcomes essay questions simply provide a less reliable measure with no compensating benefits.

At the understanding, application, and analysis levels of learning, both objective tests and essay tests are useful. Even here, though, the objective test would seem to have priority, the essay test being reserved for those situations that require the student to *give* reasons, *explain* relationships, *describe* data, *formulate* conclusions, or in some other way produce the appropriate answer. Where supplying the answer is vital, a properly constructed restricted-response question is likely to be most appropriate.

At the evaluating and creating levels of learning, both the objective test and the restricted-response test have only limited value. These tests may be used to measure some specific aspects of the total process, but the production of a complete work (such as a plan of operation) or an overall evaluation of a work (for instance, an evaluation of a novel or an experiment) requires the use of extended-response questions. It is at this level that the essay form contributes most uniquely.

2. Relate the questions as directly as possible to the learning outcomes being measured. Essay questions will not measure complex learning outcomes unless they are carefully constructed to do so. Each question should be specifically designed to measure one or more well-defined outcomes. Thus, the place to start, as is the case with objective items, is with a precise description of the performance to be measured. This will help determine both the content and form of the item and will aid in the phrasing of it.

The restricted-response item is related quite easily to a specific learning outcome because it is so highly structured. The limited response expected from the student also makes it possible for the test maker to phrase the question so that its intent is communicated clearly to the student. The extended-response item, however, requires greater freedom of response and typically involves a number of learning outcomes. This makes it more difficult to relate the question to the intended outcomes and to indicate the nature of the desired answer through the phrasing of the question. If the task is prescribed too rigidly in the question, the students' freedom to select, organize, and present the answer is apt to be infringed upon. One practical solution is to indicate to the students the criteria to be used in evaluating the answer. For example, a parenthetical statement such as the following might be added: "Your answer will be evaluated in terms of its comprehensiveness, the relevance of its arguments, the appropriateness of its examples, and the skill with which it is organized." This clarifies the task to the students without limiting their freedom, and makes the item easier to relate to clearly defined learning outcomes.

3. Formulate questions that present a clear task to be performed. Phrasing an essay question so that the desired response is obtained is no simple matter. Selecting precise terms and carefully phrasing and rephrasing the question with the desired response in mind will help clarify the task to the student. Since essay questions are to be used as a measure of complex learning outcomes, avoid starting such questions with "who," "what," "when," "where," "name," and "list." These terms tend to limit the response to the recall of knowledge outcomes. Complex achievement is most apt to be called forth by such words as "why," "describe," "explain," "compare," "relate," "contrast," "interpret," "analyze," "criticize," and "evaluate." The specific terminology to be used will be determined largely by the specific behavior described in the learning outcome to be measured (see Table 8.2).

There is no better way to check on the phrasing of an essay question than to write a model answer, or at least to formulate a mental answer, to the question. This helps the test maker detect any ambiguity in the question, aids in determining the approximate time needed by the student to develop a satisfactory answer, and provides a rough check on the mental processes required. This procedure is most feasible with the restricted-response item, the answer to which is more limited and more closely prescribed. With the extended-response form it may be necessary to ask one or more colleagues to read the question to determine whether the form and scope of the desired answer are clear.

TABLE 8.2 Types of Complex Outcomes and Related Terms for Writing Essay Questions

Outcome	Sample Terms
Comparing	compare, classify, describe, distinguish between, explain, outline, summarize
Interpreting	convert, draw, estimates, illustrate, interpret, restate, summarize, translate
Inferring	derive, draw, estimate, extend, extrapolate, predict, propose, relate
Applying	arrange, compute, describe, demonstrate, illustrate, rearrange, relate, summarize
Analyzing	break down, describe, diagram, differentiate, divide, list, outline, separate
Creating	compose, design, devise, draw, formulate, make up, present, propose
Synthesizing	arrange, combine, construct, design, rearrange, regroup, relate, write
Generalizing	construct, develop, explain, formulate, generate, make, propose, state
Evaluating	appraise, criticize, defend, describe, evaluate, explain, judge, write

4. Do not permit a choice of questions unless the learning outcome requires it. In most tests of achievement, it is best to have all students answer the same questions. If they are permitted to write on only a fraction of the questions, such as three out of five, their answers cannot be evaluated on a comparative basis. Also, since the students will tend to choose those questions they are best prepared to answer, their responses will provide a sample of their achievement that is less representative than that obtained without optional questions. As we noted earlier, one of the major limitations of the essay test is the limited and unrepresentative sampling it provides. Giving students a choice among questions simply complicates the sampling problem further and introduces greater distortion into the test results.

In some situations the use of optional questions might be defensible. For example, if the essay is to be used as a measure of writing *skill* only, some choice of topics on which to write may be desirable. This might also be the case if the essay is used to measure some aspects of creativity, or if the students have pursued individual interests through independent study. Even for these special uses, however, great caution must be exercised in the use of optional questions. The ability to organize, integrate, and express ideas is determined in part by the complexity of the content involved. Thus, an indeterminate amount of contamination can be expected when optional questions are used.

5. Provide ample time for answering and suggest a time limit on each question. Since essay questions are designed most frequently to measure intellectual skills and abilities, time must be allowed for thinking as well as for writing. Thus, generous time limits should be provided. For example, rather than expecting students to write on several essay questions during one class period, it might be better to have them focus on one or two. There seems to be a tendency for teachers to include so many questions in a single essay test that a high score is as much a measure of writing speed as of achievement. This is probably an attempt to overcome the problem of limited sampling, but it tends to be an undesirable solution. In measuring complex achievement, it is better to use fewer questions and to improve the sample by more frequent testing.

Informing students of the appropriate amount of time they should spend on each question will help them use their time more efficiently; ideally, it will also provide a more adequate sample of their achievement. If the length of the answer is not clearly defined by the problem, as in some extended-response questions, it might also be desirable to indicate page limits. Anything that will clarify the form and scope of the task without interfering with the measurement of the intended outcomes is likely to contribute to more effective measurement.

Rules for Scoring Essay Answers

As we noted earlier, one of the major limitations of the essay test is the subjectivity of the scoring. That is, the feelings of the scorers are likely to enter into the judgments they make concerning the quality of the answers. This may be a personal bias toward the writer of the essay, toward certain areas of content or styles of writing, or toward shortcomings in such extraneous areas as legibility, spelling, and grammar. These biases, of course, distort the results of a measure of achievement and tend to lower their reliability.

The following rules are designed to minimize the subjectivity of the scoring and to provide as uniform a standard of scoring from one student to another as possible. These rules will be most effective, of course, when the questions have been carefully prepared in accordance with the rules for construction.

1. Evaluate answers to essay questions in terms of the learning outcomes being measured. The essay test, like the objective test, is used to obtain evidence concerning the extent to which clearly defined learning outcomes have been achieved. Thus, the desired student performance specified in these outcomes should serve as a guide both for constructing the questions and for evaluating the answers. If a question is designed to measure "the ability to explain cause-effect relationships," for example, the answer should be evaluated in terms of how adequately the student *explains the particular cause-effect relationships presented in the question.* All other factors, such as interesting but extraneous factual information, style of writing, and errors in spelling and grammar, should be ignored (to the extent possible) during the evaluation. In some cases separate scores may be given for spelling or writing ability, but these should not be allowed to contaminate the scores that represent the degree of achievement of the intended learning outcomes.

2. Score restricted-response answers by the point method, using a model answer as a guide. Scoring with the aid of a previously prepared scoring key is possible with the restricted-response item because of the limitations placed on the answer. The procedure involves writing a model answer to each question and determining the number of points to be assigned to it and to the parts within it. The distribution of points within an answer must, of course, take into account all scorable units indicated in the learning outcomes being measured. For example, points may be assigned to the relevance of the examples used and to the organization of the answer, as well as to the content of the answer, if these are legitimate aspects of the learning outcome. As indicated earlier, it is usually desirable to make clear to the student at the time of testing the basis on which each answer will be judged (content, organization, and so on).

3. Grade extended-response answers by the rating method, using defined criteria as a guide. Extended-response items allow so much freedom in answering that the preparation of a model answer is frequently impossible. Thus, the test maker usually *grades* each answer by judging its quality in terms of a previously determined set of criteria, rather than *scoring* it point by point with a scoring key. The criteria for judging the quality of an answer are determined by the nature of the question, and thus, by the learning outcomes being measured. If students were asked to "describe a complete plan for preparing an achievement test," for example, the criteria would include such things as (1) the completeness of the plan (for example, whether it included a statement of objectives, a set of specifications, and the appropriate types of items), (2) the clarity and accuracy with which each step was described, (3) the adequacy of the justification for each step, and (4) the degree to which the various parts of the plan were properly integrated.

Typically, the criteria for evaluating an answer are used to establish about five levels of quality. Then, as the answer to a question is read, it is assigned a letter grade or a number from 1 to 5, which designates the reader's rating. One grade may be assigned on the basis of the overall quality of the answer, or a separate judgment may be made on the basis of each criterion. The latter procedure provides the most useful information for diagnosing and improving learning and should be used wherever possible.

More uniform standards of grading can usually be obtained by reading the answers to each question twice. During the first reading the papers should be tentatively sorted into five piles, ranging from high to low in quality. The second reading can then serve the purpose of checking the uniformity of the answers in each pile and making any necessary shifts in rating. Beware of student bluffing (see Box 8.4).

4. Evaluate all of the students' answers to one question before proceeding to the next question. Scoring or grading essay tests question by question, rather than student by student, makes it possible to maintain a more uniform standard for judging the answers to each question. This procedure also helps offset the *halo effect* in grading. When all of the answers on one paper are read together, the grader's impression of the paper as a whole is apt to influence the grades assigned to the individual answers. Grading question by question prevents the formation of this overall impression of a student's paper. Each answer is more apt to be judged on its own merits when it is read and

BOX 8.4 Student Bluffing and Scoring Essays

Students can obtain higher scores on essay questions by clever bluffing. Although this requires skill in writing and some knowledge of the topic, credit should not be given unless the question is specifically answered. Some common types of bluffing are listed below.

1. Student repeats the question in statement form (slightly paraphrased) and tells how important the topic is (e.g., "The role of assessment in teaching is extremely important. It is hard to imagine effective instruction without it, etc.").
2. Student writes on a well-known topic and fits it to the question (e.g., a student who knows testing well but knows little about performance assessment and is asked to compare testing and performance assessment might describe testing in considerable detail and frequently state that performance assessment is much superior for evaluating the type of learning measured by the test).
3. Student liberally sprinkles the answer with basic concepts regardless of whether they are understood (e.g., when asked to write about any assessment technique, the importance of "validity" and "reliability" is mentioned frequently).
4. Student includes the teacher's basic beliefs wherever possible (e.g., "The intended learning outcomes must be stated in performance terms before this type of test is constructed or selected").

Bluffing is most effective where plans have not been made for careful scoring of the answers.

compared with other answers to the same question than when it is read and compared with other answers by the same student.

5. Evaluate answers to essay questions without knowing the identity of the writer. This is another attempt to control personal bias during scoring. Answers to essay questions should be evaluated in terms of what is written, not in terms of what is known about the writers from other contacts with them. The best way to prevent prior knowledge from biasing our judgment is to evaluate each answer without knowing the identity of the writer. This can be done by having the students write their names on the back of the paper or by using code numbers in place of names.

6. Whenever possible, have two or more persons grade each answer. The best way to check on the reliability of the scoring of essay answers is to obtain two or more independent judgments. Although this may not be a feasible practice for routine classroom testing, it might be done periodically with a fellow teacher (one who is equally competent in the area). Obtaining two or more independent ratings becomes especially vital where the results are to be used for important and irreversible decisions, such as in the selection of students for further training or for special awards. Here, the pooled ratings of several competent persons may be needed to attain a level of reliability that is commensurate with the significance of the decision being made. See Box 8.5 for a summary checklist for evaluating essay questions.

BOX 8.5   Checklist for Evaluating Essay Questions

1. Is this type of item appropriate for measuring the intended learning outcome?
2. Does the item task match the learning task to be measured?
3. Is the question designed to measure complex learning outcomes?
4. Does the question make clear what is being measured and how the answer will be evaluated?
5. Has terminology been used that clarifies and limits the task (e.g., "describe" not "discuss")?
6. Are all students required to answer the same questions?
7. Has an ample time limit been indicated for each question?
8. Have adequate provisions been made for scoring answers (e.g., model answers or criteria for evaluating)?

Summary of Points

1. Use supply-type items whenever producing the answer is an essential element in the learning outcome (e.g., *defines* terms, instead of *identifies* meaning of terms).
2. Supply-type items include short-answer items, restricted-response essay, and extended-response essay.
3. The short-answer item can be answered by a word, number, symbol, or brief phrase.
4. The short-answer item is limited primarily to measuring simple recall of knowledge outcomes.
5. Each short-answer item should be so carefully written that there is only one possible answer, the entire item can be read before coming to the answer space, and there are no extraneous clues to the answer.
6. In scoring short-answer items, give credit for all correct answers and score for spelling separately.
7. Essay questions are most useful for measuring the ability to organize, integrate, and express ideas.
8. Essay questions are inefficient for measuring the recall of knowledge because they provide limited sampling, are influenced by extraneous factors (e.g., writing skills, bluffing, grammar, spelling, handwriting), and scoring is subjective and unreliable.
9. Restricted-response essay questions can be more easily written and scored, but due to limitations on the responses they are less useful for measuring the higher-level outcomes (e.g., integration of diverse material).
10. Extended-response essay questions provide the freedom to select, organize, and express ideas in the manner that seems most appropriate; therefore, they are especially useful for measuring such outcomes.
11. Essay questions should be written to measure complex learning outcomes, to present a clear task, and to contain only those restrictions needed to call forth the intended response and provide for adequate scoring.

12. Essay answers should be scored by focusing on the intended response, by using a model answer or set of criteria as a guide, by scoring question by question, and by ignoring the writer's identity. Be wary of student bluffing. If an important decision is to be based on the results, two or more competent scorers should be used.

References and Additional Reading

Linn, R. L., & Gronlund, N. E. *Measurement and Assessment in Teaching*, 8th ed. (Upper Saddle River, NJ: Merrill/Prentice Hall, 2000).

McMillan, J. H. *Classroom Assessments: Principles and Practices for Effective Instruction*, 3rd ed. (Boston: Allyn and Bacon, 2004).

Osterhoff, A. C. *Classroom Applications of Educational Measurement*, 3rd ed. (Upper Saddle River, NJ: Merrill/Prentice Hall, 2001).

Stiggins, R. J. *Student-Involved Classroom Assessment*, 3rd ed. (Upper Saddle River, NJ: Merrill/Prentice Hall, 2001).

Self-Assessment

MULTIPLE CHOICE

DIRECTIONS: Select the best answer for each item by circling the corresponding letter.

1. For which of the following general outcomes is the essay item least appropriate?
   (a) Remembering
   (b) Creating
   (c) Application
   (d) Evaluation

2. Essay questions are more appropriate than multiple-choice items when the specific outcome calls for
   (a) identification of concepts
   (b) identification of data
   (c) supplying the answer
   (d) matching terms to definitions

3. A weakness of short-answer questions is that they
   (a) are too easy to answer
   (b) can potentially have several answers
   (c) don't require student differentiation
   (d) require time-consuming computation

4. Short-answer items are typically limited to measuring a student's ability to
   (a) evaluate the merits of a product
   (b) carry out a procedure
   (c) reorganize elements
   (d) remember information

TRUE-FALSE

DIRECTIONS: Read each statement and record as true or false on the lines provided.

5. _____ Having two or more persons grade each essay question is the best way to check the reliability of scoring.

6. _____ Only grade spelling, grammar, and punctuation of supply-type answers when they relate to the intended learning outcome.

7. _____ According to the "Rules for Writing Essay Questions" in your textbook, it is best to limit the amount of time a student has to answer each essay.

8. _____ According to the "Rules for Scoring Essay Answers" in your textbook, it is best to grade essay tests question by question, rather than student by student.

9. _____ Asking a student to defend a position or point of view would best be assessed with an extended-response essay question.

Restricted-Response Essay

10. The authors of your textbook discuss the strengths and limitations of short-answer items. Describe each strength and limitation. Confine your answer to one page.

Box 8.1

9 | PERFORMANCE ASSESSMENTS

Studying this chapter should enable you to

1. Describe how performance assessments differ from paper-and-pencil testing.
2. Identify the strengths and limitation of performance assessments.
3. Write intended performance outcomes for a performance assessment.
4. Distinguish between restricted and extended performance assessment.
5. Describe the general procedure for making a performance assessment.
6. Describe the use of a student project for performance assessment.
7. Prepare a plan for arranging, observing, recording, and evaluating a performance task.
8. Construct a checklist that is well stated, relevant, and easy to use.
9. Construct a rating scale that is well stated, relevant, and easy to use.
10. Construct a holistic scoring rubric for some performance outcome.
11. Describe the influence of realism on performance assessment.
12. Describe how the performance assessment environment should be prepared.
13. Describe how a performance assessment is conducted to diagnose student understanding.

Paper-and-pencil tests can measure a variety of learning **tasks** from simple to complex. However, performance assessment is needed when performance skills are not adequately assessed by paper-and-pencil tests alone. These performance outcomes are important in many different types of courses. For example, science courses are concerned with laboratory skills, English and foreign-language courses are concerned with communication skills, mathematics courses are concerned with various types of problem-solving skills, and social studies are concerned with skills such as map and graph construction. In addition, skill outcomes are emphasized heavily in art and music courses, industrial education, business education, agricultural education, home economics courses, and physical education.

BOX 9.1   Performance Assessments

Strengths

1. Instructors can evaluate complex learning outcomes and skills that cannot be evaluated with traditional paper-and-pencil tests.
2. These assessments provide a more natural, direct, and complete evaluation of some types of reasoning, oral, and physical skills.
3. This form of evaluation provides greater motivation for students by clarifying goals and making learning more meaningful.
4. Performance assessments encourage the application of learning to real-life situations.

Limitations

1. This format requires considerable time and effort to use.
2. Judgment and scoring performance is subjective, burdensome, and typically has low reliability.
3. Evaluation must frequently be done individually, rather than in groups.

Thus, in most instructional areas performance assessment provides a useful adjunct to paper-and-pencil tests. Although tests can tell us whether students know what to do in a particular situation, more direct assessments are needed to evaluate their actual performance skills (see Box 9.1).

COMPONENTS OF PERFORMANCE SKILLS

Although the focus in this chapter is on the assessment of performance skills, it is important to note that successful performance typically has several components that must be considered before and during the assessment (see Figure 9.1).

In assessing writing ability, for example, we are concerned with knowledge of vocabulary, grammar, and similar basic elements needed for effective writing, as well as interests and attitudes that support good writing. In assessing laboratory skills we are concerned with the student's knowing the names and uses of the equipment and the procedures to be followed, as well as having an attitude of care and safety in handling the equipment and making accurate measurements. The knowledge components can be measured by tests before the skill is evaluated or made a part of the evaluation. The affective component is typically made a part of the skill assessment (e.g., handles equipment in a

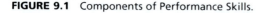

FIGURE 9.1   Components of Performance Skills.

careful manner, follows all safety precautions in operating the machine). In any event, all components of the performance must be considered when planning for the performance assessment.

STATING OBJECTIVES FOR PERFORMANCE ASSESSMENT

In planning for instruction, the objectives for performance assessment should be developed at the same time as the objectives are being prepared for the testable learning outcomes. The same two-step procedure of stating the general objectives first and then defining them with a list of specific learning outcomes is followed. A list of objectives for a test construction unit, for example, could be stated as follows.

1. Prepares a table of specifications for an achievement test.

1.1 Writes a clear description of the achievement domain to be tested.
1.2 States the intended learning outcomes in performance terms.
1.3 Lists the content areas to be covered by the test.
1.4 Constructs a twofold table of specifications that indicates the proportion of items to be devoted to each learning outcome and each area of content.
1.5 Checks the table of specifications with the achievement domain to be certain the test measures a representative sample of the desired achievement.

Statements such as these clarify what is involved in preparing a table of specifications and what the final product should be like. An evaluation can be made by using the statements as they are and adding a rating scale to each item to indicate degree of success, or by developing more specific criteria in each area (e.g., Comprehensive description of achievement domain, Intended learning outcomes are clearly stated). In either case, the objectives set the stage for performance assessment by focusing attention on what is to be assessed (see Box 9.2).

BOX 9.2 Writing Performance Objectives for Skills and Products

1. State each general objective so that it clearly describes the skill or product to be assessed.
2. List specific performance outcomes for each objective that are most relevant to a successful performance or a satisfactory product.
3. List enough specific performance outcomes to clarify what is meant by an effective performance.
4. State the specific performance outcomes in terms of observable dimensions of the skill or product.
5. State the specific performance outcomes so that they are clear to students.

RESTRICTED AND EXTENDED PERFORMANCE TASKS

Performance tasks may be restricted to fit a specific and limited skill (e.g., measure humidity) or extended to a comprehensive performance that includes numerous specific skills (e.g., predicting weather). Although this dichotomy is somewhat arbitrary, it is useful in planning performance assessments. In some cases, it may be desirable to assess specific skills before putting them together in a more complex performance. In other cases, it may be desirable to use restricted performance tasks to diagnose problems in performing a complex task. For example, students having difficulty with laboratory procedures might benefit from a restricted assessment of measurement skills, and students having difficulty constructing a wood or metal product might need a restricted assessment of how to use a particular tool. Although our major focus is the overall performance, assessing restricted aspects of it can serve as guides for its improvement. This is another example of how teaching and assessment work together to improve learning.

Restricted performance tasks are typically highly restricted and limited in scope, as shown in the following examples.

EXAMPLES

Write a one-page report describing a field trip.

Give a one-minute speech on a given topic.

Read aloud a brief selection of poetry.

Construct a graph from a given set of data.

Demonstrate how to use a measuring instrument.

By limiting the scope of the task, it is easier to focus the observation and to judge the response. It should be recognized, however, that a series of restricted tasks do not provide sufficient evidence of a comprehensive performance. For that we need more extended tasks that integrate the specific skills into a complex pattern of movements or the production of a high-quality product.

Extended performance tasks are typically less structured and broader in scope, as illustrated in the following examples.

EXAMPLES

Design and conduct an experiment.

Design and build a wood or metal product.

Write a short story.

Repair a malfunctioning motor.

Paint a picture.

Demonstrate a physical or musical performance.

Extended performance assessments typically give students greater freedom in selecting and carrying out the tasks and greater opportunity for self-assessment and self-improvement. Discussions of the ongoing performance and the final results with the teacher should focus on both the quality of the performance and the development of the students' independent learning skills.

STEPS IN PREPARING PERFORMANCE ASSESSMENTS

Effective performance assessments are most likely to result when a systematic approach is used. The following procedural steps outline the main factors to consider when making performance assessments.

1. Specifying the performance outcomes.
2. Selecting the focus of the assessment (procedure, product, or both).
3. Selecting an appropriate degree of realism.
4. Selecting the performance situation.
5. Selecting the method of observing, recording, and scoring.

Each of these steps will be described in turn.

Specifying the Performance Outcomes

If the intended learning outcomes have been prespecified for the instruction, it is simply a matter of selecting those that require the use of performance assessment. If performance outcomes are not available, they should be identified and defined for the areas of performance to be assessed. Restricted performance outcomes commonly use verbs such as *identify, construct,* and *demonstrate* (and their synonyms). A brief description of these verbs and some illustrative objectives for restricted performance outcomes are shown in Table 9.1.

The specification of performance outcomes typically includes a job or task analysis to identify the specific factors that are most critical in the performance. Because it is frequently impossible to focus on all of the specific procedures involved in a particular performance, it is necessary to obtain a representative sample of the most crucial ones. Keeping the list to a reasonable length increases the possibility of more accurate observations and judgments. The following example illustrates a realistic set of performance tasks for restricted performance assessments.

Demonstrates Skill in Oral Reporting

1. Stands in a natural manner.
2. Maintains good eye contact.
3. Uses appropriate facial expressions.
4. Uses gestures effectively.
5. Speaks clearly and with good volume.
6. Speaks at an appropriate rate.
7. Presents ideas in an organized manner.
8. Uses appropriate language.
9. Maintains interest of the group.

TABLE 9.1 Typical Action Verbs and Illustrative Instructional Objectives for Restricted Performance Outcomes

Action Verbs	Illustrative Instructional Objectives
IDENTIFY: Selects the correct objects, part of the object, procedure, or property (typical verbs: *identify, locate, select, touch, pick up, mark, describe*)	Select the proper tool. Identify the parts of a typewriter. Choose correct laboratory equipment. Select the most relevant statistical procedure. Locate an automobile malfunction. Identify a musical selection. Identify the experimental equipment needed. Identify a specimen under the microscope.
CONSTRUCT: Makes a product to fit a given set of specifications (typical verbs: *construct, assemble, build, design, draw, make, prepare*)	Draw a diagram for an electrical circuit. Design a pattern for making a dress. Assemble equipment for an experimental study. Prepare a circle graph. Construct a weather map. Prepare an experimental design.
DEMONSTRATE: Performs a set of operations or procedures (typical verbs: *demonstrate, drive, measure, operate, perform, repair, set up*)	Drive an automobile. Measure the volume of a liquid. Operate a filmstrip projector. Perform a modern dance step. Repair a malfunctioning TV set. Set up laboratory equipment. Demonstrate taking a patient's temperature. Demonstrate the procedure for tuning an automobile.

Extended performance outcomes typically involve multiple instructional objectives, and it is important to consider all of them when designing a study. A research project, for example, might include intended learning outcomes as follows:

Designs and conducts an experiment.

Writes an accurate account of the study.

States valid conclusions.

Writes a critique of the procedure and findings.

Presents and defends the study in class.

These outcomes would need to be defined in more specific terms, like the two described earlier, but stating the general objectives first and then specifying them in more detail provides a useful procedure. In defining each major outcome, it may be desirable to divide some in two (e.g., Designs an experiment, Conducts an experiment). In other cases some may be combined. For example, "States valid conclusions" may be included as part of "Writes an accurate account of the study." In any event, the final list should provide a major list of the intended learning outcomes, each clearly specified by descriptions of what students can do to demonstrate achievement of the outcomes. More detailed descriptions of how to state intended learning outcomes and define them in performance terms can be found in Gronlund and Brookhart (2009).

Selecting the Focus of the Assessment

Performance assessment can focus on the procedure, the product, or some combination of the two. The nature of the performance frequently dictates where the emphasis should be placed, but in some cases there are also other considerations.

ASSESSING THE PROCEDURE. Those types of performance that don't result in a product (e.g., speaking, reading aloud, physical skills, musical performance) require that the performance be evaluated in progress.

In many cases, both procedure and product are important aspects of a performance. For example, skill in locating and correcting a malfunction in a television set involves following a systematic procedure (rather than using trial and error) in addition to producing a properly repaired set. Frequently, procedure is emphasized during the early stages of learning and products later, after the procedural steps have been mastered. In assessing typing skill, for example, proper use of the "touch system" would be evaluated at the beginning of instruction, but later evaluation would focus on the neatness and accuracy of the typed material and the speed with which it was produced. Similarly, in such areas as cooking, woodworking, and painting, correct procedure is likely to be stressed during the early stages of instruction and the quality of the product later. Procedure evaluation may also be used during later stages of instruction, of course, in order to detect errors in procedure that might account for an inferior product.

In general, focus the performance assessment on the procedure when:

1. There is no product, or product evaluation is infeasible (e.g., unavailable or too costly).
2. The procedure is orderly and directly observable.
3. Correct procedure is crucial to later success.
4. Analysis of procedural steps can aid in improving a product.

ASSESSING THE PRODUCT. In some areas of performance, the product is the focus of attention and the procedure (or process) is of little or no significance. In evaluating a student's theme, drawing, or insect display, for example, the teacher is not likely to assess the procedures used by the student. This might be because various procedures could lead to an equally good product, or because the product was the result of a take-home project, and the process was therefore not observable by the teacher. Also, some in-class activities are nonobservable because they involve primarily mental processes (such as mathematical reasoning). Some elements of the process can be obtained by having students "think aloud" and by using oral questioning, but the main focus is on the product. The quality of the product is typically guided by specific criteria that have been prepared especially for that purpose.

Where both the procedure and product are observable, the emphasis given to each will depend on the skill being assessed and the stage of skill development. However, when the procedure has been sufficiently mastered, product evaluation is favored because it typically provides a more objective basis for judgment, it can be done at a convenient time, and judgments can be rechecked if necessary.

Performance assessment should be focused on the product when:

1. Different procedures can result in an equally good product (e.g., writing a theme).
2. The procedure is not available for observation (e.g., take-home work).
3. The procedural steps have been mastered.
4. The product has qualities that can be clearly identified and judged.

Selecting an Appropriate Degree of Realism

Performance assessment in instructional settings typically falls somewhere between the usual paper-and-pencil test and performance in real-life situations. Although we can't expect to duplicate the natural situation in which the learning will later be used, we can strive for performance assessments that approximate real-world conditions. This, then, is another dimension to consider in preparing performance assessments. How much "realism" can we incorporate into our assessment? The more the better, of course, but authenticity is a matter of degree.

The presence of varying degrees of realism in a performance assessment can be illustrated by the simple example of applying arithmetic skills to the practical problem of determining correct change while shopping in a store (adapted from Fitzpatrick & Morrison, 1971). A simulation of this situation might range from the use of a story problem (low realism) to an actual purchase in a store-like situation (high realism). The various problem situations that might be contrived for this performance measure are shown in Figure 9.2. It should be noted that even though solving a story problem is relatively low in realism, it simulates the criterion situation to a greater degree than simply asking students to subtract 69 from 100. Thus, even with paper-and-pencil testing it is frequently possible to increase the degree of realism to a point where the results are useful in assessing performance outcomes.

The degree of realism selected for a particular situation depends on a number of factors. First, the nature of the instructional objectives must be considered. Acceptable performance in paper-and-pencil applications of skill, or in other measures with a low degree of realism, might be all that the instruction is intended to achieve. This is frequently the case with introductory courses that are to be followed by more advanced courses emphasizing applied performance. Second,

Low realism

Have students solve this story problem: "If you bought a toy for 69¢ and you gave the clerk $1.00, how much change would you get?"

Demonstrate the problem situation with actual money and ask each student to judge whether the change is correct.

Pair off the students, give them actual money, and have them role-play the problem situation.

High realism

Set up a mock toy store and have each student demonstrate the "purchase" of a toy with actual money.

FIGURE 9.2 Illustration of Various Degrees of Realism in Measuring the Ability to Determine Correct Change While Making a Purchase in a Store.

the sequence of instruction within a particular course may indicate that it would be desirable to measure paper-and-pencil applications before "hands-on" performance is attempted. Locating the source of a malfunction on a diagram, for example, might precede working with actual equipment. Third, numerous practical constraints, such as time, cost, availability of equipment, and difficulties in administering and scoring, may limit the degree of realism that can be obtained. Fourth, the task itself may restrict the degree of realism in a test situation. In testing first aid skills, for example, it would be infeasible (and undesirable) to use actual patients with wounds, broken bones, and other physical conditions needed for realistic assessment. Thus, although we should strive for as high a degree of realism as the performance outcomes dictate, it is frequently necessary to make compromises in preparing performance assessments.

Selecting the Performance Situation

Performance assessments can be classified by the type of situation or setting used. The following classification system closely approximates the degree of realism present in the situation and includes the following types: (1) paper-and-pencil performance, (2) identification test, (3) structured performance test, (4) simulated performance, (5) work sample, and (6) student project. Although these categories overlap to some degree, they are useful for describing and illustrating the various approaches used in performance assessment.

PAPER-AND-PENCIL PERFORMANCE. Paper-and-pencil performance differs from the more traditional paper-and-pencil test by placing greater emphasis on the application of knowledge and skill in a simulated setting. These paper-and-pencil applications might result in desired terminal learning outcomes, or they might serve as an intermediate step to performance that involves a higher degree of realism (for example, the actual use of equipment).

In a number of instances, paper-and-pencil performance can provide a product of educational significance. A course in test construction, for example, might require students to perform activities such as the following:

Construct a set of test specifications for a unit of instruction.

Construct test items that fit a given set of specifications.

Construct a checklist for evaluating an achievement test.

The action verb "construct" is frequently used in paper-and-pencil performance testing. For instance, students might be asked to construct a weather map, bar graph, diagram of an electrical circuit, floor plan, design for an article of clothing, poem, short story, or plan for an experiment. In such cases, the paper-and-pencil product is a result of both knowledge and skill, and it provides a performance measure that is valued in its own right.

In other cases, paper-and-pencil performance might simply provide a first step toward hands-on performance. For example, before using a particular measuring instrument, such as a micrometer, it might be desirable to have students read various settings from pictures of the scale. Although the ability to read the scale is not a sufficient condition for accurate measurement, it is necessary one. In this instance, paper-and-pencil performance would be favored because it is a more convenient method of testing a group of students. Using paper-and-pencil performance as a precursor to hands-on performance might be favored for other reasons. For example, if the performance is complicated and the equipment is expensive, demonstrating competence on paper-and-pencil situations could avoid subsequent accidents or damage to equipment. Similarly, in the health sciences, skill in diagnosing and prescribing for hypothetical patients could avoid later harm to real patients.

IDENTIFICATION TEST.   The identification test includes a wide variety of situations representing various degrees of realism. In some cases, a student may be asked simply to identify a tool or piece of equipment and to indicate its function. A more complex situation might present the student with a particular performance task (e.g., locating a short in an electrical circuit) and ask him or her to identify the tools, equipment, and procedures needed in performing the task. An even more complex type of identification test might involve listening to the operation of a malfunctioning machine (such as an automobile motor, a drill, or a lathe) and from the sound, identifying the most probable cause of the malfunction.

Although identification tests are widely used in industrial education, they are by no means limited to that area. The biology teacher might have students identify specimens that are placed at various stations around the room or identify the equipment and procedures needed to conduct a particular experiment. Similarly, chemistry students might be asked to identify "unknown" substances, foreign-language students to identify correct pronunciation, mathematics students to identify correct problem-solving procedures, English students to identify the "best expression" to be used in writing, and social studies students to identify various leadership roles as they are acted out in a group. Identifying correct procedures is also important, of course, in art, music, physical education, and such vocational areas as agriculture, business education, and home economics.

STRUCTURED PERFORMANCE TEST.   A structured performance test provides for an assessment under standard, controlled conditions. It might involve such things as making prescribed measurements, adjusting a microscope, following safety procedures in starting a machine, or locating a malfunction in electronic equipment. The performance situation is structured and presented in a manner that requires all individuals to respond to the same set of tasks.

The construction of a structured performance test follows somewhat the same pattern used in constructing other types of achievement tests, but there are some added complexities. The test situation can seldom be fully controlled and standardized, it typically takes more time to prepare and administer, and it is frequently more difficult to score. To increase the likelihood that the test situation will be standard for all individuals, instructions should be used that describe the test situation, the required performance, and the conditions under which the performance is to be demonstrated. Instructions for locating a malfunction in electronic equipment, for example, would typically include the following:

1. Nature and purpose of the test
2. Equipment and tools provided
3. Testing procedure:
   a. Type and condition of equipment
   b. Description of required performance
   c. Time limits and other conditions
4. Method of judging performance

When using performance tests, it may be desirable to set performance standards that indicate the minimum level of acceptable performance. These might be concerned with accuracy (e.g., measure temperature *to the nearest two-tenths of a degree*), the proper sequencing of steps (e.g., adjust a microscope *following the proper sequence of steps*), total compliance with rules (e.g., check *all safety guards* before starting a machine), or speed of performance (e.g., locate a malfunction in electronic equipment *in three minutes*). Some common **standards** for judging performance are shown in Box 9.3.

Errors of observation and judgment can be significantly reduced when performance outcomes specify clear and definite criteria for judging the procedure or product in observable terms. Judging student performance by the time it takes to complete a procedure, the number of spelling errors made on a work sample, or the accuracy of measurements taken is highly objective. Two judges would likely not disagree when basing ratings of students on these criteria.

However, disagreement becomes more likely when criteria are more subjective. Judgments about whether a student *demonstrates caution* when operating a table saw is up to interpretation by the judge. Whether the student meets the

BOX 9.3   Some Common Standards for Judging Performance

Type	Examples
Rate	Solve ten addition problems in two minutes.
	Type 40 words per minute.
Error	No more than two errors per typed page.
	Count to 20 in Spanish without error.
Time	Set up laboratory equipment in five minutes.
	Locate an equipment malfunction in three minutes.
Precision	Measure a line within one-eighth of an inch.
	Read a thermometer within two-tenths of a degree.
Quantity	Complete 20 laboratory experiments.
	Locate 15 relevant references.
Quality (rating)	Write a neat, well-spaced business letter.
	Demonstrate correct form in diving.
Percentage Correct	Solve 85 percent of the math problems.
	Spell correctly 90 percent of the words in the word list.
Steps Required	Diagnose a motor malfunction in five steps.
	Locate a computer error using proper sequence of steps.
Use of Material	Build a bookcase with less than 10 percent waste.
	Cut out a dress pattern with less than 10 percent waste.
Safety	Check all safety guards before operating machine.
	Drive automobile without breaking any safety rules.

criteria will depend less on whether the student followed appropriate safety procedures and more on how the judge defines caution. Thus, the reliability of the performance assessment is diminished. To improve reliability, subjective terms such as *caution* should be replaced with descriptions of observable, cautious behaviors (e.g., makes certain all safety guards are in proper position).

SIMULATED PERFORMANCE.   Simulated performance is an attempt to match the performance in a real situation—either in whole or in part. In physical education, for example, swinging a bat at an imaginary ball, shadow boxing, and demonstrating various swimming or tennis strokes are simulated performances. In science, vocational, and business courses, skill activities are frequently designed to simulate portions of actual job performance. In mathematics, the use of computers in solving lifelike problems represents simulated performance. Similarly, in social studies, student role-playing of a jury trial, a city council meeting, or a job interview provides the instructor with opportunities to evaluate the simulated performance of an assigned task. In some cases, specially designed equipment is used for instructional and assessment purposes. In both driver training and flight training, for example, students are frequently trained and tested on simulators. Such simulators may prevent personal injury or damage to expensive equipment during the early stages of skill development. Simulators are also used in various types of vocational training programs.

In some situations, simulated performance testing might be used as the final assessment of a performance skill. This would be the case in assessing students' laboratory performance in chemistry, for example. In many situations, however, skill in a simulated setting simply indicates readiness to attempt actual performance. The student in driver training who has demonstrated driving skill in the simulator, for example, is now ready to apply his or her skill in the actual operation of an automobile.

WORK SAMPLE. The work sample requires the student to perform actual tasks that are representative of the total performance to be measured. The sample tasks typically include the most crucial elements of the total performance and are performed under controlled conditions. In being tested for automobile driving skill, for example, the student is required to drive over a standard course that includes the most common problem situations likely to be encountered in normal driving. The performance on the standard course is then used as evidence of the ability to drive an automobile under typical operating conditions.

Performance assessments in business education and industrial education are frequently of the work-sample type. When students are required to take and transcribe shorthand notes from dictation, type a business letter, or operate a computer to analyze business data, a work-sample assessment is being employed. Similarly, in industrial education, a work-sample approach is being used when students are required to complete a metalworking or woodworking project that includes all of the steps likely to be encountered in an actual job situation (steps such as designing, ordering materials, and constructing). Still other examples are the operation of machinery, the repair of equipment, and the performance of job-oriented laboratory tasks. The work-sample approach to assessing performance is widely used in occupations involving performance skills, and many of these situations can be duplicated in the school setting.

STUDENT PROJECT. One of the most comprehensive types of performance assessments involves the student project. This approach involves a combination of academic, communication, and thinking skills in the solving of unstructured real-world problems, the construction of a unique product, or both. It typically involves multiple outcomes and criteria for each, and student participation in developing criteria, selecting the problem to investigate, designing and carrying out the study, and evaluating the results (see Box 9.4).

To illustrate the use of projects in assessment, we will focus on a problem-solving type of project. Typically, an unstructured problem, like those in the real world, is used so that there is no simple or single solution. This increases the complexity of the problem and provides for greater focus on higher-level learning outcomes (e.g., analyzing, evaluating, creating). It also provides for the assessment of a greater range of skills useful later in life (e.g., locating resources, writing, speaking, self-assessment).

BOX 9.4   Characteristics of a Good Student Project

1. It focuses on multiple learning outcomes.
2. It includes the integration of understanding, skills, and strategies.
3. It is concerned with problems and activities that relate to out-of-school life.
4. It involves the active participation of students in all phases of the project.
5. It provides for student self-assessment and independent learning.
6. It requires performance skills that are generalizable to similar situations.
7. It is feasible within the constraints of the students' present knowledge, time limits, and available resources and equipment.
8. It is both challenging and motivating to students.
9. It is fair and doable by all students.
10. It provides for collaboration between the students and the teacher.

A common outline for a problem-solving project includes the following items.

1. Establishing criteria and standards.
2. Selecting and stating the problem.
3. Locating and selecting resources.
4. Writing the report.
5. Designing and completing a research study or making a product.
6. Orally presenting and defending the project.

Each of these steps is guided by the teacher and involves considerable student–teacher collaboration.

Establishing Criteria and Standards.   Because of the multiple outcomes expected from a project, criteria must be established in many areas. For example, criteria for each of the major areas (i.e., problem selection, research skills, report writing, product design and construction, and oral presentation). Throughout these areas, or as separate categories, criteria must also be established for level of thinking shown and general problem-solving skills. These criteria may be developed by the teacher or they may be cooperatively prepared with the students. The latter procedure tends to provide greater understanding of the criteria by students and tends to be more motivating. The final list of criteria should be checked against the instructional objectives to be sure they are in agreement.

Standards that describe levels of success on each criterion should be set at the same time as the criteria are prepared. These may be stated for use in holistic scoring rubrics or may be included as part of a rating scale to be used in evaluating the project (see Box 9.5).

Selecting and Stating the Problem.   Students should be free to select a problem that interests them, but the selection may require considerable help from the teacher. In a traditional classroom, many students are in the "tell me what to do" mode; and one or two conferences may be needed to help them think about possible problems to study. In helping students select a problem, it is

Box 9.5   Characteristics of Sound Performance Criteria

1. They describe the components that are most crucial to satisfactory completion of the performance (e.g., beware of peripheral activities that are trivial).
2. They focus on observable aspects of the performance (e.g., "Follows safety procedures," not "Demonstrates safety consciousness").
3. They apply in various contextual settings (e.g., "skill in computation" is applicable in all contexts).
4. They represent aspects of performance that experts would agree are necessary for a successful performance (e.g., "Good organization" would be recognized by experts as basic in all types of writing).
5. They are stated in terms that are readily understood and usable by students in evaluating performance (e.g., for self-evaluation and peer evaluation).
6. They are in harmony with the instructional objectives and the use to be made of the assessment results (e.g., criteria used in judging writing skills and their improvement over time).

important to keep in mind how suitable the problem is for the student. Is it too difficult or too easy for the student? Does it provide an opportunity for new learning, or is it one the student already has studied? Will the problem be motivating to the student or one that is done grudgingly? Will the problem provide significant learning experiences that are in harmony with the intended learning outcomes? These and similar concerns will aid in helping the student select an appropriate and worthwhile problem to study.

Students also typically need help in phrasing the problem so that it is clear, objective, and realistic. Stating the problem in question form usually provides the crux of the problem most effectively. For example, changing "Study of the Environment" to "How Can We Improve the Environment?" helps provide a focus on a major problem. From here it is possible to go to more specific statements, such as "How Can We Improve the Air or Water?" Asking students to put their topics in question form forces them to pose problems. It is then just a matter of helping them refine the statements until they are clear and realistic.

If criteria for selecting and stating a problem have been developed beforehand, as should be done, they can be stated in evaluation form and serve as an aid in the process. They can also, of course, provide a basis for later assessment of the project. Criteria such as the following can be combined with other project criteria and used as a basis for a rating scale.

1. Selects and states a realistic problem.

   1.1 Is the problem in harmony with the student's present knowledge and skill?
   1.2 Does the problem provide opportunities for the student to learn new knowledge and skills?
   1.3 Does the problem provide opportunities for assessing cognitive and communication skills?
   1.4 Does the problem relate to real-world situations?

1.5 Does the problem have more than one possible solution?
1.6 Is the problem stated clearly?
1.7 Is the statement of the problem free from bias and distortion?

In stating the criteria, it is important that they be understandable to the students. This can be accomplished by having the students help develop the criteria. If the problem requires teacher-prepared criteria, they can be presented to the students for clarification and rewording as needed. In any event, criteria should be clear to students and available to them at the beginning of the project. This will provide a focus for doing the project and a guide for self-assessment and peer assessment later.

Locating and Selecting Resources.   After stating the problem clearly, the student is expected to go to reference books and other sources to gather information. Other sources might include interviews with knowledgeable people in the community (e.g., banker, accountant, doctor, scientist), observation of a process (e.g., council meeting, trial, bakery operation), or writing a letter to a congressional representative requesting information. The point is, students are expected to obtain information from any source that can provide help with the problem—as we do in real life.

This phase of the project might include criteria similar to the following.

2. Selects appropriate resource material.

2.1 Has a variety of resources been selected?
2.2 Is the resource material relevant to the problem?
2.3 Do the resources provide various possible solutions to the problem?
2.4 Does the resource material include evidence supporting the suggested solutions?
2.5 Is there enough resource material to provide for valid conclusions?

Writing the Report.   The written report provides an opportunity for students to combine ideas from various sources, analyze and interpret the findings, and summarize and draw conclusions. The criteria for judging the report should be used as a guide for writing it. The written report provides an important means of assessing higher-order thinking skills and, thus, they should be reflected in the criteria.

The following list illustrates how criteria might be stated for the written report.

3. Writes a clear and effective report.

3.1 Has the problem been clearly stated?
3.2 Have the study procedures been adequately described?
3.3 Has the material from various sources been analyzed, compared, and evaluated?
3.4 Have the findings been integrated into a well-organized report?
3.5 Have the findings been supported by adequate and relevant information?
3.6 Does the summary include the main points?

3.7 Are the conclusions in harmony with the findings and the limits of the study?

3.8 Does the report exhibit good reasoning ability?

The specific nature of the criteria will, of course, be influenced by the content, instructional objectives, and level of the instruction. Emphasis on reasoning ability might require more specific criteria on the quality of the questions raised, the relevance of the arguments, and distinctions between supported and unsupported statements. Emphasis on communication skills might call for criteria on the clarity of the writing, on grammar, and on spelling. At lower grades, the criteria would, of course, need to be modified to fit the age level of the students. Our illustrative criteria are general and simply show how the intended learning outcomes might be stated so that they are most useful for instruction, learning, and assessment. If properly stated, they can be easily converted to a rating scale by adding numbers from 1 to 4, representing different levels of performance.

In any event, the student should be aware of the completed list of criteria before writing this report, use them to evaluate the report, and then to revise the report as needed. It is helpful for the teacher to evaluate the report and compare the ratings with those of the student in a conference before the student revises the report. Peer evaluations, of course, may also be used.

Designing and Completing a Research Study or Making a Product. In some cases the written report may serve as a basis for a research study. In others, the written report may serve as a basis for constructing a product. This might be a map, poster, chart, graph, model, or some other type of exhibit illustrating the findings. Or it might be a wood or metal product, as in the vocational area. In this case, the focus of the project may be on designing and constructing the product, but the study phase is still important. For a woodworking project, for example, the study phase may involve a comparison of different types of wood, various construction procedures, or a history of the product (e.g., making a replica of an antique chair). The study phase provides for the combining of academic and vocational skills in carrying out the project and increases the opportunity for including higher-level thinking skills in the project.

Criteria for assessing the research or product should be stated in the same manner as those listed earlier. The specific nature of the criteria for a research study will depend on the type of problem being studied. However, there are some general criteria that should be considered, such as the use of proper procedures, control of variables, selection and use of equipment, accuracy of measurements, adequacy of interpretation of results, and validity of conclusions. Adapting these and similar criteria to the specific research project and phrasing them in terms the students can understand provide a sound basis for conducting the research and for its later assessment.

The criteria for a product will depend on the type of product that is being constructed and its relation to the written report. If an exhibit, such as a graph or poster, is being constructed as part of the project, for example, the criteria will include how well it illustrates the findings, its ease of interpretation, and the like.

For a woodworking project, the criteria might be concerned with both the procedure (e.g., selection of tools and materials, the use of tools and machines, etc.) and the product (e.g., appearance, meeting specifications, and functioning properly). As indicated earlier, the criteria should be known to students before starting on the construction project. It is also helpful to put the criteria in rating form, as illustrated later in the chapter to clarify how they will be used in the assessment.

Orally Presenting and Defending the Project.   Upon completion of the project, it may be desirable to have each student describe the procedures and findings to a group of students, parents, or members of the community. The nature of the group depends on the purpose of the assessment, the type of project, and how the school is organized.

The final presentation gives the student practice in public speaking and in defending his or her work. This, of course, also provides another opportunity to evaluate higher-order thinking skills through use of questions that require the student to defend the procedures, findings, and products of the project. As with other phases of the project, evaluation of the presentation is guided by a set of criteria developed at the beginning of the project and fully shared with the students.

The expanded project described here includes multiple outcomes, such as research skills, writing skills, speaking skills, thinking skills, self-assessment skills, and, in some cases, vocational skills. The specific nature of such a project will, of course, vary with the area of instruction and the purpose of the project. It is helpful to review descriptions of how this and other types of expanded performance assessments are functioning in the schools. The list of references at the end of the chapter provides numerous descriptions and examples of performance assessment in action.

Selecting the Method of Observing, Recording, and Scoring

Whether judging procedures, products, or some combination of the two, some type of guided observation and method of recording and scoring the results is needed. Commonly used procedures include (1) systematic observation and anecdotal records, (2) checklists, (3) rating scales, and (4) scoring rubrics.

SYSTEMATIC OBSERVATION AND ANECDOTAL RECORDS.   Observing students in natural settings is one of the most common methods of assessing performance outcomes. Unfortunately, the observations are typically unsystematic, and frequently no record is made of the observation. For minor performance tasks that are easily corrected, like how to hold a paintbrush or how to label a graph, informal observation may be all that is needed. For more comprehensive performance situations, however, the observations should be systematic and typically some record of the observation should be made. This will enhance their objectivity, meaningfulness, and usefulness at a later date.

Observations are frequently guided by checklists or rating scales, but there is some advantage in making and recording less structured observations. For example, noting how students approach a task, how persistent they are in completing it, and how carefully they work has significance for evaluating their success in performing the task. Similarly, one student may need assistance on every step of the performance, while another student completes the task early and turns to help others. These important aspects of performance are apt to be overlooked by more structured observational devices but can be described in anecdotal records.

An **anecdotal record** is a brief description of some significant event. It typically includes the observed behavior, the setting in which it occurred, and a separate interpretation of the event. Although keeping anecdotal records can be time consuming, the task can be kept manageable by limiting the records to certain types of behavior (e.g., safety) and to those individuals needing the most help (e.g., slow, careless). The records are likely to be most useful when (1) they focus on meaningful incidents, (2) they are recorded soon after the incident, (3) they contain enough information to be understandable later, and (4) the observed incident and its interpretation are kept separate. What is desired is a brief, objective, self-sufficient description of a meaningful incident and a separate interpretation (if needed) of what the incident means. As these records of events accumulate for a particular individual, a typical pattern of behavior is obtained.

CHECKLISTS. The **checklist** is basically a list of measurable dimensions of a performance or product, with a place to record a simple "yes" or "no" judgment. If a checklist were used to evaluate a set of procedures, for example, the steps to be followed might be placed in sequential order on the form; the observer would then simply check whether each action was taken or not taken. Such a checklist for evaluating the proper use of an oral thermometer is shown in Figure 9.3. A checklist for evaluating a product typically contains a list of the dimensions that characterize a good product (size, color, shape, and so on), and a place to check whether each desired characteristic is present or absent. Thus, the checklist simply directs attention to the elements to be observed and provides a convenient means of recording judgments.

Construction of a checklist for performance assessment involves the following steps.

1. List the procedural steps or product characteristics to be evaluated.
2. Add common errors to the list, if such is useful in diagnosing poor performance.

Directions: Place a check in front of each step as it is performed.

_____ 1. Removes thermometer from container by grasping nonbulb end.
_____ 2. Wipes thermometer downward from nonbulb end with fresh wiper.
_____ 3. Shakes thermometer down to less than 96° while holding nonbulb end.
_____ 4. Places bulb end of thermometer under patient's tongue.
_____ 5. Tells patient to close lips but to avoid biting on thermometer.
_____ 6. Leaves thermometer in patient's mouth for three minutes.
_____ 7. Removes thermometer from patient's mouth by grasping nonbulb end.
_____ 8. Reads temperature to the nearest *two-tenths* of a degree.
_____ 9. Records temperature reading on patient's chart.
_____ 10. Cleans thermometer and replaces in container.

FIGURE 9.3 Checklist for Evaluating the Proper Use of an Oral Thermometer.

3. Arrange the list in some logical order (e.g., sequence of steps).
4. Provide instructions and a place for checking each item.
5. Add a place for comments at the bottom of the form, if needed.

RATING SCALES. The **rating scale** is similar to the checklist and serves somewhat the same purpose in judging procedures and products. The main difference is that the rating scale provides an opportunity to mark the degree to which an element is present instead of using the simple "present-absent" judgment. The scale for rating is typically based on the frequency with which an action is performed (e.g., always, sometimes, never), the general quality of a performance (e.g., outstanding, above average, average, below average), or a set of descriptive phrases that indicates degrees of acceptable performance (e.g., completes task quickly, slow in completing task, cannot complete task without help). Like the checklist, the rating scale directs attention to the dimensions to be observed and provides a convenient form on which to record the judgments.

A sample rating scale for evaluating both procedures and product is shown in Figure 9.4. Although this numerical rating scale uses fixed alternatives, the same scale items could be described by descriptive phrases that vary from item to item. A sample rating scale for a student project is presented in Box 9.6. Although this scale is not complete, it indicates how to arrange a scale for convenient recording and scoring.

The construction of a rating scale for performance assessment typically includes the following steps.

1. List the procedural steps or product characteristics to be evaluated.
2. Select the number of points to use on the scale and define them by descriptive terms or phrases.

Directions: Rate each of the following items by circling the appropriate number. The numbers represent the following values: 5—outstanding; 4—above average; 3—average; 2—below average; 1—unsatisfactory.

PROCEDURE RATING SCALE

How effective was the student's performance in each of the following areas?

5 4 3 2 1   (a) Preparing a detailed plan for the project.
5 4 3 2 1   (b) Determining the amount of material needed.
5 4 3 2 1   (c) Selecting the proper tools.
5 4 3 2 1   (d) Following the correct procedures for each operation.
5 4 3 2 1   (e) Using tools properly and skillfully.
5 4 3 2 1   (f) Using materials without unnecessary spoilage.
5 4 3 2 1   (g) Completing the work within a reasonable amount of time.

PRODUCT RATING SCALE

To what extent does the product meet the following criteria?

5 4 3 2 1   (a) The product appears neat and well constructed.
5 4 3 2 1   (b) The dimensions match the original plan.
5 4 3 2 1   (c) The finish meets specifications.
5 4 3 2 1   (d) The joints and parts fit properly.
5 4 3 2 1   (e) The materials were used effectively.

FIGURE 9.4 Rating Scale for a Woodworking Project.

BOX 9.6   Sample Rating Scale Form for a Student Project

Directions: Rate each item by circling the appropriate number. The numbers represent the following values: 4—excellent; 3—good; 2—satisfactory, 1—weak (needs modification).

Selecting and Stating the Problem

4 3 2 1   (a) Is the problem in harmony with the student's present knowledge and skill?

4 3 2 1   (b) (add others)

Locating and Selecting Resources

4 3 2 1   (a) Has a variety of resources been selected?

4 3 2 1   (b) (add others)

Writing the Report

4 3 2 1   (a) Has the problem been clearly stated?

4 3 2 1   (b) (add others)

Conducting a Research Study

4 3 2 1   (a) Have proper procedures been followed?

4 3 2 1   (b) (add others)

Building a Product

4 3 2 1   (a) Did the product match the specifications?

4 3 2 1   (b) (add others)

Oral Presentation of Project

4 3 2 1   (a) Did the oral presentation reflect understanding of the problem studied?

4 3 2 1   (b) (add others)

3. Arrange the items on the rating scale so that they are easy to use.
4. Provide clear, brief instructions that tell the rater how to mark items on the scale.
5. Provide a place for comments, if needed for diagnostic or instructional purposes.

Analytic Versus Holistic Scoring.   Rating scales are especially useful for **analytic scoring.** That is, when we want a judgment on each criterion by which the performance or product is to be judged. In evaluating writing skill, for example, such things as organization, vocabulary, style, ideas, and mechanics might be judged separately. The rating scale then becomes an instrument for directing observation to these criteria and provides a convenient means of recording and scoring our judgments.

Holistic scoring is based on an overall impression of the performance or product rather than a consideration of the individual elements. The global judgment is made by assigning a numerical score to each performance or product. Typically, between 4 and 8 points are used, and an even number of points is favored to avoid a "middle dumping ground." Evaluation consists of quickly examining the performance or product and assigning the number that matches the general impression of the performance or product. In the case of writing assessment, for example, the reader will read each writing sample quickly for overall impression and place it in one of the piles ranging from 4 to 1. It is assumed that good writing is more than a sum of the individual elements that go into writing and that holistic scoring will capture this total impression of the work.

SCORING RUBRICS.   Holistic scoring can be guided by scoring rubrics that clarify what each level of quality is like. **Scoring rubrics** (i.e., scoring guides) for writing and a psychomotor skill are shown in Boxes 9.7 and 9.8. These descriptions of each level do not provide for analysis of the product or the performance but simply list the criteria to keep in mind when making the overall judgment. Another way to clarify the meaning of each score level for a product is to use a *product scale*. This consists of a series of sample products that represent various degrees of quality. In writing assessment, for example, a writing sample representing each level of quality from 4 to 1 are reviewed, and each writing product is compared to the sample models and assigned the number of the sample it matches most closely. Product scales are especially useful where the quality of the product is difficult to define (e.g., art, creative writing).

For most instructional purposes, both holistic and analytic scoring are useful. One gives the global judgment of the performance or product and the other

---

BOX 9.7   Sample Scoring Rubric for Writing

4—	Interesting throughout Flows smoothly, good transitions Well-organized for topic Good use of mechanics and sentence structure
3—	Interesting most of the time Flows smoothly but some poor transitions Organized but some weaknesses Minor mechanical errors
2—	Interest lowered by lapses in focus Flow is interrupted by many poor transitions Organization weak, strays from topic Some serious mechanical errors
1—	No clear focus Jerky and rambling Poorly organized Many mechanical errors and weak sentence structure

BOX 9.8   General Scoring Rubric for a Psychomotor Skill

EXCELLENT	Uses procedure rapidly and skillfully
	Explains function of each step in procedure
	Modifies procedure to fit changing conditions
GOOD	Uses procedure correctly but with some hesitation
	Gives general explanation of steps in procedure
	Modifies procedure but needs some instructor guidance
ACCEPTABLE	Uses procedure correctly but is slow and clumsy
	Explanation of procedure is limited
	Modifies procedures but only after demonstration by instructor
INADEQUATE	Fails to use procedure correctly
	Explanation of procedure shows lack of understanding
	Uses trial and error in adjusting procedure

provides diagnostic information useful for improving performance. Where both are used, the global judgment should be made first so some specific element does not distort the general impression of the product.

MAKING PERFORMANCE ASSESSMENTS MORE AUTHENTIC

Performance assessments can be made more authentic by presenting performance tasks more like those in the real world. Real-world problems are open-ended, have no set strategies for solving them, and provide for the integration of cognitive, communication, and problem-solving skills.

This broader conception of performance assessment and its role in the teaching–learning process is supported by the more recent conceptions of how students learn. Modern learning theory emphasizes the need for focusing on more complex learning outcomes, using more comprehensive student activities, engaging students in the activities and obtaining meaning from them, and using more realistic types of problem solving. This emphasis requires more elaborate performance assessments that integrate the various skills and ideas imbedded in the activities. Properly done, these expanded assessments can make a significant contribution to the improvement of students' understanding and to their general educational development, in addition to their improvement of the particular skill activity (see Box 9.9).

PREPARING FOR PERFORMANCE ASSESSMENTS

Performance assessments can provide useful information concerning student achievement, but they are subject to all of the errors of observation and judgment. If performance assessments are to provide valid information, special care must be taken to improve the objectivity, reliability, and meaningfulness of the results.

BOX 9.9   Skill Execution Versus Authentic Assessment

Performing a Skill	**Authentic Assessment**
1. Write a short story on a given topic.	1. Plan a short story, outline the plot and characters, write the story, review and critique the story, and rewrite it.
2. Construct a bar graph from a given set of data.	2. Analyze a set of data and select the best type of graph to illustrate it. Construct the graph and give reasons for selecting this type of graph.
3. Set up laboratory equipment and follow the steps of an assigned exercise.	3. Design an experiment for comparing two products, complete the experiment, and write a summary of the findings. Make recommendations concerning the two products and give reasons.
4. Construct a birdhouse to fit a given set of plans.	4. Make a study of the birds that are most prevalent in your area. Design and build a birdhouse for one of the most common types. Explain to the class why you selected this model and where would be the best place to locate it.

Clearly, intended performance outcomes that are specified in observable terms and well-developed rating scales enhance the usefulness of the results. However, consideration must also be given to properly preparing (1) the environment in which the performance assessment will take place, (2) the student being assessed, and (3) those observing and judging the performance.

Prepare the Environment

By its very nature, a performance assessment requires the student to interact with his or her environment. For example, a driving test requires the student to interact with controls, pedals, and the steering wheel inside the vehicle, as well as the road, traffic, and pedestrians outside the vehicle. An assessment of typing skill requires the student to interact with the keyboard and the written material being typed, as well as the seat, desk, and lighting. Obviously, then, the environment cannot be divorced from the performance assessment. The performance task that the student is required to complete and the environment in which the student completes the task are intertwined.

As noted in the previous chapter, the higher the degree of realism in the performance assessment, the better. Determining driving ability by placing a student in a vehicle is considered a more valid method of assessment than a paper-and-pencil test. However, as the degree of realism increases, environmental factors become more difficult to anticipate and control. For example, an assessment of driving ability on a closed course (moderate realism) allows for the inclusion of obstacles the student may someday face. But, an assessment on an actual public street (high realism) may present many obstacles that were unexpected by both the student and the observer.

In some assessment situations, this degree of uncertainty on the part of the student is desirable and intended. For example, it is valuable to determine during a flight simulation how the student reacts to a sudden engine malfunction. But in this simulated situation, the engine malfunction was planned and the method and criteria of recording performance was established in advance. When environmental factors and events present themselves unexpectedly, objectively judging and comparing a student's performance to a criterion, or to others, becomes much more difficult.

Regardless of whether the performance assessment is conducted in a simulated environment or in the real world, steps must be taken to control or eliminate as many undesirable events as possible. Failure to do so may result in conditions that unfairly handicap the performance of some students while benefiting others. Box 9.10 provides some guidelines when preparing the environment for the performance assessment.

Prepare the Student

Historically, assessment in public education has centered on paper-and-pencil tests. By the time students reach the sixth grade, they have likely completed hundreds of written tests, quizzes, and homework assignments. Students have become accustomed to the ways tests are administered, scored, and returned by the teacher. They likely need little instruction regarding where to place their name, how to record their answers, and how they should behave during the exam. In essence, test taking becomes standardized through the limited, common, and routine practices among teachers and the consistent experiences

---

BOX 9.10   Guidelines When Preparing the Environment

1. Make certain that all tools, equipment, and instruments to be used by each student during the performance assessment are available and in good working condition.
2. Ensure that conditions that may handicap performance (e.g., weather, climate, temperature, lighting, time of day, etc.) are the same for each student.
3. Provide students with adequate space to perform.
4. Eliminate unnecessary conditions that may distract a student during performance (e.g., ringing telephone, disruptive students, conversation, etc.).
5. Allow sufficient time to observe performance, record observations, and provide feedback to the student.
6. Create activities for students waiting to perform. These activities should have educational value and occupy their time. However, the activities should be unrelated to the performance task so that they do not unfairly benefit from the activities compared to other students.
7. Create activities for students who have completed the performance assessment. Again, these activities should have educational value and occupy their time. However, these students should not have the opportunity to discuss the assessment with those students waiting to be assessed and, therefore, who may unfairly benefit from this counsel.

among students. As a result, student errors due to misunderstandings about how to complete the assessment are less of a concern.

While the use of performance assessments has become more common in public education, most students do not experience formal performance assessments until high school. For many students the performance assessment is a new experience. They have not had a prior history to guide behavior and form expectations. Thus, regardless of a student's competence, there is a concern that the novelty of the performance assessment process itself could cause the student to be apprehensive and confused, negatively impacting his or her performance.

To reduce student apprehension and eliminate confusion, teachers need to discuss with the students the purpose, process, and expected outcomes of the performance assessment. The following rules should be applied to guide the discussion.

1. In clear and concise language, explain what the student is expected to do. Whether provided to the student in writing, orally, or both, the student should be made aware what he or she will be expected to accomplish during the performance assessment. The performance outcomes and, more specifically, the instructional objectives that define what the student will be required to identify, construct, or demonstrate should be shared with the student prior to beginning the assessment. The students should also be given the opportunity to ask questions. The assessment should not begin until all of the students' questions concerning expectations have been answered.

2. Explain and show what tools, equipment, instruments, and other resources will be available to the student. To orient students to the conditions in which they will be expected to perform the task, the teacher should present to the students those items that will be made available during the assessment. Tools, equipment, and instruments should be shown to the student, and written materials should be at the proper reading level.

3. Explain how performance will be assessed. As discussed, the assessment of performance may be based on observing the student completing a task, the product that the student produces, or both. Students should be informed in advance how they will be assessed. If by observation, then students should know who will be observing, when observation will begin, and when observation will end. Also, students should know how performance will be judged. If a rating scale will be used, then the student should be made aware of the levels of performance that will be rated (e.g., 5 — outstanding; 4 — above average; 3 — average; 2 — below average; 1 — unsatisfactory). The students should also know the areas in which they will be rated. If a product, then the student should know how and when the product is to be submitted to the teacher and the criteria that will be used to assess the product.

4. Explain when and how feedback will be provided. Feedback should be given to students in a timely manner. Ideally, feedback should be provided as soon as students have completed the performance assessment. Doing so helps students to more effectively learn from any mistakes made. But, teachers should be sensitive not to embarrass students when they perform poorly. Students should be told that feedback will be provided privately to each student and that both strengths and weaknesses of their performance, as well as corrective action, will be discussed.

Prepare the Observer

In most instances, the teacher who develops the performance assessment procedures and rating instruments is the sole person who observes the students. However, this is not always the case. When the number of students is many and the time to conduct the performance assessment is extensive, teachers may need the assistance of additional observers. Multiple observers are also necessary to establish the reliability of the performance assessment (see Chapter 4). In these cases, it is imperative that each observer is adequately prepared. Failure to do so may result in inaccurate or biased judgments.

PROVIDE WRITTEN INSTRUCTIONS TO THE OBSERVER. Regardless of whether multiple observers are used, written instructions should be prepared to ensure that the administration procedures are consistent for all the students. These instructions should be detailed and include directions regarding what instructions, tools, equipment, and materials should be provided to the student; how much time the student should be given to perform the task; and when feedback should be given to the student.

DISCUSS POTENTIAL ERRORS IN OBSERVATION AND JUDGMENT. Objective assessment of performance can be threatened by *personal bias* and the *halo effect*. Personal bias is the tendency to rate all students relatively equally. Because of their predisposition, observers may be unjustly generous, severe, or neutral with their ratings of the students. The halo effect refers to errors in judgment due to a preestablished attitude toward a particular student. A favorable attitude toward a student may result in unjustly favorable ratings. Likewise, an unfavorable attitude toward a student may result in unjustly poor ratings. Observers should be made aware of these common errors in observation and judgment and reminded to remain objective.

CONDUCT A PRACTICE SESSION. Before placing the observer in the position of rating a student's performance, a practice session should be conducted. After being given the written instructions, each observer should take a turn performing the task that will be expected of the students and also judging the performance of another. Doing so will allow the observers to clarify questions related to the procedure and understand the expected student performance prior to the actual administration of the assessment.

PROVIDE EXAMPLES OF PERFORMANCE AND RATINGS. To clarify how performance should be rated, observers should be shown examples of various levels of student performance. Ideally, observers should view video recordings of prior students performing the task. At a minimum, one recording should show exceptional performance, while another should show unacceptable performance. The ratings of these students should be shared with the observers, and the reasoning behind the ratings should be discussed in detail.

DIAGNOSTIC PERFORMANCE ASSESSMENTS

As noted in earlier, the value of observing and assessing a student performing a procedure, as opposed to a product, is that specific errors are more easily detectable. When the product serves as the sole focus of assessment, it may be evident that an error occurred when producing the product. But, it may be difficult to ascertain precisely what error the student made. For instance, it would be difficult to determine whether a cake (the product) that is dry was the result of the wrong proportion of ingredients, baking too long, or some other reason. Had the student been observed measuring the ingredients and baking the cake, then the error would have been evident.

Yet, procedure evaluations do have their diagnostic limitations. While focusing the assessment on the procedure will more readily indicate what specific errors occurred, it may provide little information that can be used to explain "why" the error occurred. Was the student simply careless and missed a critical step? Or, does the student not understand why the step must be performed?

To find the answers to these questions, students could be asked to explain each step they are performing and what purpose the step serves. By requiring students to "think aloud," the observer is in a better position to assess the student's depth of understanding about which tools, equipment, and materials are most appropriate to use and what will result from performing each step correctly.

Summary of Points

1. Performance assessments provide direct evidence of valued learning outcomes that cannot be adequately assessed by traditional paper-and-pencil testing, but they are time consuming to use and require greater use of judgment in scoring.
2. Performance tasks contain knowledge and affective components as well as the skill component. All three components must be considered when planning performance assessments.
3. Writing performance objectives involves stating each general objective so that it describes a skill or product and then defining it by a list of specific performance outcomes that are relevant, clarify an effective performance, and are stated in observable terms that are easily understood by students.
4. Restricted performance tasks are highly structured and limited in scope (e.g., construct a graph). Extended performance tasks are typically less well structured and broad in scope (e.g., design and conduct an experiment).

5. The first step in performance assessment is to specify the intended performance outcomes.

6. Performance assessment may focus on a procedure (e.g., giving a speech), a product (e.g., a theme), or both (e.g., using tools properly in building a bookcase).

7. In some cases, it may be desirable to emphasize procedure evaluation during the early stages of instruction (e.g., touch system in typing) and product evaluation later (typed letter).

8. There are varying degrees of realism in performance assessment, and the aim is to obtain as high a degree of realism as possible within the various constraints operating (e.g., time, cost, availability of equipment).

9. Paper-and-pencil performance assessment is useful as a terminal measure in many areas (e.g., writing, drawing, problem solving) and can serve as a first step toward hands-on performance in others (e.g., procedure for repairing an automobile engine).

10. The identification test is typically concerned with identifying the tools, equipment, and procedures needed for a performance task and serves as an *indirect* measure of performance, or as an instructional device to prepare students for actual performance.

11. A structured performance test provides for an assessment under standard, controlled conditions (e.g., locating a malfunction in electronic equipment). The tools, equipment, conditions, and standards of performance are all carefully prescribed.

12. Performance assessment based on simulated performance (e.g., driver's training simulator) and the work sample (e.g., analyze business data on a computer) has a high degree of realism. Many performance skills in laboratory courses, business education, and industrial education can be evaluated at this level.

13. Student projects provide for the assessment of multiple learning outcomes (e.g., research, writing, speaking, thinking, and self-assessment skills), are adaptable to various areas of instruction, and typically use realistic problems.

14. A problem-solving project includes establishing criteria and standards for assessing the project, selecting and stating the problem, locating and selecting resources, writing the report, designing and completing a research study or making a product (e.g., model), and orally presenting and defending the project.

15. Observing students in natural settings and keeping anecdotal records can aid in evaluating aspects of performance that are likely to be overlooked by more structured methods (e.g., work habits).

16. Rating scales provide for analytic scoring, direct attention to the performance dimensions to be observed, and provide a convenient form on which to record the judgments.

17. Holistic scoring rubrics and product scales are especially useful where global judgments are being made (e.g., creative writing, works of art).

18. Improving performance assessments involves making clear what is to be observed, how it is to be observed, how the observations are to be recorded, and how the results are to be scored and used. In addition, any

procedure that contributes to more objective observations and records will aid in increasing the reliability and meaningfulness of the results.

19. The more authentic the performance assessment setting, the more likely unexpected and undesirable events will occur.

20. Before the assessment begins, steps should be taken to control or eliminate undesirable events.

21. Students should be prepared for the performance assessment in order to reduce any apprehension and confusion.

22. Preparing those individuals who will observe and rate student performance is recommended in order to increase the likelihood of objective ratings.

23. The diagnostic capability of performance assessments is enhanced by asking students to explain during the assessment what they are doing and why the procedures are necessary.

References and Additional Reading

Arter, J., & McTighe, J. *Scoring Rubrics in the Classroom* (Thousand Oaks, CA: Corwin Press, 2001).

Bott, P. A. *Testing and Assessment in Occupational and Technical Education* (Boston: Allyn and Bacon, 1996).

Fitzpatrick, R., & Morrison, E. J. "Performance and Product Evaluation." Chapter 9 in R. L. Thorndike, Ed., *Educational Measurement,* 2nd ed. (Washington, DC: American Council on Education, 1971).

Gronlund, N. E., & Brookhart, S. M. *Gronlund's Writing Instructional Objectives,* 8th ed. (Upper Saddle River, NJ: Pearson/Merrill/Prentice Hall, 2009).

Johnson, B. *Performance Assessment Handbook: Volume 2, Performances and Exhibitions* (Princeton, NJ: Eye on Education, 1996).

Nitko, A. J. *Educational Assessment of Students,* 4th ed. (Upper Saddle River, NJ: Merrill/Prentice Hall Pearson Education, 2004).

Oosterhoff, A. C. *Classroom Applications of Educational Measurement,* 3rd ed. (Upper Saddle River, NJ: Merrill/Prentice Hall, 2001).

Taylor, C. S., & Nolen, S. B. *Classroom Assessment: Supporting Teaching and Learning in Real Classrooms* (Upper Saddle River, NJ: Merrill/Prentice Hall, Pearson Education, 2005).

Self-Assessment

MULTIPLE CHOICE

DIRECTIONS: Select the best answer for each item by circling the corresponding letter.

1. An advantage of restricted performance tasks over extended performance tasks is that they
   (a) include numerous instructional objectives
   (b) are more valid
   (c) are more reliable
   (d) are easier to judge performance

2. A major advantage of specifying the performance outcomes prior to administering the task is that they can
   (a) help students understand what is expected
   (b) prevent bias from creeping into scoring
   (c) reduce the scoring burden for teachers
   (d) restrict the range of student performance

3. Constructing a graph from a given set of data is an example of
   (a) a restricted performance task
   (b) an extended performance task
   (c) an aptitude task
   (d) a knowledge task

4. When a specific procedure is not necessary to produce a product, the focus of assessment should be on the
   (a) product
   (b) procedure
   (c) procedure and product
   (d) instructional effectiveness

5. When preparing the environment for a performance assessment, activities should be created for students waiting to perform that
   (a) are related to the performance task
   (b) are unrelated to the performance task
   (c) allow students to interact with students who have been assessed
   (d) allow observation of students being assessed

6. One method to diagnose a student's depth of understanding during a performance assessment is to
   (a) focus the assessment on a product produced
   (b) require the student to explain the purpose of each step
   (c) not allow students to use any tools, equipment, or materials
   (d) require the student to perform steps in reverse order

TRUE-FALSE

DIRECTIONS: Read each statement and record as true or false on the lines provided.

7. _____ Restricted performance outcomes typically require students to identify, construct, or demonstrate completion of a simple task.

8. _____ Analytic scoring is most appropriate when it is desired to provide the student with feedback on performance of each step in a process.

9. _____ The "halo effect" occurs when a judgment of a student's performance is influenced by preexisting feelings toward the student.

Restricted-Response Essay

10. The authors of your textbook discuss the ways to make performance assessments more authentic. Compare, contrast, and provide examples of approaches that would assess skill performance in a more real-world context. Confine your answer to one page.

10 | ASSESSMENT IN DISTANCE EDUCATION

Studying this chapter should enable you to

1. Distinguish between asynchronous and synchronous assessments.
2. Describe the common assessment types used in distance education.
3. Describe the advantages of using a portfolio as a means of assessment.
4. Distinguish between a developmental portfolio and a showcase portfolio.
5. List the types of portfolio entries that should be considered in your teaching area.
6. Describe the factors to consider in planning a portfolio.
7. Describe a procedure for getting started in the use of a portfolio in the classroom.
8. Prepare a rating scale for the structural evaluation of a portfolio in your teaching area.
9. Prepare a rating scale for evaluating a student's learning progress shown in a portfolio in your teaching area.
10. Prepare a holistic scoring rubric for evaluating a student's final level of performance shown in a portfolio in your teaching area.
11. Describe the common methods of online cheating and ways to prevent them.

The number of secondary and postsecondary education institutions offering distance learning courses through online instruction continues to grow. In 2003, the Sloan Consortium reported that 1.6 million students were taking at least one online course during the fall of 2002 (Allen & Seaman, 2003). By the fall of 2005, the number of students who received online instruction had doubled (Allen & Seaman, 2006). This growth and reliance by education institutions to provide online delivery of instruction has led researchers and scholars to write numerous articles and books that define the best practices in curricula development and teaching online. But, comparatively less has been written about the best practices when conducting online assessments of student achievement.

In previous chapters, we discussed the methods used to develop valid and reliable pencil-and-paper achievement tests and performance assessments. However, the administrations of these assessment tools were discussed within the context of use in a traditional face-to-face classroom setting. This chapter departs from assessment in the typical classroom. Instead, the focus of this chapter is on a discussion of the (1) various forms of assessment in a distance learning environment and (2) benefits and limitations of online assessment.

ASYNCHRONOUS VERSUS SYNCHRONOUS ONLINE ASSESSMENT

Distance learning is characterized as a learning environment where there is a geographical and/or temporal separation between the teacher and the student. The earliest form of distance learning was the correspondence course in which students would receive in the mail print-based course materials. The students were required to review the materials in a time period designated by the teacher and complete and return to the teacher some form of assessment such as an achievement test and/or perhaps a written term paper to demonstrate cognitive mastery of the material. Students were geographically separated from the teacher, and interaction between the student and the teacher was **asynchronous** (i.e., occurred at different points in time). As a result, answers to student questions and the feedback the student received from the teacher on assessments were not immediate, but delayed.

While asynchronous correspondence courses remain in existence today, course materials once delivered to the student solely as print-based are often now available to the student online. Online streaming video and graphics supplement textbook and teacher-developed content to engage the individual learning styles of students and enhance learning. Further, the use of email and discussion boards has reduced the temporal delay in communication between the student and the teacher.

In Chapter 1, we discussed that the purpose of a summative assessment is to determine the *extent to which students have achieved the intended outcomes of instruction.* Through a summative assessment, the teacher determines the degree to which each student has mastered the course content and assigns the appropriate grade. Summative assessments typically involve the student submitting to the teacher a completed achievement test or some other end-of-unit or course assessment. The teacher then reviews and grades the assessment, and feedback on assessment performance is provided to the student at a later point in time. Therefore, assessments that are summative are viewed as asynchronous.

Due to the limitations of timely communication between the student and the teacher inherent in asynchronous delivery of instruction, the use of **synchronous** (i.e., occurring at the same point in time) distance learning technology is now available and has become more commonplace. Live video conferencing and telephone conference calling are being incorporated into distance learning courses to allow the degree of responsiveness to students that are observed in a face-to-face teaching–learning environment.

As we discussed in Chapter 2, an essential component of effective assessment is that feedback of assessment results *should be given immediately following or during the assessment.* When instruction is delivered synchronously, immediate feedback is possible. But when interaction with the student is solely asynchronous, then adherence to this guideline is not possible. The goal, then, for the teacher is to utilize available technologies and incorporate into the instruction synchronous assessment tools that will allow immediate feedback to students.

TYPES OF ONLINE ASSESSMENTS

There are a number of methods to assess students completing a distance education course. To follow is a discussion of several types that are used most often.

Achievement Tests

Achievement tests are arguably the most commonly used summative assessment tool. While the process involved in developing the test (e.g., test items) is the same regardless of whether the test is administered in a classroom or online, there are threats unique to unproctored online tests, specifically cheating. The potential for cheating on a test regardless of whether it is administered face-to-face or online is always present. But, the opportunity for students to cheat is greater when a test is administered online without a proctor. When opportunities to cheat are more prevalent, how then can a teacher know that a student's performance on an unproctored online achievement test is a true measure of how much the student has learned? The teacher can't know for certain. But, the first line of defense is for teachers to be aware of the methods that can be used by students to cheat. Potential methods of cheating identified by Rowe (2004) are described in Box 10.1. Methods to deter cheating are presented in a later section of this chapter.

BOX 10.1   Common Methods of Cheating

Potential Threat	Potential Outcome
1. Students complete the test at different points in time.	Students provide answers to other students.
2. The security of the test is not adequately maintained.	Students gain access to the test via unauthorized use of the instructor's password.
3. Unauthorized collaboration occurs among students and/or with outside consultants.	Students consult with each other during the test to arrive at correct answers.
4. Teachers lack of verification of student identity.	An imposter completes the test.
5. Unauthorized outside resources are available.	Students resort to online resources and print material to identify correct answers on the test.

Achievement tests administered online for formative and diagnostic purposes are typically synchronous. These tests are used by students to gauge their level of understanding content and progression throughout the course. At the end of each instructional unit, the students would be required to take an online test consisting of selection-type items relating to the learning outcomes of the unit. When students answer a question correctly, they are given immediate affirmative feedback through the testing software. When students answer incorrectly, they are notified and forwarded to the section of the instructional unit that relates to the question so that they can see where they went wrong. This form of assessment is effective in promoting student-centered, self-directed learning. But, teachers can also monitor student performance and make corrections in instruction when necessary.

Oral Presentations

Two-way interactive video conferencing offers many of the same benefits when assessing an oral presentation as those delivered by a student in the classroom. The student is provided a live audience, the length of the presentation can be controlled by the teacher, and feedback is immediate. In the absence of two-way interactive video technology to observe and provide synchronous feedback to a student delivering an oral presentation, the student could record him/herself delivering the presentation, and then the teacher would view the recording and assess the student's presentation at a later point in time. However, it is typical that the oral presentation assessment rubric will include rating criteria such as nonverbal skills (e.g., eye contact with the audience, body language), organization and demonstrated mastery of presentation content, and verbal skills (e.g., pronunciation, projection of voice) among others. The value of a face-to-face oral presentation is that the assessment is more authentic and aligned with the rubric criteria. Specifically, with a face-to-face oral presentation an audience is present, voice projection must be adequate for the size of the audience, and the presenter has only one opportunity to deliver the presentation. With a prerecorded oral presentation, there may not be an audience. Eye contact and projection, therefore, become less relevant; and there is no assurance that the teacher is viewing the first and only presentation attempt.

Threaded Class Discussions

Email or discussion boards included in a learning management system serve several useful purposes. First, they provide a convenient means for students to communicate and remain connected with the teacher and other students. Second, questions a student may have regarding a course assignment or content can be shared with other students, as well as the instructor. Other students may be solicited to respond to the questions, thereby involving them more directly in the teaching and learning process. Also, the answers to the questions, either from the teacher or students, are available to all the students, which will benefit those who may have had a similar question but didn't think or weren't comfortable to ask. Finally, class discussions can be a useful tool to assess student achievement. But to be useful the discussion topic must have sufficient breadth and depth in order to encourage meaningful participation and contributions from students.

In Chapter 8, we discussed the types of essay questions (restricted-response questions versus extended-response questions) as well as their strengths and limitations. One of the strengths noted is that essay questions provide a means to measure student attainment of the highest level of learning outcomes (analyzing, evaluating, creating). Extended-response questions in particular provide the greatest freedom to analyze, evaluate, and/or create a response. It is precisely for this reason that the topic for a threaded discussion should be posed as an extended-response essay question. Specifically, the topic of the essay should be sufficiently broad enough to allow each student the ability to make a unique contribution to the discussion. For instance, asking students to "describe the approaches used to establish the validity of an achievement test" would likely be too restrictive to elicit a unique but correct contribution from each student. More appropriate, for example, would be a topic that requires the students to discuss the implications and provide examples of the application of theory in practice, a social phenomenon, or a legislative policy such as the No Child Left Behind Act.

Synchronous class discussions through electronic chat rooms, two-way video, or phone conferencing provide the benefit of immediate feedback to students. However, there are several advantages to asynchronous discussions that teachers should keep in mind. First, as with face-to-face classroom discussions, some students may be reluctant to participate in the discussion. Discussion boards and email have the distinct advantage of adding a layer of separation from the teacher and other students that make those who are shy more comfortable and apt to actively participate. Second, discussion boards and email provide students the opportunity to think carefully about the best way to craft a question or respond to a discussion before pressing the submit button. With a synchronous discussion, students may feel pressured to participate and not give sufficient thought to their contribution to the discussion. Finally, asynchronous discussions are not restricted to a specific time when all students are expected to go online and participate. Most students who enroll in online courses do so because they don't have a personal or work schedule that will allow them to attend the course in a classroom. Therefore, it may be too restrictive for some students to participate in a classroom discussion at a particular time.

Electronic Portfolios

Electronic portfolios are becoming an important means of assessment in many schools. In some cases, they are used as a basic, or sole, method of performance assessment. In others, they provide another useful tool in the teacher's assessment kit. An electronic portfolio is a collection of student work saved electronically that has been selected and organized to show student learning progress (developmental portfolio) or to show samples of the student's best work (showcase portfolio). A common practice is to use the developmental portfolio throughout an instructional program and the showcase portfolio at the end.

Thus, the showcase portfolio provides a collection of work that indicates the student's final level of performance. Some schools have used the showcase portfolio as a basis for high school graduation. Some states have used them on a statewide basis as a means of assessing performance in basic skills. Our focus will be on **portfolio assessment** in the online instructional program.

The assessment value of portfolios is found in the variety of types of evidence that are available for judging student performance. They typically include various types of independent work (e.g., writing samples, drawings, research reports, computer worksheets, projects) as well as assessment results in the form of written comments, checklists, rating scales, test scores, and conference reports. The assessment data is also likely to include the student's self-assessments, peer assessments, and teacher's assessments. See Box 10.2 for what portfolios can show.

Students play an active role in selecting the entries and maintaining the portfolio. This provides for another important item to be included in a portfolio—that is, the student's reflections on such things as why the entry was chosen, what it illustrates, what was learned, and what might be done to improve performance. These written reflections cause students to focus on the learning process, the changes taking place, and the growth in their learning.

The active participation of students in selecting entries for the portfolio helps them focus on the criteria of successful performance, and their reflections on the criteria provides a basis for developing critical thought and deeper understanding. The criteria also make students aware of their responsibility for participating fully in the learning process, an important step toward becoming independent learners.

ADVANTAGES OF USING ELECTRONIC PORTFOLIOS.   Portfolios have a number of specific advantages as a means of assessing learning.

1. Learning progress over time can be clearly shown (e.g., changes in writing, thinking, or research skills).
2. Focus on students' best work provides a positive influence on learning (e.g., best writing samples, best examples of reasoning, and problem solving).

BOX 10.2   What a Student Portfolio Can Show

1. Learning progress over time.
2. Student's current best work.
3. Comparison of best work to past work.
4. Development of self-assessment skills.
5. Development of reflective learning.
6. Individual's level and pace of work.
7. Clear evidence of learning to parents and others.
8. The amount of teacher–student collaboration involved.

3. Comparing work to past work provides greater motivation than comparison to the work of others (e.g., growth in knowledge and skills).
4. Self-assessment skills are increased due to the student selection of best samples of work (e.g., focus is on criteria of good performance).
5. Reflective learning is encouraged as students are asked to comment on each portfolio entry (e.g., why do you consider this your best work?)
6. Adjustments can be made to provide for individual differences (e.g., students work at their own levels but work toward common goals).
7. Clear communication of learning progress is provided to students, parents, and others (e.g., work samples obtained at different times can be shown and compared).
8. Teacher–student collaboration in the teaching–learning–assessment process is increased.

Despite the numerous advantages of using portfolios, they are time consuming to maintain and use. Assisting students in the selection of portfolio entries, providing feedback on the students' work, and periodically reviewing the students' learning progress requires considerable student–teacher conference time. Simply collecting samples of student work and putting it in a file does not constitute a portfolio. Much greater care is required in the development of a portfolio that will be useful in instruction and assessment.

PLANNING FOR THE USE OF PORTFOLIOS.   There are a number of factors to keep in mind when planning for the use of portfolios. A careful consideration of them will increase a portfolio's value as an instructional and assessment tool. The major tasks are to:

1. Define the purpose of the portfolio.
2. Select the types of entries to include.
3. Develop methods to evaluate the entries.
4. Establish means to maintain and use the portfolio.
5. Evaluate the portfolio.

Each of these will be discussed in turn.

   Define the Purpose of the Portfolio.   The main purpose of the assessment portfolio is to improve student learning. But a secondary purpose is to help students become responsible for their own learning. This means active participation of the students in selecting the samples to be included in the portfolios, in assessing the quality of entries, in reflecting on what was learned and how to improve performance, in maintaining the portfolio, and in evaluating it. Each entry should be accompanied by the students' reflections on the entry. A brief form can be designed that provides questions and a space for answering. For example, What did I do? What did I learn? How would I improve it? Such questions cause students to think about their learning and their need to take responsibility for it. All of this is done under the guidance of the teacher, of course, but there should be a weaning away of control as students become increasingly capable of independent learning.

Select the Types of Entries to Include. The selection of entries for the portfolio is guided by the purpose, the intended learning outcomes, and the use to be made of the results. If the portfolio is limited to a specific area such as writing skill, the entries might be limited to one type of writing (e.g., narrative) or include different types of writing tasks (e.g., letters, essays, poetry). They might also include writing on different topics or in specific content areas (e.g., scientific writing). Both the first draft of the writing and later revisions also might be included. The specific types of entries will depend on the goals of instruction, how the information is to be used in the instructional programs, and with whom the information will be shared.

A more comprehensive portfolio will include samples of various types of student work, depending on the area of instruction. In math, for example, entries might include samples of problem solving, written explanations of how to solve problems, mathematical charts and graphs, and computer printouts of problem solving. Science entries might include examples of experimental studies, laboratory skills, evidence of conceptual understandings, student-designed projects, and field studies. The types of entries to include will, of course, vary with the purpose of the portfolio, the grade level, the instructional objectives, and any school requirements concerning the nature of the portfolio.

The portfolio should not be a repository for all of the student's work. If this is done, it becomes too cumbersome and unmanageable. Its content should be a sample of the student's best work, or latest work in progress, in selected areas. The areas may be determined by the teacher or by school requirements. In any event, the selection and evaluation of the portfolio entries should be determined by guidelines such as those in Box 10.3.

Develop Methods to Evaluate the Entries. The procedure for developing criteria for evaluating the portfolio entries is the same as for any performance task, like those discussed in Chapter 9. The criteria should specify the types of

---

BOX 10.3   Guidelines for Selecting Entries

1. Entries should be in harmony with the goals of instruction and the use to be made of the portfolio (e.g., to improve learning, for use in parent–teacher conferences, as part of a schoolwide assessment).
2. Entries should provide a variety of types of evidence (e.g., written, oral, exhibits, projects).
3. Entries should be selected in terms of the criteria to be used in judging them.
4. Entries should be selected by students, or at least they should be involved in the process.
5. Entries should be complex enough to allow for students' self-evaluations and their reflections on the learning that resulted.
6. Entries should be started early in the instructional program to better show growth in learning.
7. Entries should be evaluated by using the criteria and standards established for the performance tasks.

performance we are willing to accept as evidence of a quality product, and the standards should identify the various levels of acceptable performance. These are then used in preparing rating scales or holistic scoring rubrics to be used in the assessments.

The criteria can aid students in selecting, preparing, and evaluating the samples to be entered in the portfolio by focusing their attention on the elements to be included in the product. In working on a problem-solving project, for example, criteria like those discussed in Chapter 9 make clear to the students that the project requires a realistic problem, the selection and use of various resources, a written report, the preparation of an exhibit, and an oral report to a group. The specific criteria in each area make clear how the project will be judged and thus provide direction for student learning. Within the framework provided by the criteria, the students are still free to select a problem that interests them.

Our discussion makes clear why the criteria and standards must be shared with students at the beginning of the instruction. They provide guidelines for the preparation of the portfolio entries, for the students' self-assessments and reflections, and for the final assessment of the performance.

Establish Means to Maintain and Use the Portfolio. The portfolio entries are typically saved as an electronic document as part of a learning management system. As noted earlier, it is important to keep the portfolio entries down to a manageable number, so that they can be arranged in an orderly and useful manner. A hodgepodge collection of material is apt to defeat the purpose of using portfolios. Arranging the entries by sections and placing a table of contents in front of the file makes it easier to maintain the file and to locate material when evaluating learning progress or reporting to parents. Each entry should be dated and labeled before saving it in the file.

Students should actively participate in the maintenance of the portfolio. It is a collection of their work, so they should aid in setting the guidelines for what goes into the portfolio, selecting the portfolio samples, and evaluating the progress reflected in the samples of work. Unless a student is an active participant, he or she is likely to feel that it is not a personal portfolio.

The portfolio is to also be reviewed periodically by the teacher. The advantage of an electronic portfolio saved through the learning management systems used in the online program is that teachers have access to the portfolio as well. Here, the teacher can view the content and discuss with the student the strengths in learning progress and areas where improvement is needed. The portfolio is also used in parent–teacher conferences to demonstrate and discuss student achievement. There is no better way to make clear to parents what a student is learning than by the use of actual samples of student work.

Evaluate the Portfolio. As noted earlier, criteria for each performance task that is to serve as an entry should be clearly specified beforehand, as is done with any performance assessment. The criteria provide guidelines for preparing and evaluating the entry and should be shared with students early in the process. They are typically converted to rating scales or other scoring rubrics that can be used in self-assessment, peer assessment, and teacher assessment. The specification of criteria and their use in task assessment have been discussed and illustrated earlier and need not be repeated here. In addition to these specific performance assessments, however, there is a need to evaluate the portfolio structure and the students' overall performance.

EVALUATING THE PORTFOLIO STRUCTURE. The criteria for evaluating the structure of the portfolio should clarify the main features of an effective portfolio. Although these will vary somewhat with the content and level of instruction, there are some general criteria that should apply to all portfolios. The list in Box 10.4 includes some of main ones to be considered.

General criteria, such as these, provide guidelines both for developing a portfolio and for detecting shortcomings in its makeup. Criteria for evaluating a portfolio in a given content area could be made more specific and content oriented. For example, in a science course, item 2 might be stated as "Does the portfolio provide evidence of understandings, laboratory skills, and research skills?" Thus, the general criteria can serve as a guide for developing a more content-relevant set of criteria.

EVALUATING THE STUDENT'S OVERALL PORTFOLIO PERFORMANCE. In addition to the evaluation of individual samples as they are entered in the portfolio, there is a need to evaluate the student's overall performance. Criteria concerning the improvement in performance during the year and the final level of performance can provide the basis for a rating scale or holistic scoring rubric.

BOX 10.4   General Criteria for Evaluating the Portfolio's Structure

1. Has the purpose of the portfolio been clearly stated?
2. Does the portfolio provide evidence of various types of student learning?
3. Does the portfolio include evidence of complex learning in realistic settings?
4. Does the portfolio include enough entries in each area to make valid judgments?
5. Does the portfolio include students' self-evaluations and their reflections on what was learned?
6. Does the portfolio enable one to determine learning progress and current level of learning?
7. Does the portfolio provide clear evidence of learning to users of the portfolio?
8. Does the portfolio provide for student participation and responsibility?
9. Does the portfolio provide guidelines for student participation?
10. Does the portfolio present the entries in a well-organized and useful manner?
11. Does the portfolio include assessments based on clearly stated criteria of successful performance?
12. Does the portfolio provide for greater interaction between instruction and assessment?

EVALUATING STUDENT IMPROVEMENT. For evaluating student's improvement over the school year, a rating scale is typically favored because it can focus attention on the student's strengths and weaknesses. A rating scale based on general criteria is shown in Box 10.5.

The items in our illustrative rating scale are, obviously, very general, but they illustrate the types of items to consider when preparing this form of assessment instrument. The specific items to include would be determined by the instructional area, the intended learning outcomes of the instruction, and the purpose of the portfolio. A set of items for a writing portfolio, for example, would focus on the improvement of specific writing skills (e.g., word choice, sentence structure, organization, flow of ideas). A language arts portfolio would include specific items not only on writing skills but also on reading skills, reading comprehension, and speaking and listening skills. In addition to the specific items needed to fit the nature of the instruction, however, some of the general criteria still should be considered. Growth in self-assessment skills, reflective skills, and independent learning should be of interest in all areas of instruction.

The unique advantage of the portfolio in assessing student growth is that the entries over the school year provide sequential evidence of changes in student performance that can be examined and reexamined, if needed, when judging the degree of improvement. The rating scale simply provides a convenient place to record the judgments. As with the assessment of individual

---

BOX 10.5   Portfolio Ratings of Student Improvement

Directions: Rate each of the following items by circling the appropriate number. The numbers represent the following values: 4—outstanding progress; 3—good progress; 2—satisfactory progress; 1—unsatisfactory progress.

To what extent does the student show improvement in:

4	3	2	1	Understanding of concepts
4	3	2	1	Application of information
4	3	2	1	Reasoning ability
4	3	2	1	Writing skills
4	3	2	1	Speaking skills
4	3	2	1	Problem-solving skills
4	3	2	1	Performance skills
4	3	2	1	Computational skills
4	3	2	1	Computer skills
4	3	2	1	Self-assessment skills
4	3	2	1	Reflection skills
4	3	2	1	Work-study skills
4	3	2	1	Independent learning

entries, the students can also use the rating scale to rate their own overall improvement and, if desired, compare it with the teacher's ratings.

EVALUATING THE STUDENT'S FINAL LEVEL OF PERFORMANCE. For an evaluation of the student's final level of performance, a holistic scoring rubric is preferred. Here we are interested in an overall impression of each student's terminal performance. If the portfolio is focused on one limited area of instruction such as narrative writing, a single scoring rubric may suffice. However, for most courses of instruction several scoring rubrics would be needed. In science, for example, a separate scoring rubric for understanding science concepts, application of concepts and methods, scientific research skills, and process skills might be needed. In math, separate scoring rubrics for conceptual understanding, problem solving, reasoning ability, and using math in communications might be needed.

The preparation of scoring rubrics for an overall evaluation of a student's final level of performance is time consuming but the following outline of steps should help.

1. **Prepare a list of criteria for each scoring rubric to be prepared.** A review of the instructional objectives and the criteria used for portfolio entries should help here. For overall assessment of a student's final level of performance in the portfolio, however, there is a problem of selecting a limited number of criteria. A list of six or fewer is desirable so that the scoring rubric does not become too cumbersome. This means focusing on the most important criteria for judging the quality of the performance. A common procedure is to state the criteria you think are most important and then consult the literature to get help on how to combine them into a list of major criteria.

2. **Select the number of categories of performance to be used.** A good procedure is to start with four categories and expand it to six or eight if finer distinctions are needed. It is frequently difficult to describe more than four discrete levels of performance. A guide for preparing holistic scoring rubrics, using four categories, is presented in Box 10.6. The commonly used category labels and the frequently used terms for stating criteria were gleaned from currently used scoring rubrics in various content areas. The lists are not meant to be exhaustive and should not be used in a perfunctory manner, but they should be helpful in getting started.

3. **Adapt scoring rubrics from published sources.** The literature on portfolios and scoring rubrics provides numerous examples of scoring rubrics in various areas of instruction that might be adapted for use in an overall evaluation of student performance. Because of the difficulty of preparing holistic scoring rubrics, selecting those rubrics that seem most appropriate and then adapting them by modifying the criteria to fit your particular instructional situation and type of portfolio can provide a good way to start. When completed, check to be sure they are appropriate for your use.

BOX 10.6 Guide for Preparing Holistic Scoring Rubrics

Level Number	Category Labels	Frequently Used Terms When Stating Criteria	
4	Exemplary	Sophisticated	Thorough
	Superior	Extensive	Deep
	Distinguished	Comprehensive	Elegant
	Excellent	Unique	Perceptive
		Clear	Efficient
3	Satisfactory	Appropriate	Mostly
	Adequate	Consistent	Clear
	Competent	Relevant	Accurate
	Good	Acceptable	Broad
		Detailed	Variety
2	Minimal	Paraphrases	Inconsistent
	Borderline	Shallow	Incomplete
	Marginal	Limited	Basic
	Fair	Weak	Minor
		Minimal	Conventional
1	Unsatisfactory	Trivial	Incoherent
	Inadequate	Unclear	Lacks
	Incomplete	Vague	Disorganized
	Poor	General	Irrelevant
		Inaccurate	Superficial

4. **Check your prepared scoring rubrics to see if they work as intended.** When you have completed the sets of scoring rubrics, try them out by evaluating students' sample portfolios. This will help you determine whether the criteria focus on the most important areas of performance and provide clear distinctions between the various levels of performance. At this point you might just need some fine-tuning.

WAYS TO IDENTIFY OR REDUCE CHEATING IN ONLINE ASSESSMENT

Can teachers trust the results of an online assessment? In the absence of safeguards and methods to deter student cheating, often teachers cannot fully trust the results from all students. Of course, not all students will take the opportunity to cheat—many will not. But studies have shown that the prevalence of cheating has grown over the years, particularly on assessments administered online.

Can cheating be prevented? Perhaps it can't in all instances and with all students. But Cizek (1999) provides several suggestions later adapted by Rowe (2004) that may prove helpful to deter cheating on online assessments. These suggestions are discussed below.

Establish an Honor Policy

Typically, schools and universities have an established honor code addressing cheating and other forms of academic dishonesty that each student is required to follow. These codes explain to the student the conduct that is expected and the consequences of violating the code. However, these codes may have been presented to students only upon entry into the education institution and, therefore, can easily become less effective in deterring cheating over time. At the beginning of each course, the teacher should require students to reread the existing honor code, or they should develop their own code, and have students sign that they pledge to comply.

Continuously Monitor the Typical Performance of Each Student

In this chapter we have discussed the importance of including the frequent use of multiple types of synchronous and asynchronous assessments throughout an online course. The use of achievement tests, oral presentations, threaded discussions, and portfolio artifacts provide the means to determine the overall performance level that is typical for each student. Having a wealth of assessment evidence allows teachers the ability to identify performance that seems atypical for a student, given his or her prior performance. For instance, use of sentence structure and terminology that is much more advanced than those a student has presented in earlier written assignments is a clue that he or she may have plagiarized earlier published work. However, it is important that the teacher do not jump immediately to the conclusion that cheating has occurred. The teacher should investigate further by discussing the concerns with the student and gathering additional evidence to determine whether actual cheating has occurred.

Keep Assessment Materials and Grades Secure

Online learning management systems provide a layer of password security. Both students and teachers must submit a personalized password to gain access to the course content. The teacher can also gain access to the achievement tests and scoring rubrics that will be used during the course, and an electronic grade book used to record student grades, among other sensitive materials. For obvious reasons, the teacher's password should be difficult for students to guess. Further, intrusion-detection software should be used to reveal attacks or help prevent attacks before they occur. As an added measure of protection, the teacher should keep duplicate copies of assessment materials and student grades in a secure location other than the computer server housing the course just in case the server is compromised.

Proctor Achievement Tests

Earlier in Box 10.1, we presented the common methods that students use to cheat on unproctored online achievement tests. Knowing the potential for cheating, many education institutions have entered into contractual agreements with public libraries, high schools, community colleges, universities, and private organizations across the country to provide a place where students can go in their local area to complete an online assessment in a secure, proctored, and monitored environment. These proctors ensure that students complete the assessment at a designated time, without the assistance of others, and without the use of materials not authorized by the instructor. Further, the proctor can verify the identity of the student before the assessment begins.

Administer Alternative Versions of the Achievement Test

Finally, the teacher should consider varying the order of questions on the exam or randomly selecting test items from a pool of items so that all students do not receive the same test items on the exam. However, if the teacher chooses to randomly select items from a pool, then it is important that the varying versions of the tests be balanced in the number of items relating to each learning outcome. Also, each version should have acceptable reliability and should be equal in item difficulty and discriminating power. At a minimum, the teacher should follow the procedures discussed in Chapters 4 and 5 to (1) develop a table of specifications that lists the number of test items in the pool that relate to each learning outcome, (2) establish the equivalent-forms reliability of the alternative versions, and (3) conduct a simple item analysis to ensure that, on average, the versions of the test are essentially equal in levels of difficulty and ability to discriminate between high-performing and low-performing students.

Summary of Points

1. When planning for assessment in a distance education course, synchronous as well as asynchronous assessments should be used to ensure that students receive immediate feedback regarding their academic progress.
2. Teachers should be aware of the opportunities that students have to cheat when completing an unproctored achievement test and should reduce the likelihood of cheating by establishing an honor code, monitoring typical student performance, keeping course materials password secure, contracting proctors, and administering to students alternative versions of a test.
3. A portfolio is a collection of student work that has been selected and organized to show learning progress (developmental portfolio) or to show the student's best work (showcase portfolio).
4. Both types of portfolios are useful in the classroom—the developmental to show student's growth during the school year and the showcase to indicate final level of learning.

5. The assessment value of portfolios is found in the vast array of evidence of learning they provide, the actual use of students' samples of work, the active participation of students in selecting entries and maintaining the portfolio, and the variety of types of assessment data included.
6. The specific advantages of using a portfolio in the classroom are that it shows actual samples of student work, provides for comparisons of work in different areas and growth over time, provides students with an opportunity to evaluate and reflect on their work, provides clear evidence of learning to all interested persons, and provides for increased participation of students in the teaching-learning-assessment process.
7. Planning for the use of portfolios involves determining the purpose, the types of entries to include, the guidelines for selecting and evaluating the entries, the procedures for maintaining and using the portfolio, and the criteria for an overall evaluation of the portfolio.
8. Although the main purpose of using a portfolio is to improve student learning, a secondary purpose is to encourage students to participate more actively in the learning process and become more responsible for their own learning. This is an important step in becoming independent learners.
9. The structural evaluation of a portfolio can be accomplished by considering a series of questions concerning its makeup, organization, and content.
10. The overall evaluation of student progresses shown in the portfolio can be determined by a rating scale that focuses on the learning outcomes being assessed by the portfolio.
11. The final level of student performance can best be determined by holistic scoring rubrics for each of the major areas of instruction included in the portfolio.

References and Additional Reading

Allen, E. I., & Seaman, J. (2006). Making the Grade: Online Education in the United States, *Report from the Sloan Consortium* [Online], Available: http://www.sloan-c.org/publications/survey/index.asp

Allen, E. I., & Seaman, J. (2003). Seizing the Opportunity: The Quality and Extent of Online Education, *Report from the Sloan Consortium* [Online], Available: http://www.sloan-c.org/publications/survey/survey03.asp.

Arter, J., & McTighe, J. *Scoring Rubrics in the Classroom* (Thousand Oaks, CA: Corwin Press, 2001).

Cizek, G. J. (1999). *Cheating on Tests: How to Do It, Detect It, and Prevent It.* Mahwah, NJ: Lawrence Erlbaum.

Cole, D. J., Ryan, C. W., Kick, F., & Mathies, B. K. *Portfolios Across the Curriculum and Beyond,* 2nd ed. (Thousand Oaks, CA: Corwin Press, 2000).

Johnson, B. *Performance Assessment Handbook: Volume 1, Portfolios and Socratic Seminars* (Princeton, NJ: Eye on Education, 1996).

Linn, R. L., & Gronlund, N. E. *Measurement and Assessment in Teaching,* 8th ed. (Upper Saddle River, NJ: Merrill/Prentice Hall, 2000).

McMillan, J. H. *Classroom Assessment: Principles and Practices for Effective Instruction*, 3rd ed. (Boston: Allyn and Bacon, 2004).

Rowe, N. C. (2004). Cheating in Online Student Assessment: Beyond Plagiarism, *Online Journal of Distance Learning Administration*, VII (II), Available: http://www .westga.edu/distance/ojdla/summer72/rowe72.html

Taylor, C. S., & Nolen, S. B. *Classroom Assessment: Supporting Teaching and Learning in Real Classrooms* (Upper Saddle River, NJ: Prentice Hall, Pearson, 2005).

Self-Assessment

MULTIPLE CHOICE

DIRECTIONS: Select the best answer for each item by circling the corresponding letter.

1. Which of the following would be best considered an asynchronous assessment?
   (a) Threaded discussion
   (b) Chat room discussion
   (c) Telephone conference call discussion
   (d) Audio-video discussion

2. A collection of student work selected to show student learning progress is called a
   (a) developmental portfolio
   (b) showcase portfolio
   (c) formative assessment
   (d) work sample

3. When planning for the use of portfolios, one major consideration is
   (a) whether selection-type items will be used
   (b) the construct-related validity of portfolio entries
   (c) the criteria used to score portfolio entries
   (d) whether a table of specifications will be constructed

4. Sharing with students the criteria and standards used to assess portfolio entries at the beginning of the instruction helps to
   (a) diagnose potential learning disabilities
   (b) improve the reliability of assessment results
   (c) reduce the likelihood of cheating
   (d) guide the preparation of portfolio entries

5. Evaluating a student's final level of overall performance on a portfolio requires
   (a) an analytic scoring rubric
   (b) anecdotal records
   (c) a holistic scoring rubric
   (d) a process assessment

TRUE-FALSE

DIRECTIONS: Read each statement and record as true or false on the lines provided.

6. _____ The selection of portfolio entries is typically guided by the intended learning outcomes.

7. _____ It would be inappropriate to include test scores from paper-and-pencil tests as an indication of cognitive mastery in a student's portfolio.

8. _____ Ideally, portfolios should only include entries that are of one type (e.g., writing samples only).

9. _____ Portfolio entries should only include the work students completed at the end of an instructional program.

Restricted-Response Essay

10. The authors of your textbook discuss the common methods that students cheat on an online assessment. Describe each method and ways that cheating can be reduced. Confine your answer to one page.

11 GRADING AND REPORTING

Studying this chapter should enable you to

1. Distinguish between absolute grading and relative grading.
2. Describe how to select a proper frame of reference, or standard, for assigning grades.
3. Explain why learning ability, improvement, and effort provide a poor basis for grading.
4. Describe and defend the grading system you would use in your area of instruction.
5. Demonstrate how to properly weight components to be included in a grade.
6. Describe a rationale for making the pass-fail decision.
7. Write a statement, to be given to students, that describes your grading procedures.
8. Report learning progress to students and parents.

Grades assigned to student work should represent the extent to which the instructional objectives (i.e., the intended learning outcomes) have been achieved and should be in harmony with the grading policies of the school. Some schools have both clearly defined objectives and grading policies; many schools have neither. With or without the guidance of clear-cut policies and procedures, the assigning of grades is a difficult and frustrating task. It is somewhat easier if valid evidence of achievement has been gathered throughout the course.

Assessment of learning during instruction might include the use of objective and essay tests, ratings, papers, and various types of performance assessment. The problem of grading is that of summarizing this diverse collection of information into a single letter grade or brief report. Because the single letter grade (e.g., A, B, C, D, F) is the most widely used grading system, we shall focus on how best to assign such grades. This involves several important considerations: (1) What frame of reference, or standard, should be used to report level of performance? (2) How should the performance data be combined for grading? (3) What guidelines should be followed to provide the most effective and fair grading system? Each of these will be discussed in turn.

SELECTING THE BASIS FOR GRADING

Letter grades are typically assigned by comparing a student's performance to a prespecified standard of performance (absolute grading) or to the performance of the members of a group (relative grading). In some cases, grades are based on or modified by the learning ability of the student, the amount of improvement shown over a given instructional period, or student effort. As we shall see later, these factors provide an inadequate basis for assigning grades.

Absolute Grading

A common type of absolute grading is the use of letter grades defined by a 100-point system. Whether assigning grades to an individual set of test scores or as a basis for the final grades in a course, the set of grades might be expressed as one of the following:

Points	Points	Points
A = 90–100	95–100	91–100
B = 80–89	85–94	86–90
C = 70–79	75–84	81–85
D = 60–69	65–74	75–80
F = below 60	below 65	below 75

In the case of an individual test, this 100-point system might represent the percentage of items correct or the total number of points earned on the test. When used as a final grade, it typically represents a combining of scores from various tests and other assessment results. In any event, it provides an absolute basis for assigning letter grades.

Which set of points provides the best basis for assigning grades? There is no way of knowing. The distribution of points is arbitrary. Whatever distribution is used, however, should be based on the teacher's experience with this and past groups of students, knowledge concerning the difficulty of the intended learning outcomes, the difficulty of the tests and other assessments used, the conditions of learning, and the like. These are all subjective judgments, however, and shifts in the proportion of students getting the letter grade of A or F are difficult to evaluate. Do a larger number of grades of A represent improved instruction and better study habits by students, or easier tests and less rigid grading of papers and projects? Do more failures indicate poor teaching, inadequate study, or assessments that have inadvertently increased in difficulty?

Despite the problem of setting meaningful standards for an absolute grading system, this method is widely used in schools. It is most appropriate in programs where the set of learning tasks has been clearly specified, the standards have been defined in terms of the learning tasks, and the tests and other assessment techniques have been designed for criterion-referenced interpretation. All too frequently, however, absolute grading is based on some hodgepodge of ill-defined achievement results. When the distribution of points does not fit the grading scale, the points are adjusted upward or downward by some obscure formula to get a closer fit. Needless to say, such grades do not provide a meaningful report of the extent to which the intended learning outcomes have been achieved.

Relative Grading

When assigning grades on a relative basis, the students are typically ranked in order of performance (based on a set of test scores or combined assessment results), and the students ranking highest receive a letter grade of A, the next highest receive a B, and so on. What proportion of students should receive each grade is predetermined and might appear as one of the following:

	Percent of Students	Percent of Students
A	15	10–20
B	25	20–30
C	45	40–50
D	10	10–20
F	5	0–10

The percent of students to be assigned each grade is just as arbitrary as the selection of points for each grade in the absolute grading system. The use of a range of percents (e.g., A = 10–20 percent) should probably be favored because it makes some allowance for differences in the ability level of the class. It does not make sense to assign 15 percent As to both a regular class and a gifted class. Likewise, in an advanced course a larger proportion of As and Bs should be assigned and fewer (if any) Fs because the low-achieving students have been "weeded out" in earlier courses. When these percentages have been set by the school system, one has little choice but to follow the school practice—at least until efforts to change it are successful.

Older measurement books recommended using the normal curve to assign grades. This resulted in the same percent of As and Fs (e.g., 7 percent) and Bs and Ds (e.g., 38 percent). Although some teachers may still use such a system, its use should be discouraged. Measures of achievement in classroom groups seldom yield normally distributed scores. Also, to maintain the same proportion of grades, especially failures, at different grade levels does not take into account that the student population is becoming increasingly select as the failing students are held back or drop out of school.

The relative grading system requires a reliable ranking of students; thus, it is most meaningful when the achievement measures provide a wide range of scores. This makes it possible to draw the lines between grades with greater assurance that misclassifications will be kept to a minimum. Ideally, of course, the spread of scores should be based on the difficulty and complexity of the material learned. For example, an A should not simply represent more knowledge of factual material, but a higher level of understanding, application, and thinking skills. Thus, although norm-referenced interpretation is being utilized, the real meaning of the grades comes from referring back to the nature of the achievement that each grade represents. See Box 11.1 for a summary comparison of absolute and relative grading.

Learning Ability, Improvement, and Effort

In some cases, attempts are made to base grades on achievement in relation to learning ability, the amount of improvement in achievement, or the amount of effort a student puts forth. All of these procedures have problems that distort the meaning of grades.

Grading on the basis of *learning ability* has sometimes been used at the elementary level to motivate students with less ability. At first glance, it seems sensible to give a grade of A to students who are achieving all that they

---

BOX 11.1   Absolute Grading and Relative Grading

ABSOLUTE GRADING

Strengths

1. Grades can be described directly in terms of student performance, without reference to the performance of others.
2. All students can obtain high grades if mastery outcomes are stressed and instruction is effective.

Limitations

1. Performance standards are set in an arbitrary manner and are difficult to specify and justify.
2. Performance standards tend to vary unintentionally due to variations in test difficulty, assignments, student ability, and instructional effectiveness.
3. Grades can be assigned without clear reference to what has been achieved (but, of course, they should not be).

RELATIVE GRADING

Strengths

1. Grades can be easily described and interpreted in terms of rank in a group.
2. Grades distinguish among levels of student performance that are useful in making prediction and selection decisions.

Limitations

1. The percent of students receiving each grade is arbitrarily set.
2. The meaning of a grade varies with the ability of the student group.
3. Grades can be assigned without clear reference to what has been achieved (but, of course, they should not be).

are capable of achieving. There are two major problems with this procedure, however. First, it is difficult, if not impossible, to get a dependable measure of learning ability apart from achievement. Both tests have similar type items and measure similar concepts. Second, the meaning of the grades becomes distorted. A low-ability student with average performance might receive an A, whereas a high-ability student with average performance receives a grade of C. Obviously, the grades are no longer very meaningful as indicators of achievement.

Using the amount of *improvement* as a basis for grading also has its problems. For one, the difference scores between measures of achievement over short spans of time are very unreliable. For another, students who score high on the entry test cannot possibly get a high grade because little improvement can be shown. Students who know about this grading procedure ahead of time can, of course, do poorly on the first test and be assured of a fairly good grade. This is not an uncommon practice where grades are based on improvement. Finally, the grades lack meaning as indicators of achievement when increase in achievement becomes more important than level of achievement. For example, a low-achieving student with considerable improvement might receive an A, while a high-achieving student with little improvement receives a B or C.

Grading on the basis of *effort*, or adjusting grades for effort, also distorts the meaning of the results. Low-achieving students who put forth great effort receive higher grades than their achievement warrants and high-achieving students who put forth little effort are likely to receive lower grades than deserved. Although such grading seems to serve a motivational function for low-achieving students, the grades become meaningless as measures of the extent to which students are achieving the intended learning outcomes.

In summary, assigning grades that take into account learning ability, amount of improvement, or effort simply contaminates the grades and distorts their meaning as indicators of student achievement. A letter grade is most useful when it represents achievement and only achievement. Other factors may be rated separately on a report card, but they should not be allowed to distort the meaning of the letter grade.

A Combination of Absolute and Relative Grading

Grades should represent the degree of which instructional objectives (i.e., intended learning outcomes) are achieved by students. Some of the objectives of instruction are concerned with minimum essentials that must be mastered if a student is to proceed to the next level of instruction. Other objectives are concerned with learning outcomes that are never fully achieved but toward which students can show varying degrees of progress. The first are called minimal objectives and the second developmental objectives.

Minimal objectives are concerned with the knowledge, skill, and other lower-level learning outcomes that represent the minimum essentials of the course. In order to receive a passing grade, a student must demonstrate that this basic knowledge and skill, which are prerequisite to further learning in the area, have been learned to a satisfactory degree. *Developmental objectives* are concerned with higher-level learning outcomes such as understanding, application, and thinking skills. Although we can identify degrees of progress toward these objectives, we cannot expect to ever fully achieve them. In science, for example, we might expect all students to master basic terms, concepts, and skills, but encourage each student to proceed as far as he or she can in understanding and applying the scientific process and in developing the intellectual skills used by scientists. Similarly, all students in math might be expected to master the fundamental operations, but show wide diversity in problem-solving ability and mathematical reasoning. In all instructional areas there are lower-level objectives that should be mastered by all students and higher-level objectives that provide goals that never can be fully achieved. Thus, with minimal objectives we attempt to obtain a uniformly high level of performance for all students, and with developmental objectives we encourage each student to strive for maximum development.

As indicated earlier, the pass-fail decision should be based on whether the minimal objectives have been mastered. Students demonstrating that they have achieved the minimal objectives, and thus have the necessary prerequisites for success at the next level of instruction, should be passed. Those who do not should fail. This requires an *absolute* judgment, not a relative one. Students should not be failed simply because their achievement places them near the bottom of some group. It is the nature of the achievement that is significant.

Above the pass-fail cutoff point, grades should be assigned on a relative basis. This is because students' scores will tend to be spread out in terms of their degree of development beyond the minimal level. Students cannot be expected to master the more complex learning outcomes described by developmental objectives, but they can show varying degrees of progress toward their attainment. Although it would be ideal to have a scale of achievement ranging from simple to complex so that absolute grading could be used, this is not possible at this time. The best we can do is obtain a spread of student achievement scores in terms of the complexity of the learning outcomes attained and use relative grading. If properly done, a grade of A would represent greater achievement of the higher-level learning outcomes and not simply a high relative position in the group. This would assume, of course, that tests and other assessment techniques would measure a range of achievement from simple to complex, and not just knowledge of factual information and simple skills.

In most cases the school will dictate the grading policy, including the basis on which the grades are to be assigned. Regardless of the system used, it is important to relate the grades back to student achievement so that different grades represent different levels of performance. Letter grades without an achievement referent tend to have little meaning.

COMBINING DATA FOR GRADING

Assigning grades typically involves combining results from various types of assessment, including such things as tests, projects, papers, and laboratory work. If each element is to be included in the grade in terms of its relative importance, the data must be combined in a way that proper weights are used. For example, if we want test scores to count 50 percent, papers 25 percent, and laboratory work 25 percent of the grade, we need a method that will result in grades that reflect this emphasis. The process is simplified if all assessment results are converted to numerical scores first. It is then simply a matter of following a systematic procedure of combining scores.

The method of combining scores so that proper weights are obtained for each element is not as simple as it seems. A common procedure is simply to add scores together if they are to have equal weight and to multiply by 2 if an element is to count twice as much as the other. This typically will not result in each element receiving its proper weight, even if the highest possible score is the same for all sets of scores. How much influence each element has in a composite score is determined by the spread, or variability, of scores and not the number of total points.

The problem of weighting scores when combining them can be best illustrated with a simple example. Let's assume we only have two measures of achievement and we want to give them equal weight in a grade. Our two sets of achievement scores have score ranges as follows:

Test scores	20 to 100
Laboratory work	30 to 50

If we simply added together a student's test score and score on laboratory work, the grade the student received would be determined largely by the test score because of its wide spread of scores. This can be shown by comparing a student who had the highest test score and lowest laboratory score (Student 1) with a student who had the lowest test score and highest laboratory score (Student 2).

	Student 1	Student 2
Test score	100	20
Laboratory score	30	50
Composite score	130	70

It is quite obvious from the difference in composite scores that the weighting is not equal.

With sets of scores like those for our test and laboratory work, it is not uncommon for teachers to attempt to give them equal weight by making the top possible score equal. This can be done, of course, by multiplying the score on laboratory work by 2, making the highest possible score 100 for both measures. Here is how the two composite scores for our hypothetical students would compare under this system:

	Student 1	Student 2
Test score	100	20
Laboratory score (×2)	60	100
Composite score	160	120

Our composite scores make clear that equalizing the maximum possible score does not provide equal weights either. As noted earlier, the influence a measure has on the composite score depends on the spread, or variability, of scores. Thus, the greater the spread of scores, the larger the contribution to the composite score.

We can give equal weight to our two sets of scores by using the **range** of scores in each set. Because our test scores have a range of 80 (100 – 20) and our laboratory scores have a range of 20 (50 – 30), we must multiply each laboratory score by 4 to equalize the spread of scores and, thus, given them equal weight in the composite score. Here are the composite scores for our two hypothetical students:

	Student 1	Student 2
Test score	100	20
Laboratory score (×4)	120	200
Composite score	220	220

At last we have a system that gives the two measures equal weight in the composite score. Note that if we wanted to count our test score *twice* as much as the laboratory score, we would multiply it by 2 and the laboratory score by 4. However, if we wanted to have our laboratory score count twice as much as the test score, we would have to multiply each laboratory score by 8. Thus, when we originally multiplied our laboratory scores by 4, we simply adjusted the spread of those scores to match the spread of the test scores. When the two sets of scores have the same range of scores, we can then assign additional weights in terms of their relative importance (Box 11.2).

The range of scores provides only a rough approximation of score variability but it is satisfactory for most classroom grading purposes. A more

BOX 11.2   Computing Composite Scores for Grading

1. Select assessments to be included in the composite score and assign percentages.
2. Record desired weight for each assessment.
3. Equate range of scores by using multiplier.
4. Determine weight to apply to each score by multiplying "desired weight" by "multiplier to equate ranges."

Components		Desired Weight	Range of Scores	Multiplier to Equate Ranges	Weight to Apply to Each Score
1. Test score	50%	2	20 to 100	1	2 × 1 = 2
2. Laboratory work	25%	1	30 to 50	4	1 × 4 = 4
3. Homework	25%	1	0 to 10	8	1 × 8 = 8

Computing The Composite Scores

Students	Raw Scores			Weighted Scores			Composite
	1	2	3	1(×2)	2(×4)	3(×8)	1(w)+2(w)+3(w)
Nguyen	93	42	8	186	168	64	418
Derek	84	45	10	168	180	80	428
Maria	85	47	7	170	188	56	414
Jonus	95	35	10	190	140	80	410

Note that Derek had the highest composite score but would have had the lowest if the raw scores were simply added together, or even if the test score was multiplied by 2 (the desired weight). That is because the measure with the biggest range of scores has the greatest influence on the combined scores unless adjustments are made to equate the spread of scores. Compare Jonus's raw scores and composite scores to Derek's.

dependable basis for weighting grade components can be obtained with the standard deviation.

Some teachers obtain a composite grade by converting all test scores and other assessments to letter grades, converting the letter grades to numbers (e.g., A = 4, B = 3, C = 2, D = 1, F = 0) and then averaging them for a final grade. When this procedure is followed, information is lost because the data are reduced to only five categories. For example, a student with a high A and high B would receive the same average grade as a student with a low A and a low B. To overcome this problem, pluses and minuses are sometimes added (e.g., A+ = 12, A = 11, A− = 10, B+ = 9, B = 8, B− = 7, etc.). This provides more categories but some information is still lost. A better solution is to use numerical scores on all assessments and then combine these numerical scores into a composite score before assigning grades.

ELECTRONIC GRADING

The use of a computer can aid in the process of grading. This may be done with the use of a simple spreadsheet program that can be used to set up your own grading system for recording, combining, and reporting grades. There are also a number of gradebook computer programs that provide spreadsheets that are set up with a place to record students' names, test scores, and grades. They provide for the calculation of average scores and print reports. The gradebook programs vary considerably, however, in the type of calculations they provide. The one you select should fit your grading system or be easily adapted to it. Some school districts provide gradebook programs that teachers are expected, or required, to use. In that case you will, of course, have to adapt your grading procedure to fit the gradebook program.

GUIDELINES FOR EFFECTIVE AND FAIR GRADING

Assigning grades that provide a valid measure of student achievement, that have a meaning beyond the classroom in which they are given, and that are considered to be fair by students is a difficult but important part of teaching. The following guidelines provide a framework that should help clarify and standardize the task.

1. **Inform students at the beginning of instruction what grading procedures will be used.** This should include what will be included in the final grade (e.g., tests, projects, laboratory work) and how much weight will be given to each element. It should also include a description, in achievement terms, of what each letter grade represents. A descriptive handout may be helpful.

2. **Base grades on student achievement, and achievement only.** Grades should represent the extent to which the intended learning outcomes were achieved by students. They should *not* be contaminated by student effort, tardiness, misbehavior, or other extraneous factors. These can be reported on separately, but they should not influence the achievement grade. If they are permitted to become a part of the grade, the meaning of the grade as an indicator of achievement is lost.

3. **Base grades on a wide variety of valid assessment data.** All too frequently, grades are based primarily, if not entirely, on test scores. If grades are to be sound indicators of achievement, all important learning outcomes must be assessed and the results included in the final grade. Evaluations of papers, projects, and laboratory work are not as reliable as objective test scores but to eliminate them lowers the validity of the grades.

4. **When combining scores for grading, use a proper weighting technique.** As noted earlier, the influence of a component on the overall grade is determined by the spread, or variability, of the scores. Thus, in combining scores to obtain a composite for assigning grades, be sure the spread of scores is equalized before weighting and combining them.

5. **Select an appropriate frame of reference for grading.** If the entire instruction is based on mastery learning, it is necessary to use an *absolute* standard for grading and to define the grades in mastery terms. For conventional classroom instruction, the pass-fail distinction should be described in absolute terms and the grades above that determined by relative position in the group. However, these relative letter grades should have achievement referents representing learning outcomes ranging from simple to complex.

6. **Review borderline cases by reexamining all achievement evidence.** When setting cutoff points for each grade, there is typically a student or two just below the cutoff line. Measurement errors alone might be responsible for a student being just below (or above) the line. Also, the composite score may contain a clerical error, or one low test score contributing to the composite score may be due to illness or some other extraneous factor. In any event, it is wise to review the data for borderline cases and make any needed adjustments. When in doubt, fair grading would favor giving the student the higher grade.

Although in this chapter we focused on assigning grades, it does not imply that all student assignments and activities should be graded. Using brief tests, written assignments, and projects as learning tools is frequently more effective if the focus is on detecting and overcoming learning errors rather than on assigning grades. Formative assessment emphasizes this function of assessment results. Whether graded or not, however, all assessments of student achievement should include plans for the effective feedback of results along with suggestions for improving learning. Grading is an important and necessary task in teaching but it is secondary to our main purpose—improving student learning.

REPORTING TO STUDENTS AND PARENTS

The letter grade is typically required for school records, but a more elaborate report is needed for describing achievement to students and parents. One method is to use a reporting system that provides a rating of performance on each of the major learning outcomes of a course of instruction. The example of a Science Performance Report shown in Box 11.3 illustrates a form for this purpose. The report could be made more informative by listing the specific learning outcomes for each major outcome. If the instructional objectives and specific learning outcomes are specified at the beginning of instruction, as they should be, the report form can be easily arranged and shared with students when instruction begins. Just don't make the list so long and cumbersome that it overwhelms students and confuses parents. It may be helpful to have a committee of teachers, students, and parents work out a satisfactory report form for your grade level, department, or the entire school.

A comprehensive report form should contain a place for an achievement grade (uncontaminated by effort, tardiness, misbehavior, or similar factors), a separate grade for effort (if desired), and a list of the intended learning

---

BOX 11.3 Science Performance Report

The circled number indicates the student's level of performance on each of the major learning outcomes being evaluated. The numerical ratings are defined as follows:

4—Outstanding performance.

3—Good performance, some improvement needed.

2—Inadequate performance, needs additional work.

1—Did not achieve the intended outcome.

4 3 2 1 (a) Knows scientific terms and facts.

4 3 2 1 (b) Understands science concepts and processes.

4 3 2 1 (c) Applies science learning to new situation.

4 3 2 1 (d) Demonstrates reasoning ability.

4 3 2 1 (e) Demonstrates research skills.

4 3 2 1 (f) Demonstrates laboratory proficiency.

4 3 2 1 (g) Solves math problems needed in science.

outcomes, work habits, and personal characteristics to be rated. The letter grade is useful as an overall measure of achievement and is easily recorded for administrative uses. But the ratings of intended learning outcomes and related characteristics provide the most valuable information for improving learning and instruction, and reporting progress to students and parents.

Using a Portfolio

As noted in Chapter 10, there is no better way of reporting student achievement than the use of a portfolio. The collected samples of work make clear to students and parents alike what students are learning and how well they are learning it. In conference with students and parents, you can present a summary of the students' achievements and then support it by showing actual samples of the students' work. This provides as comprehensive and complete a report of student achievement as is possible. The conference also provides for two-way communication that permits the student or parent to ask for clarification and to discuss ways to improve performance.

If portfolios are not used in the school, it is still wise to use samples of student work when discussing learning progress and level of achievement with students and parents. Combined with a report form, like the one described earlier, work samples can be very useful in clarifying student achievement.

Summary of Points

1. Grades should represent achievement of the intended learning outcomes and be uncontaminated by other factors.
2. Grades should be assigned in accordance with the grading policies and procedures of the school.
3. Absolute grading requires predetermined standards based on clearly specified learning tasks and measures designed for criterion-referenced interpretation.
4. If instruction is based on a mastery learning program, absolute grading should be used with defined cutoff points and a stated rationale for the selection of the cutoff points.
5. Relative grading is based on the ranking of individuals in a group, but relative grades also should have content meaning. Higher grades should represent higher levels of understanding, application, thinking skills, and performance skills.
6. Where relative grading is used, the pass-fail decision still should be determined on an absolute basis. The important question is: Does this student have the minimum knowledge and skill needed to succeed at the next level of instruction?
7. A grading system based on minimal objectives (to determine the pass-fail decision) and developmental objectives that spread students out in terms of the difficulty and complexity of the material learned provides a good compromise between absolute and relative grading for use in conventional classroom instruction.

8. Basing grades on achievement in relation to learning ability, amount of improvement, or effort will only distort the meaning of grades as measures of achievement.

9. Grades should be based on valid measures of achievement. Validity is built in during the construction of tests and other assessment procedures by designing instruments that measure the intended outcomes of instruction.

10. Grades should be based on a variety of achievement assessments. Test scores should be supplemented by various types of performance assessment that measure the intended outcomes of instruction more directly (e.g., writing samples, laboratory work).

11. Components entering into an overall grade should be adjusted for the spread of scores before weighting them in terms of their importance.

12. Borderline cases should be given the benefit of the doubt and assigned the higher grade, unless a review of the achievement data indicates otherwise.

13. Attitude, effort, misbehavior, and other nonachievement factors might be rated separately but should not be allowed to influence the achievement grade.

14. Some tests and assessment procedures can be used for learning purposes and need not be assigned a grade (e.g., formative use of learning assessments).

15. Reporting to students and parents involves informing them of the extent to which the intended learning outcomes are being achieved. Both detailed performance reports and portfolios are useful for this purpose.

16. Whatever grading and reporting system is used, the procedures should be made clear to students at the beginning of instruction. A descriptive handout may be useful for this.

References and Additional Reading

Airasian, P. W. *Classroom Assessment*, 4th ed. (New York: McGraw-Hill, 2001).

Brookhart, S. M. *Grading* (Upper Saddle River, NJ: Merrill/Prentice Hall, 2004).

Linn, R. L., & Gronlund, N. E. *Measurement and Assessment in Teaching*, 8th ed. (Upper Saddle River, NJ: Merrill/Prentice Hall, 2000).

McMillan, J. H. *Classroom Assessment: Principles and Practices for Effective Instruction*, 3rd ed. (Upper Saddle River, NJ: Merrill/Prentice Hall, 2004).

Oosterhoff, A. C. *Classroom Applications of Educational Measurement*, 3rd ed. (Upper Saddle River, NJ: Merrill/Prentice Hall, 2001).

Self-Assessment

MULTIPLE CHOICE

DIRECTIONS: Select the best answer for each item by circling the corresponding letter.

1. Assigning grades by comparing student performance with a prespecified standard is referred to as
   (a) performance grading
   (b) absolute grading

    (c) relative grading

    (d) standardized grading

2. Relative grading applies a
   (a) norm-referenced approach
   (b) objective-referenced approach
   (c) criterion-referenced approach
   (d) illustrative-referenced approach

3. A point system used to assign grades is an example of
   (a) relative grading
   (b) correcting for guessing
   (c) standardized testing
   (d) absolute grading

4. One criticism of basing the percentage of classroom students who receive each letter grade (i.e., A, B, C, D, F) on the normal curve is that
   (a) the distribution is often skewed
   (b) students can't be ranked
   (c) too many students would get As
   (d) relative grading is unreliable

5. Basing grades on the amount of improvement in learning that a student demonstrates may penalize students who perform
   (a) high on the entry test
   (b) low on the entry test
   (c) high on the final test
   (d) the same on both tests

TRUE-FALSE

DIRECTIONS: Read each statement and record as true or false on the lines provided.

6. _____ Relative grades indicate a student's ability to meet performance standards.

7. _____ Absolute grading guarantees that at least one student will get a grade of A.

8. _____ Unless adjustments are made, the measure with the largest range of scores has the greatest influence on the composite score.

9. _____ If the range of scores on a test is 50 to 90, the range on a project is 60 to 80, and the desired weight for both is 1, then the weight to apply to the project scores would be 4.

Restricted-Response Essay

10. The authors of your textbook discuss why learning ability, improvement, and effort should not be used to base grading. Describe why each of these should not be used. Confine your answer to one page.

12 | INTERPRETING STANDARDIZED ACHIEVEMENT TEST SCORES

Studying this chapter should enable you to

1. Distinguish between norm-referenced and criterion-referenced interpretation of standardized test results.
2. Describe the basic features of a standardized achievement test.
3. Explain the meaning of each of the scores used in norm-referenced interpretation and list the cautions when interpreting each one.
4. Describe how standard scores are derived from the mean and standard deviation.
5. Convert standard scores to each other and to percentile ranks, using the normal curve.
6. Explain the stanine system and describe the advantages of using stanine scores.
7. Describe the procedures for making criterion-referenced interpretations with standardized tests.
8. List the cautions to observe when making criterion-referenced interpretations with standardized tests.

Standardized achievement tests have been widely used in the schools as a means of determining how well schools are doing. These tests have been primarily norm-referenced tests that compared local student performance to the performance of a representative sample of students in a norm group (e.g., a group of students at the national, regional, or state level). In the past, the test items were selection-type items, primarily multiple choice. In recent years, the tests have been modified to provide for criterion-referenced interpretations as well (e.g., by including more items per task, using open-ended tasks, and providing for interpretation by clusters of tasks). Both types of interpretation will be discussed in turn.

Being able to interpret the various types of norm-referenced test scores and understand how criterion-referenced interpretations are used in standardized tests is important, if the tests are to play a role in the instructional program.

It is also important, of course, to understand them well enough to be able to explain them to students and parents. To start with, it is important to keep in mind that norm-referenced interpretation indicates a student's relative level of performance in comparison to others and criterion-referenced interpretation describes the tasks a student can perform.

FEATURES OF STANDARDIZED ACHIEVEMENT TESTS

Standardized achievement tests are designed to determine how well students are achieving a common set of broadly based goals. Well-constructed standardized achievement tests typically have the following features.

1. The content of the test is based on widely used textbooks and curriculum guides.
2. The test items are written by test experts in consultation with subject-matter experts and are based on a clear set of specifications.
3. The test items are tried out, reviewed, analyzed for difficulty and discriminating power, and either revised or eliminated.
4. The final set of items is selected on the basis of the test specifications.
5. Directions for administering and scoring the test are rigidly prescribed.
6. The test is administered to select groups of students to establish national, regional, or statewide norms for interpretation of the test scores.
7. The final version of the test is published along with a test manual that describes the test's technical qualities and the procedures for administering, scoring, interpreting, and using the results.

Thus, a standardized test measures a standard set of broadly based educational outcomes, uses standard directions and standard scoring procedures, and provides for a comparison of a student's score to that of similar students who have taken the same test under the same conditions. If a **battery of tests** is used, and all tests have been standardized on the same norm group, a student's performance on the different tests can also be compared. On a basic skill battery, for example, we can determine a student's relative level of performance in reading, language, and mathematics. With comparable forms of the test, we can also examine learning progress over a series of grade levels. All of these norm-referenced interpretations and comparisons of standardized test scores requires an understanding of the various types of test scores that are used in describing students' test performance.

INTERPRETING NORM-REFERENCED SCORES

The score a student receives when a test has been scored according to the directions is called the **raw score.** On a classroom test, this is typically the number of items a student answers correctly. Although raw scores are used in classroom testing, the interpretations and comparisons made with standardized tests require that the raw scores be converted to some type of **derived score.** Comparison of performance on two different tests (e.g., reading and math), for example, require that both tests be on the same scale. Raw scores won't work because the two tests may differ in the number of items in the test and the difficulty of the items. By converting both sets of raw scores to the same derived score scale, we provide a common basis for comparing relative performance. Although there are many different types of derived scores, the most common types used in school achievement testing are

1. Percentile ranks.
2. Grade equivalent scores.
3. Standard scores.

The raw scores on a standardized test are converted to derived scores during the norming of the test. Attempts are made to obtain norm groups that contain a sample of students like those for whom the test is intended. National **norms,** for example, typically include students from the various geographic regions of the United States, urban and rural schools, and schools of different size. A balance of boys and girls, socioeconomic levels, and ethnic groups is also sought. Thus, national norms should approximate as closely as possible the student population throughout the United States. The same care is typically also followed in obtaining regional, state, and special group norms (e.g., private schools). Despite the care in obtaining norm groups, however, the obtained sample of students only approximates the ideal sample, due to such constraints as the needed cooperation of selected schools to administer the tests and the time limits for obtaining the norm sample.

After the norm groups have been selected and the tests administered and scored, the raw scores are converted to derived scores and presented in the test manual in tables of norms. These tables present the raw scores and derived scores in columns so that a raw score can be converted into a derived score by going across the parallel columns from the raw score to the derived score. Of course, the printout from machine scoring will give both the raw score and the derived score.

Before using the derived scores from a standardized test, it is wise to consider the nature of the norm group. Does the norm group provide a relevant basis for interpreting student performance? How was the norm group obtained ? When were the norms obtained? We can obtain the most meaningful norm-referenced interpretation of test scores when the norms are relevant, representative, and up to date.

A final caution. The scores in the norm group should not be viewed as goals or standards. They are simply the scores that a representative group of students have earned on the test. They aid in interpreting and comparing test performance, but they do not represent levels of performance to strive for. They are average or typical scores obtained in average or typical schools.

Percentile Ranks

The percentile rank is one of the easiest scores to understand and to interpret to parents. A percentile rank indicates a student's relative position in a group in terms of the percentage of group members scoring at or below the student's raw score. For example, if a raw score of 33 equals a percentile rank of 80, it means 80 percent of the group members had raw scores equal to or lower than 33. By converting raw scores to percentile ranks, the raw scores are put on a scale that has the same meaning with different size groups and for different length tests.

To further clarify the meaning of percentile ranks, Table 12.1. illustrates how raw scores are converted to percentile ranks. The following steps illustrate the procedure.

1. The raw scores are ranked from high to low (column 1).
2. The number of students obtaining each score is listed in the frequency column (column 2).
3. The score frequencies are added from the bottom up (i.e., adding each score frequency to the total frequency of all lower scores) to obtain the cumulative frequency (column 3).

TABLE 12.1 Frequency Distribution and Percentile Ranks for an Objective Test of 40 Items

1 Test Score	2 Frequency	3 Cumulative Frequency	4 Percentile Rank[*]
38	1	30	98
37	1	29	95
36	0	28	93
35	2	28	90
34	1	26	85
33	2	25	80
32	3	23	72
31	2	20	63
30	1	18	58
29	4	17	50
28	2	13	40
27	2	11	33
26	2	9	27
25	3	7	18
24	1	4	12
23	0	3	10
22	1	3	8
21	1	2	5
20	0	1	3
19	1	1	2
	$N = 30$		

*Rounded to nearest whole number.

4. Apply the following formula at each score level to get the percentile rank for that raw score (column 4).

$$PR = \frac{CF \text{ below score} + 1/2 \text{ of frequency at score}}{\text{number in group } (N)} \times 100$$

where PR = percentile rank
     CF = cumulative frequency

To illustrate the computation, let's compute the percentile ranks for two scores.

$$\text{Score 33} \quad PR = \frac{23 + 1}{30} \times 100 = 80$$

$$\text{Score 30} \quad PR = \frac{17 + .5}{30} \times 100 = 58.3$$

Percentile ranks are rounded to the nearest whole number, so the percentile rank for the raw score of 30 is listed in Table 12.1 as 58. To be sure you understand this procedure, you can compute the percentile ranks of other raw scores in the table and check your answers.

When interpreting percentile ranks, there are a number of cautions to be kept in mind. (1) Percentile ranks describe test performance in terms of the *percentage of persons* earning a lower score and *not* the percentage of items answered correctly. The **percentage correct score** is a criterion-referenced interpretation; **percentile rank** indicates relative standing and, therefore, is a norm-referenced score. (2) Percentile ranks are always specific to a particular group. For example, a percentile rank of 90 in a gifted group represents higher test performance than a percentile rank of 90 in an average group. Thus, whenever we are describing a student's relative performance, knowing the nature of the group is just as important as knowing the student's relative standing. (3) Percentile ranks are not equally spaced on the scale. A difference of 5 percentile ranks near the middle of the distribution of scores represents a smaller difference in test performance than a 5-percentile-rank difference at the ends of the distribution. This is because percentile ranks are based on the percentage of persons being surpassed and there is a larger percentage of persons in the middle of a score distribution to surpass than at the ends of the distribution. For example, at the high end of the distribution, a raw score difference of several points will make little difference in percentile rank because there are so few high scores. Although this limits some uses of percentile ranks (e.g., they can't be directly averaged), they remain one of the most useful and easiest to interpret types of derived scores.

PERCENTILE BANDS.   Some test manuals use **percentile bands** in presenting test norms. Instead of a specific percentile rank for each raw score, a range of percentile ranks is presented. For example, a table of norms may show that a raw score of 52 has a percentile band of 60–64. This allows for the possible error in the test score. The band tells us that we can be fairly certain that a student who earns a raw score of 52 on the test has a relative standing that falls somewhere between the 60th and 64th percentile rank. We cannot be more precise than this because our estimates of test performance (i.e., raw scores) always contain some error, due to such factors as fluctuations in attention, memory, effort, and luck in guessing during testing.

The width of the percentile band is determined by the reliability of the test. With a highly reliable test, the band is narrow. With a test of low reliability, the band is wide. The width of the band is computed by using the **standard error of measurement.** This is a statistic computed from the reliability coefficient and used to estimate the amount of error in an individual test score (see Chapter 4). These *error* bands can, of course, be computed for raw scores or for any type of derived score. They are sometimes called *confidence* bands because they indicate how much confidence we can have in the score representing a person's test performance. With a narrow band, we are more confident that the score represents the person's "true" or "real" level of achievement.

In addition to using percentile bands to interpret an individual's test performance, percentile bands can also be used to interpret differences in test performance on a battery of tests. In comparing percentile bands for the different tests, we can conclude that where the bands do *not* overlap there is probably a "real" difference in test performance and where they do overlap, the differences are likely to be due to error. For example, the following percentile bands from a test battery for Maria indicate that there is no "real" difference in her performance in reading and language, but she is lower in math.

	Reading	Language	Math
Maria's percentile bands	70–75	74–79	63–68

The use of percentile bands prevents us from overinterpreting small differences in test scores. Test publishers that use percentile bands typically plot them as bars on students' test profiles, making it easy to determine when the ends of the bands overlap and when they don't.

Grade Equivalent Scores

Grade equivalent scores provide another widely used method of describing test performance. They are used primarily at the elementary school level. With these scores, a student's raw score on the test is converted to the grade level at which the score matches the average raw score of students in the norm group. As with other derived scores, tables in the test manual present parallel columns of raw scores and grade equivalents. Thus, all we need to do is consult the table and obtain the grade equivalent for any given raw score. Although it is easy to obtain and is apparently easy to interpret, it is probably one of the most misinterpreted types of score. Let's take a look at what the grade equivalent score means and what it doesn't mean.

To clarify the meaning of grade equivalents, let's assume that we obtained the following grade equivalent scores from a test battery for Dave, who is in the middle of the fourth grade.

Reading	4.5
Language	6.5
Math	7.8

First note that the grade equivalent score is expressed in terms of the grade level and the month in that school year. Thus, Dave's score in reading is equal to the average score earned by students (in the norm group) in the middle of the fourth grade. Because Dave is in the middle of the fourth grade, we interpret his performance in reading as average. In language, Dave is two years advanced, and in math, he is more than three years advanced. Does that mean that Dave can do the work at these levels? No, it most likely means that he does fourth-grade work in these areas faster and more efficiently than other fourth-graders. The tests probably did not include sixth- and seventh-grade material. The same misinterpretations can occur with low grade equivalents. If Dave had a math score of 2.0, for example, it wouldn't mean he could only do second-grade math problems. It would more likely mean that he did fourth-grade problems slower and with more errors than other fourth-graders. High and low grade equivalent scores are typically obtained by extrapolation and do not represent average scores earned by those groups. This is often necessary because students at lower grade levels may not have the knowledge and skill needed to take the test, and students at higher grade levels may have moved beyond the types of skills measured by the test.

Grade equivalent scores provide a simple method of interpreting test performance, but when using them and interpreting them to parents, the following common misinterpretations should be avoided.

1. They are *not* standards to be achieved but simply the average scores of students in the norm group.
2. They do *not* indicate the grade level at which a student can do the work.
3. Extremely high and low grade equivalent scores are *not* as dependable indicators of test performance as those near the student's grade level.

In addition to these cautions to be observed when interpreting an individual's grade equivalent scores, a comparison of scores on tests in a test battery requires an additional caution. Growth in basic skills, for example, is uneven. In reading, growth is more rapid than in math, which depends more directly on the skills taught in school. Thus, a difference of a year in grade equivalent scores represents a larger difference in achievement on a reading test than on a math test. In addition, growth in achievement tends to slow down at different times for different skills, and when growth slows down, the differences in achievement between grade equivalent scores become smaller. Both the variations in growth of skills from one area to another and the variations in patterns of growth over time contribute to the unevenness of the units on our grade equivalent score scale. In comparing a student's grade equivalent scores on different tests from a test battery, it may be wise to look at the norm table to see how the raw scores spread out on each test. A high or low grade equivalent score might be discounted if the difference from other grade equivalent scores is based on relatively few raw score points.

Standard Scores

A **standard score** describes test performance in terms of how far a raw score is above or below average. It is expressed in units that are computed from the mean and the standard deviation of a set of scores. We are all familiar with the use of the **mean** as an average. It is obtained by summing the test scores and dividing by the number of scores. The standard deviation indicates the spread of scores in a set. The computation for obtaining the standard deviation is shown in Box 12.1, but that does not help us understand its meaning or its use in interpreting standard scores. This can best be done by describing its properties and showing how it is used as the basic unit for the various types of standard scores.

The standard deviation (*SD* or *s*) is an important and widely applicable statistic in testing. In addition to its use as a basic unit in standard scores, it also serves as a basis for computing reliability coefficients and the standard error of measurement, as we saw in the Chapter 4.

BOX 12.1   Computation of the Standard Deviation Using a Hand Calculator

Steps to Follow

1. Square each score in the set.
2. Add these squared values to obtain a total.
3. Divide the total by the number of scores in the set.
4. Square the mean of the set of scores.
5. Subtract the squared mean in step 4 from the result obtained in step 3.
6. Take the square root of the difference obtained in step 5. This is the standard deviation (*SD* or *s*).

Formula for the Computational Steps

$$SD = \sqrt{\frac{\Sigma X^2}{N} - M^2}$$

where Σ = "sum of"
X = a test score
N = number of scores
M = mean
$\sqrt{}$ = "square root of"

THE MEAN, STANDARD DEVIATION, AND NORMAL CURVE.   The mean and the standard deviation can probably be best understood in terms of the **normal curve,** although a normal distribution is not required for computing them. The normal curve is a symmetrical bell-shaped curve based on a precise mathematical equation. Scores distributed according to the normal curve are concentrated near the mean and decrease in frequency the further one departs from the mean. A sample normal curve is presented in Figure 12.1.

It will be noted in Figure 12.1 that the mean falls at the exact center of a normal distribution. Note also that when the normal curve is divided into standard deviation (*SD*) units, which are equal distances along the baseline of the curve, each portion under the curve contains a fixed percentage of cases. Thus, 34 percent of the cases fall between the mean and +1 SD, 14 percent between +1 SD and +2 SD, and 2 percent between +2 SD and +3 SD. Since the curve is symmetrical, the same percentages, of course, apply to the intervals below the mean. These percentages have been rounded to the nearest whole number, but only a small fraction of a percent (0.13 percent) of the cases fall above and below three standard deviations from the mean. Thus, from a practical standpoint, a normal distribution of scores falls between −3 and +3 standard deviations from the mean.

To aid in understanding the meaning of standard deviation, a set of raw scores with a mean of 40 and a standard deviation of 5 has been placed below the baseline of the curve in Figure 12.1. Note that the mean raw score of 40 has been placed at the zero point and that the distance of one standard deviation is 5 raw score points everywhere along the baseline of the curve. Thus, the point one standard deviation above the mean equals 45 (40 + 5) and the point one standard deviation below the mean equals 35 (40 − 5). In this particular set of scores, then, approximately 68 percent of the scores (about two-thirds) fall between 35 and 45, approximately 96 percent fall between 30 and 50, and approximately 99.7 percent fall between 25 and 55 (the figure shows 100 percent because numbers are rounded).

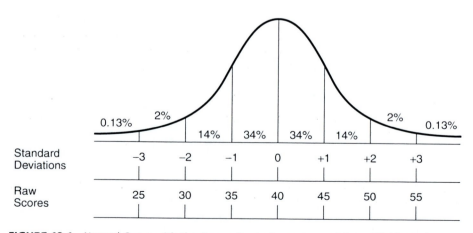

FIGURE 12.1   Normal Curve with the Approximate Percentage of Cases Within Each Interval (Percentages Have Been Rounded).

When the standard deviation is being computed for a set of normally distributed scores, we are essentially determining how far we need to go above (or below) the mean in raw score points to include 34 percent of the cases. The scores obtained with standardized tests typically approximate a normal distribution or are normalized by statistical means and thus permit the types of interpretations we are making here.

Z-SCORES.   A number of standard scores are based on the standard deviation unit. The simplest of these and the one that is basic to the others is the z-score. This score simply indicates, in standard deviation units, how far a given raw score is above or below the mean. The raw score of 45 in Figure 12.1, for example, would be assigned a z-score of 1.0 because it is one standard deviation above the mean. The raw score of 30 in Figure 12.1 would be given a z-score of −2.0 because it is two standard deviations below the mean. The formula for z-scores is:

$$z\text{-}score = \frac{\text{Raw score} - \text{Mean}}{\text{Standard deviation}}$$

For example, z-scores for raw scores of 47 and 36 in Figure 12.1 would be computed as follows:

$$z\text{-}score = \frac{47 - 40}{5} = 1.4 \qquad z\text{-}score = \frac{36 - 40}{5} = -.8$$

Thus, a raw score of 47 is 1.4 standard deviations above the mean and a raw score of 36 is .8 of a standard deviation below the mean.

While used in research, z-scores are seldom used directly in test interpretation because of the use of decimal points and minus signs. Instead, z-scores are converted to other types of standard scores that use only whole numbers and positive values. Such scores are more convenient to use and avoid the possibility of misinterpretation due to a forgotten minus sign.

There are a number of different types of standard scores used in test interpretation. All one needs to do is select an arbitrary mean and standard deviation and convert the z-scores into the standard score units. To illustrate, we will describe the procedure for some common standard scores.

T-SCORES.   **T-scores** have a mean of 50 and a standard deviation of 10. They are obtained from z-scores by multiplying the z-score by 10 and adding the result to 50, as shown in the following formula.

$$T\text{-}score = 50 + 10 \,(z\text{-}score)$$

Applying the formula to the various z-scores discussed earlier (1.0, −2.0, 1.4, −.8) we would obtain T-scores as follows:

$$T = 50 + 10 \,(1.0) = 60 \qquad T = 50 + 10 \,(-2.0) = 30$$
$$T = 50 + 10 \,(1.4) = 64 \qquad T = 50 + 10 \,(-.8) = 42$$

T-scores can be easily interpreted because they always have the same mean and standard deviation. A T-score of 60 always means one standard deviation above the mean and a T-score of 30 always means two standard deviations below the mean. Thus, with the use of T-scores, an individual's performance on different tests can be directly compared, and the scores can be combined or averaged without the distortion of different size standard deviations, which occur with the raw scores.

Where a normal distribution can be assumed, T-scores can also be interpreted in terms of percentile ranks because, in this case, there is a direct relationship between the two as shown in Figure 12.2. Note that a T-score of 30 is equivalent to a percentile rank of 2, a T-score of 40 is equivalent to a percentile rank of 16, and so on. This relationship makes it possible to use standard scores for those purposes where equal units are needed and to use percentile ranks when interpreting test performance to students and parents.

Because T-scores and percentile ranks both have a mean of 50 and use similar two-digit numbers, the two types of scores are often confused by

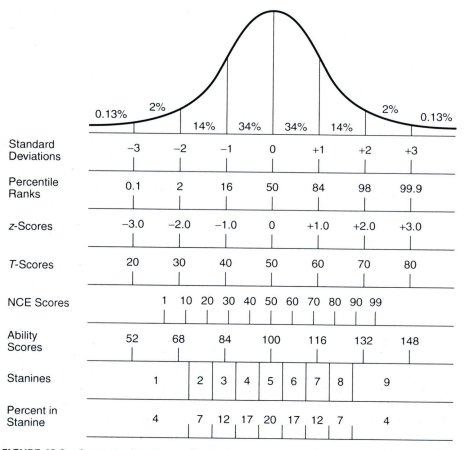

FIGURE 12.2 Corresponding Percentile Ranks, z-Scores, T-Scores, NCE Scores, Ability Scores, and Stanines in a Normal Distribution.

those inexperienced in test interpretation. Thus, it is important to keep in mind that percentile rank indicates the percentage of individuals who fall at or below a given score, while a T-score indicates how many standard deviation units a given score falls above or below the mean. Note in Figure 12.2 that although percentile ranks and T-scores have the same mean value of 50, below the mean percentile ranks are smaller than T-scores and above the mean they are larger than T-scores. This is accounted for, of course, by the fact that percentile ranks are crowded together in the center of the distribution and spread out at the ends, while T-scores provide equal units throughout the distribution of scores.

NORMAL-CURVE EQUIVALENT (NCE) SCORES. Another standard score that might be confused with both T-scores and percentile ranks is the **normal-curve equivalent** (NCE) score. This set of scores also has a mean of 50, but a standard deviation of 21.06. This provides a set of scores with equal units, like the T-score, but the scores range from 1 to 99. Percentile ranks also range from 1 to 99, but they do not provide equal units. As can be seen in Figure 12.2, percentile ranks are smaller at the middle of the distribution (e.g., one SD = 34 percent) than at the ends (e.g., one SD = 2 percent). Thus, when interpreting NCE scores, don't confuse them with T-scores, which have a more restricted range of scores (typically 20 to 80), or with percentile ranks that have the same range of scores (1 to 99) but are based on unequal units.

ABILITY SCORES. Publishers of achievement test batteries typically administer a test of learning ability (also called cognitive ability, school ability, or intelligence) to the same norm groups as the achievement battery to make comparisons of learning ability and achievement possible. The scores on these tests are now reported as standard scores with a mean of 100 and standard deviation of 16 (15 on some tests). These scores are to be interpreted like any other standard score (see Figure 12.2). A score of 116 means one standard deviation above the mean (percentile rank = 84). These scores were originally called deviation IQs, because they replaced the old ratio IQ (i.e., $\frac{MA}{CA} \times 100$). More recently, however, to avoid the confusion surrounding IQ scores, they have been given more appropriate names, such as school ability scores and standard age scores.

STANINE SCORES. Test scores can also be expressed by single-digit standard scores called stanines (pronounced *stay-nines*). The stanine scale divides the distribution of raw scores into nine parts (the term **stanine** was derived from *standard nines*). The highest stanine score is 9, the lowest is 1, and stanine 5 is located in the center of the distribution. Each stanine, except 9 and 1, includes a band of raw scores *one-half of a standard deviation wide*. Thus, stanines are standard scores with a mean of 5 and a standard deviation of 2. The distribution of stanines and the percentage of cases in each stanine are shown in Figure 12.2.

The nine-point scale is simple to interpret to students and parents because of the single-digit score. It is easy to visualize where a person falls on a nine-point scale, where 5 is average. Because each stanine includes a band of raw scores, there is also less chance that test performance will be overinterpreted. When comparing scores on two different tests in a test battery, a difference of two stanines is typically significant. Thus, in interpreting the following scores for a student, we would conclude that the student is higher in math but there is no difference between reading and language.

$$\text{Reading stanine} = 5$$
$$\text{Language stanine} = 4$$
$$\text{Math stanine} = 7$$

In addition to the ease of interpretation, stanines provide a simple method for combining and averaging test scores. The conversion of raw scores to stanines puts the scores from different tests on the same standard score scale, with equal units. Thus, they have uniform meaning from one part of the scale to another and from one test to another. A difference between stanine 5 and stanine 7 is the same as a difference between a stanine of 4 and a stanine of 6. A difference of two stanines is also the same, if we are referring to a reading test, a language test, a math test, or any other test. Like other standard scores, they provide equal units that can be readily combined. Unlike other standard scores, they are easy to interpret and to explain to others. See Box 12.2 for suggestions on how to interpret test results.

BOX 12.2 Interpreting Standardized Test Results to Students and Parents

1. Describe in general terms what the test measures and how it relates to the local curriculum (e.g., The test measures computational skills only. It does not include measures of math reasoning, which is the main focus of our curriculum.).
2. When interpreting percentile ranks, keep the description simple (e.g., The percentile rank of 87 means 87 percent of students in the norm group had lower scores. It is not a percentage-correct score.).
3. When interpreting grade equivalents, make statements that are unlikely to be misinterpreted (e.g., The grade equivalent of 6.5 for a fifth-grader means he can do fifth-grade work as rapidly and efficiently as students in the middle of the sixth grade.).
4. When interpreting stanines, use brief, simple statements (e.g., The stanine of 6 on the reading test is one stanine above average on a scale from 1 to 9, and the stanine of 4 on the math test is one stanine below average.).
5. When interpreting differences between test scores, use percentile bands or other ways to take error into account (e.g., The percentile bands for reading and math do not overlap, so there is probably a "real" difference in performance. Or, the stanines indicate a "real" difference because they differ by two stanines.).

CRITERION-REFERENCED INTERPRETATION

To make standardized achievement test batteries more useful for instructional purposes, some test publishers have modified the multiple-choice items to include more real-life situations, added open-ended performance tasks, and made provisions for criterion-referenced interpretation of test performance.

One of the best-known methods of reporting criterion-referenced test results is the *percentage-correct score*. This simply reports the percentage of test items in a test, or subtest, answered correctly. The report can be for individual students, the class, the school, or the entire school district. Percentage-correct scores for the various school groups are compared with the percentage-correct scores in the national norm sample as one basis for evaluating the schools.

Scores for individuals can also be presented by clusters of items representing a content area, skill, or objective, with an indication of the level of performance (e.g., above average, average, below average). Care must be taken in interpreting these results where a small number of items is included in the item clusters.

Some test batteries provide reports that include standards of performance. The standards are typically set by panels of educators and the report indicates a student level of performance by categories ranging from lack of mastery to superior performance.

When making criterion-referenced interpretations of test performance there are a number of questions to keep in mind.

1. Do the objectives the tests were designed to measure match the school's objectives for these subjects (e.g., routine skills versus reasoning)?
2. Are the skills and content measured by the tests appropriate for the grade levels tested?
3. Did elimination of the easy items from the test, to obtain greater discrimination among students for norm-referenced interpretation, result in inadequate description of what low-achieving students can do?
4. Was there a sufficient number of test items in each item cluster to permit criterion-referenced interpretation?
5. Was the procedure in setting performance standards adequate for this type of interpretation?

Criterion-referenced interpretation of standardized tests can be useful in classroom instruction but they must be cautiously made.

Summary of Points

1. Standardized achievement tests have been widely used in the schools to determine how student performance compared with that of a sample of students (i.e., a norm group) at the national, regional, or state level.
2. Standardized tests were carefully constructed to fit a set of test specifications, tried out and improved, and administered to a norm group for norm-referenced test interpretation.

3. The most common types of norm-referenced scores used with standardized tests are percentile ranks, grade equivalent scores, and various types of standard scores.

4. A percentile rank indicates relative position in a group in terms of the percentage of group members scoring at or below a given score. It should not be confused with the percentage of items answered correctly (a criterion-referenced interpretation).

5. Percentile bands are used in reporting test performance to allow for possible error in test scores. The width of the band indicates the amount of error to allow for during interpretation, and it prevents the overinterpretation of small differences in test scores.

6. A grade equivalent score indicates relative test performance in terms of the grade level at which the student's raw score matches the average score earned by the norm group. Thus, a grade equivalent score of 4.5 indicates performance equal to the average student in the middle of the fourth grade. Grade equivalent scores are easy to interpret but they are subject to numerous misinterpretations.

7. Standard scores are based on the mean (M) and standard deviation (SD) of a set of scores. To fully understand them it is necessary to understand the meaning of these statistics.

8. Standard scores indicate the number of standard deviations a raw score falls above and below the mean. They are more difficult to understand and interpret to others but they have the advantage of providing equal units.

9. The standard scores discussed in this chapter have the following means (M) and standard deviations (SD). The third column shows the score for one standard above the mean.

	M	SD	+ 1SD
z-scores	0	1	1
T-scores	50	10	60
NCE scores	50	21.06	71
Ability scores	100	16	116
Stanines	5	2	7

10. In a normal distribution, any standard score can be converted to percentile rank for easy interpretation. For example, one standard deviation above the mean (see column 3) has a percentile rank of 84, no matter what type of standard score is used to express test performance.

11. Because T-scores, NCE scores, and percentile ranks all have a mean of 50 and use similar two-digit numbers, care must be taken not to confuse them when interpreting test performance.

12. Stanines are single-digit standard scores that range from 1 to 9. They are easily explained to students and parents and a difference of two stanines typically indicates a significant (i.e., "real") difference in test performance.

13. Stanines and percentile ranks using percentile bands are the two types of scores that are favored when interpreting test results to others and judging differences between test scores.
14. Criterion-referenced interpretations of test performance have been added to many standardized tests. These include percentage correct scores, the use of performance standards, and interpretation by item clusters representing a content area, skill, or objective.
15. Criterion-referenced interpretations of standardized tests require a check on how well the objectives, content, and skills of the test match the local instructional program; whether the construction of the test favors criterion-referenced interpretation; whether there is a sufficient number of test items for each type of interpretation; and how the performance standards are determined.

References and Additional Reading

American Educational Research Association. *Standards for Educational and Psychological Testing* (Washington, DC: AERA, 1999).
Chase, C. I. *Contemporary Assessment for Educators* (New York: Longman, 1999).
Linn, R. L., & Gronlund, N. E. *Measurement and Assessment in Teaching*, 8th ed. (Upper Saddle River, NJ: Merrill/Prentice Hall, 2000).
Lyman, H. B. *Test Scores and What They Mean*, 6th ed. (Boston: Allyn and Bacon, 1998).
Nitko, A. J., & Brookhart, S. M. *Educational Assessment of Students*, 5th ed. (Upper Saddle River, NJ: Merrill/Prentice Hall, Pearson Education, 2007).
Oosterhoff, A. C. *Classroom Applications of Educational Measurement*, 3rd ed. (Upper Saddle River, NJ: Merrill/Prentice Hall, 2001).

Self-Assessment

MULTIPLE CHOICE

DIRECTIONS: Select the best answer for each item by circling the corresponding letter.

1. A percentile score of 50 on an achievement test indicates that
   (a) this person failed the test
   (b) this person did as good or better than half the class
   (c) the raw score was at least 50 out of 100
   (d) this person guessed on at least half the items

2. A population of students whose demographic characteristics approximate those of the students being tested is called
   (a) a norm group
   (b) a criterion group
   (c) an inference group
   (d) a comparison group

3. Which of the following is NOT a derived score?
   (a) Percentile rank
   (b) Mean
   (c) Mode
   (d) **Raw score**

SUPPLY-TYPE ITEMS

DIRECTIONS: Using the listed test scores below, solve for the mean, median, mode, and standard deviation. Additionally, compute the percentile rankings for raw scores of 75 and 99; and a z-score and T-score for a raw score of 92. Place your answers on the lines provided.

$$99, 97, 92, 89, 85, 83, 82, 79, 76, 75, 73, 69, 65, 59$$

4. Mean   _____

5. Median   _____

6. Mode   _____

7. Standard Deviation   _____

8. Percentile Rank (75) _____

9. T score (92)   _____

Restricted-Response Essay

10. The authors of your textbook discuss the interpretation of norm-referenced scores. List and describe the interpretation of each score. Confine your answer to one page.

13

USING ASSESSMENT IN ACTION RESEARCH

Studying this chapter should enable you to

1. Explain the differences in purpose between basic, applied, and action research.
2. Explain how the characteristics of action research differ from other forms of research.
3. Describe the sampling methods used in research.
4. List the steps for conducting action research.
5. Explain the use of the table of specifications as a diagnostic tool.
6. Define the research terms presented in the chapter.
7. Describe the methods used to collect qualitative data.
8. Describe the methods/instruments used to collect quantitative data.
9. Explain the steps for designing a questionnaire.
10. Construct the appropriate research design given a research question.

Good teaching involves more than developing curriculum, delivering instruction, and assessing student attainment of learning outcomes. Teaching also involves continuously monitoring student progress, identifying those areas in which a student exceeds expectations and those areas in which a student is struggling, and modifying instruction when necessary. The teacher must be a researcher who analyzes, interprets, and makes judgments about the data gathered through assessment in order to make informed decisions about the best course of action to help solve student academic or behavioral problems.

The goal for all researchers is to advance current knowledge about something, but the underlying reason for conducting a research study differs and will fall into one of three categories. **Basic** (also called fundamental) **research** is conducted to advance our understanding of a phenomenon, but there need not be any immediate, practical application of the research to give it value. One example is the research conducted with the Hubble Space Telescope. Scientists are learning a tremendous amount about other solar systems, and this research helps us to better understand the origins of our own solar system. **Applied research** is conducted for the purpose of testing a theory that can be generalized to a common group, or population, in other settings. For example, research findings that identify those factors affecting intrinsic motivation to learn can be universally applied to students beyond those who participated in the study. The third category, and the focus of this chapter, is **action research**. Action research is conducted for the purpose of solving a specific, current problem. Here the intent is not to test a theory that can be generalized. Rather, teachers and school administrators use action research to determine whether an intervention has fixed a school-based problem.

CHARACTERISTICS OF ACTION RESEARCH

Action research shares many of the methods used in basic or applied research. However, there are some characteristics unique to action research. Adapting the work of Gall, Gall, and Borg (2007), McMillan and Schumacher (2010) differentiate action research from traditional research by the characteristics of the researcher and research setting, extensiveness of the literature review, methods and instruments used to collect data, sampling methods, and data analysis methods.

Researcher and Setting

As discussed earlier, action research in education is typically conducted by teachers and school administrators seeking to find solutions to problems they face on a day-to-day basis. The research they conduct may be informal and is typically limited in scope to a single student, classroom, school, or school district. While applied research may also take place in a school setting, applied research studies are more controlled than action research studies. Applied research relies on carefully crafted research designs, sophisticated instruments to collect data, and complex statistical analyses. As we will discuss, action research typically uses less complex designs, data collection instruments that are readily available to teachers and principals, and simple statistics to analyze the data. Therefore, it is not necessary for action researchers to have the educational preparation and training in research methods and statistics that traditional education researchers, university professors, and scholars possess.

Literature Review

Action researchers should conduct a review of the literature before implementing an intervention and beginning the research. The goal for the action researcher is to identify from the literature the most appropriate intervention that will solve the problem. Therefore, the focus is on literature written more for the practitioner rather than the research scholar. The review by a traditional researcher is comparably more extensive. Traditional researchers rely heavily on existing literature that details previous research findings to guide their own study. An extensive review of the literature assists these researchers when forming research questions, stating hypotheses, framing the theoretical/conceptual framework for the research, and establishing research protocols, among others. It is necessary that traditional researchers conduct a thorough review and discuss the existing literature when presenting their own research if they hope to have the findings published in a scholarly journal.

Data Collection Methods and Instruments

All forms of research (basic, applied, action) apply methods and instruments to collect quantitative and qualitative data. However, the methods and instruments used in action research to collect data are generally less complex and sophisticated than those used in the other forms. Specifically, **quantitative research** involves the objective collection and statistical analyses of numbers to draw conclusions and make inferences about the characteristics of one group of subjects compared with others, the differences between groups due to the presence or absence of certain conditions, or the relationships between certain variables. The instruments used to collect the numerical data vary in sophistication, ease of use, cost, and availability. Traditional researchers rely on instruments that have been shown through prior research to have acceptable psychometric properties (i.e., validity and reliability). However, these instruments are often complicated to score, expensive, and difficult to obtain for use. The instruments used to collect data in action research are often those that are accessible, affordable, easy to score, and are likely already in use by the teacher to assess students.

Qualitative research has many of the same goals as quantitative research, but the conclusions drawn are not based on the statistical analyses of numbers. Rather, they are based on a researcher's observations and/or conversations held with subjects. The qualitative researcher seeks to understand a phenomenon through the personal experiences of those who have experienced it. When gathering qualitative data, the traditional researcher must adhere to specific observation and interview protocols in order for the study to be accepted by the scholarly community. However, the action researcher whose interest is to solve a day-to-day problem and not publish the research in a scholarly journal is not bound by these protocols.

Sampling Methods

As noted earlier, a defining characteristic of action research is that the study is limited in scope, with the goal of solving a specific problem. Action research, therefore, need not use sampling methods that would allow the findings to be generalized beyond those participating as subjects of the study. In order to explain this further, it is first necessary to define a few terms and to describe the various sampling methods used in research.

A **population** is a group of individuals that shares some common element that is the focus of the research. For example, in a study of secondary-school teachers' attitudes toward standardized testing, the population for the research might be secondary-school teachers. Or, perhaps the researcher is only interested in the attitudes of those secondary-school teachers in Illinois. In this case, the population will consist of only those secondary-school teachers in Illinois. It is often the case, however, that it simply isn't feasible or practical to include in a study all of the individuals in a population. For example, the postage may simply be too expensive to survey all the teachers in Illinois. In such instances, the researcher will select a **sample** of individuals from the population in such a manner that the sample is representative of the population (i.e., the characteristics of the individuals in the sample do not differ significantly from those in the population). Depending on the outcome of the statistical analyses conducted, the findings from the data collected from the sample would then be generalized to the population. Table 13.1 describes the various sampling techniques common in traditional research.

Not shown in Table 13.1 is **nonprobability sampling**. We have not included it in the table because, technically, it is not a sampling method at all. The subjects who make up a nonprobability sample have not been randomly selected from the population and, therefore, it is not automatically assumed that the sample is representative of the population.

One method of nonprobability sampling is **convenience sampling**. In this sampling, a group of individuals are selected to participate in a study because they are accessible and available. An example would be an intact class of college students who are solicited by their professor to participate as subjects in his or her research. Because the students in the class were not randomly selected from a population of college students, it is not appropriate to generalize the results beyond these students. In essence, this sample IS the population. The second type is **purposeful sampling** in which the researcher seeks out subjects who have a particular characteristic that is of interest to study (e.g., students diagnosed with dyslexia). These nonprobability sampling methods are used in action research. Again, the focus of action research is on solving a particular problem pertaining to a particular student or group of students, and not generalizing the results or testing a theory. Therefore, nonprobability sampling is adequate.

Data Analysis Methods

The statistical analyses performed on quantitative data fall into two general categories: **descriptive statistics** and **inferential statistics**. Descriptive statistics

TABLE 13.1 Common Sampling Methods

Simple Random Sampling	Subjects are chosen from the population at random so that each subject has an equal chance of being chosen.
Systematic Sampling	Every *n*th subject is chosen from a list of individuals in the population.
Stratified Random Sampling	The population is divided into subgroups based on a characteristic such as gender or ethnicity and subjects are randomly chosen from each subgroup to ensure that the subgroups are proportionately represented in the sample.
Cluster Sampling	The population is divided into subgroups based on, for example, geographic location and subjects are randomly chosen from each subgroup.

describe the data through calculations and reporting measures of central tendency (e.g., mean, median, mode), measures of variability (e.g., standard deviation, range), and measures of relationship (e.g., correlation). Inferential statistics indicate whether or not the findings from data collected from a sample of subjects can, and should, be generalized to the population from which they were selected. In other words, inferential statistics answer the question of whether we can infer with an acceptable level of confidence that, for example, the relationships found between variables in the sample also exists in the population. A deeper discussion of the purpose and methods of inferential statistics is beyond the scope of this book. And, a deeper discussion is not necessary in this chapter given that action research, by its very nature, does not require inferential statistics. Why? The reason is that, as mentioned earlier, action research does not involve randomly selecting a sample of subjects from a population. Nonprobability samples are used in action research and, therefore, there is no need to apply inferential statistics in order to make inferences to the population. Instead, descriptive statistics are used.

PROCESS FOR CONDUCTING ACTION RESEARCH

Before action research begins, the researcher should plan the study. Careful consideration should be given to the problem to be investigated, the research questions to be answered, the methods that will be used to gather the data needed to answer the research questions, and the way in which the research is designed. Each of these will be discussed in more detail.

Identify the Research Problem

Research begins by identifying a problem that requires further investigation. The problem may become immediately evident to the teacher through observation and personal experience in the classroom. For example, the teacher may observe that students are demonstrating aggressive behaviors toward other students, not completing their work on time, or not following directions. In other instances, the problem becomes evident only after an assessment. An achievement test, for instance, may reveal that students can remember the meaning of terms but that they can't apply principles. Further, the assessment will reveal whether the problem exists among all of the students or the problem is specific to a few students.

As a practice, teachers should use assessment results as a diagnostic tool to identify problem areas. In addition to considering student performance on a test as a whole, the overall performance of each student on an achievement test should be separated into his or her performance on test items pertaining to each learning outcome. You will recall that in Chapter 5 we discussed building a table of specifications. This two-way chart shows the number of test items that relate to each learning outcome specific to an area of course content. This table can also serve as a useful diagnostic tool to identify a specific weakness of a student. To illustrate this diagnostic approach, the table of specifications example that was presented in Chapter 5 is reproduced below (see Table 13.2), but with a few modifications.

TABLE 13.2 Table of Specifications for a Summative Test on a Unit for Achievement Testing

Student Name: John Doe   **Course:** Assessment of Student Achievement
Date: 10/15/2012

Outcomes	Remembers					Total Number of Items Correct
Content	Terms	Facts	Procedures	Understands Principles	Applies Principles	
Role of Tests in Instruction	75% (3/4)	50% (2/4)		100% (2/2)		70% (7/10)
Principles of Testing	50% (2/4)	100% (3/3)	100% (2/2)	33% (2/6)	20% (1/5)	50% (10/20)
Norm-Referenced versus Criterion-Referenced	100% (4/4)	66% (2/3)	100% (3/3)			90% (9/10)
Planning the Test	100% (3/3)	100% (5/5)	80% (4/5)	50% (1/2)	0% (0/5)	65% (13/20)
Total Number of Items Correct	80% (12/15)	80% (12/15)	90% (9/10)	50% (5/10)	20% (1/10)	65% (39/60)

The table of specifications in Table 13.2 represents a 60-item achievement test. The column headings show the learning outcomes measured and the row headings show the areas of course content covered on the test. Added to this table is a place to record the student's name, the name of the course, and the date of the assessment. On the table, the teacher would record the number of test items within each cell that the student answered correctly out of the total number of items, as is shown in the example. For instance, under the learning outcome *remembers terms* within the content area of *roles of tests in instruction* the student answered 3 out of 4 items correctly (3/4). Note that the number of total items varies from cell to cell. Therefore, to allow more meaningful comparisons of performance between cells, and between students, the number correct out of the total number of items is converted to percentages. These percentages are recorded in each cell as well (e.g., 75 percent). The column farthest to the right shows the percentages correct within each content area, and the row at the bottom of the table shows the percentages correct within each learning outcome. Inspection of the column shows that this student had the most difficulty with test items relating to the *principles of testing* (50 percent answered correctly). The student performed best on test items relating to *norm-referenced versus criterion-referenced testing* (90 percent answered correctly). However, note that the test items within this content area were all written at the lowest level (i.e., remember) of the cognitive taxonomy, which are generally easier to answer. The bottom row indicates that this student performed well overall on items written at the lowest level, but had difficulty answering items at higher levels of the cognitive taxonomy, which require students to demonstrate the ability to *understand* or *apply principles.*

Once the analysis described above is completed for each student, the teacher can determine whether a problem in achievement of certain learning outcomes is isolated to a particular few students or the problem exists among the majority of students. The finding from the analysis indicates the nature and magnitude of the problem. If the problem exists among only a few students, then the appropriate intervention may be remedial work. If the problem exists among the entire class, then a change in the curriculum may also be necessary.

Form a Research Question

Once the research problem has been identified, the teacher reframes the problem in the form of a research question. The research question provides focus for the research and should be stated in such a way that the **independent variable** and **dependent variable** under investigation are operationally defined. The independent variable is the intervention introduced by the teacher. The dependent variable is what the teacher measures to determine the effects of the intervention.

As an example, let's suppose that test scores indicate a lack of reading comprehension as a problem among the students in a teacher's fourth-grade classroom. In an effort to improve reading comprehension, the teacher identifies a newly developed reading program. She then forms the following research question: *What is the effect of the new reading program on my fourth-grade students' reading comprehension test scores?* In this example, the independent variable is the new reading program and the dependent variable is the scores on the reading comprehension test.

Note that the population serving as the focus of this research is also defined in the question. Defining the population is necessary in order to make clear that the intervention should only be considered effective or not effective for this particular group of students. As discussed earlier, an important distinction of action research, apart from other purposes and forms of research, is that the focus of the study is on solving a problem specific to a particular situation and group of people. Therefore, the findings from action research should not be generalized beyond those who participated in the study. In this example, the effects of the new reading program on test scores pertain only to these fourth-grade students. Although the new reading program may produce similar effects of other students, the teacher should not make that assumption without further study. It is quite possible that these particular fourth-grade students are unique and do not share the same characteristics of other students. Box 13.1 provides a checklist for forming research questions.

BOX 13.1   Checklist for Forming Research Questions

1. Does the research question directly relate to the research problem?
2. Is the study population identified?
3. Does the independent variable define the intervention?
4. Is the dependent variable measurable?
5. Does the research question have sufficient clarity to indicate how the research will be conducted?

Select Data Collection Methods

Next in the action research process is to collect data in order to answer the research question. Earlier in this chapter, we introduced qualitative and quantitative data collection methods. The collection of qualitative data may involve observations, interviews, questionnaires, and/or document reviews. The collection of quantitative data may involve the administration of achievement assessments, surveys, aptitude tests, and/or an instrument to measure a psychological type or trait. The nature of the research question determines whether a qualitative, quantitative, or combination of methods (mixed) is used. Each of these methods will now be discussed in more detail.

QUALITATIVE DATA COLLECTION.   Suppose the principal of a school has observed students being bullied by others on numerous occasions. To combat the problem, the principal provides the teachers with an inservice program that instructs them in how to recognize bullying when it occurs and how to best intervene and counsel the bully and the victim. The principal is interested in knowing whether the inservice program has been helpful in curbing bullying behavior and forms the following research question: *What effect has the bullying intervention inservice program had on the attitudes and behaviors of the teachers and students toward bullying?* Following a qualitative perspective, data to answer this question could be collected in a variety of ways.

    Observation.   A common method to collect qualitative data is through observation. Observation provides a means to unobtrusively record naturally occurring behaviors exhibited by the subjects of the study in a particular setting. In a traditional qualitative study, the observer is often a person outside of the setting and is not familiar to the subjects. This can create some problems for the observer. First, the observer would need to gain approval to have free access to the site. In many circumstances, this is usually not a major problem. But, in the light of recent violence in schools, an outside observer may find it difficult to gain approval to roam the classrooms, halls, and schoolyard unaccompanied. The second problem is that the presence of an observer who is unfamiliar to the subjects may cause the subjects to act differently than they normally would (i.e., the **Hawthorne effect**). The result is observation data that is not a true reflection of typical behaviors. In an action research study, the Hawthorne effect shouldn't be a problem since the observer will likely be an individual already familiar to the student such as a teacher, guidance counselor, or principal.

While students may temper bad behavior when a person of authority is present, it is more likely that their attention would be drawn to a stranger than to a person whom they have seen on a day-to-day basis.

Recordings of behavior collected through observation are referred to as **field notes**. Field notes should include a detailed description of the setting, as well as the date and time when the observations are collected. The names of those being observed should be recorded as well. The importance of recording the names of those who exhibit specific behaviors can't be overstated. The observer will want to note patterns of behaviors among specific individuals and may wish to conduct a follow-up interview with an individual to gain a better understanding of why the individual was exhibiting the behaviors. However, when the names of students are recorded, the observer must be cautious to ensure that the records are kept confidential and secure from those not involved in the action research.

Interviews. Interviews may be conducted in a variety of ways from informal to highly structured. An **informal interview** proceeds much as a conversation would. The interviewer may begin by asking a predetermined, open-ended question relating to the research topic, but the questions that follow are unstructured with no predetermination of topic or wording. Instead, the interviewer formulates questions on the fly, drawn from the responses of the subject. The advantage of this informal approach is that it helps to create a comfortable situation for the subject, which may lead to more free-flowing and detailed responses. The disadvantage is that the lack of structure may make it difficult to find patterns in responses among multiple subjects. Specifically, the questions asked in separate interviews with two subjects may be substantively different, thereby making direct comparisons of responses impossible. At the other extreme is the **structured interview**. Here, the interviewer has predetermined the exact wording of the open-ended questions, as well as the sequence in which they will be asked. In between these two is the **semi-structured interview** in which the topics of questions are predetermined, but the interviewer may alter the sequence and wording of questions as the interview proceeds.

Questionnaires. A drawback to observations and interviews is that they are time consuming to complete. To thoroughly gain an understanding of the patterns of behavior among subjects, the observer may need to spend weeks, months, or even years in some instances to interpret the behaviors observed. An interview with a single subject among many may last an hour or more. As an alternative, questionnaires could be used to gather data related to the attitudes and motivations that influence behaviors and to the experiences of subjects. In its qualitative form, a questionnaire consists of open-ended questions. These may be the same questions that would otherwise be asked in an interview. However, the obvious drawback to using questionnaires in lieu of observation and interviews is that the validity of the data may be questionable. Specifically, the subject may not understand or may misinterpret the question being asked. In an interview, there is the opportunity to clarify the question and ask follow-up questions when the response is unclear. Also, the subject may not answer truthfully. Of course, this may also occur during an interview. But an experienced interviewer would likely be able to identify when a subject is being less than truthful by his or her body language or responses to follow-up questions.

Review of Existing Documents.   Documentation may exist that provides insight into the behaviors and attitudes of individuals. Within a school, for example, there will be documentation in a student's file that describes incidences of disruptive behavior and any disciplinary action taken. Mental or physical health conditions influencing student behavior will be noted. Discussions that a school counselor had with a student will also be contained in the file, as well as evidence of academic progress. Documents are used by the action researcher to provide meaning to, and an explanation for, observed behaviors and attitudes of subjects.

Returning to the example presented at the beginning of this section, any one or more of the qualitative data collection methods discussed can be used to answer the principal's research question regarding the effect of the inservice workshop. In fact, it is advisable that multiple methods be used to permit **triangulation** of the data collected. Triangulation refers to determining the degree to which data collected using multiple methods converge and confirm the credibility of the findings. For example, the principal could observe students in the classroom, hallway, and playground to establish the frequency and nature of aggressive behavior, as well as observing teachers' intervention tactics and the outcome. The principal could also interview students and teachers to gather further evidence that attitudes and behaviors toward bullying have changed as a result of the program. Questionnaires could also be administered as a method to determine the changes in behavior and attitude. And, existing documentation could be examined to identify potential reasons why aggressive behavior is persistent among certain students.

QUANTITATIVE DATA COLLECTION.   Suppose a teacher administers a math test and finds that the students in her class have failed the section of the test that requires students to demonstrate the ability to solve certain algebraic equations. To combat the problem, the teacher requires students to complete an online tutorial program offered from an outside vendor. The program includes streaming video clips of an instructor demonstrating how to solve various algebraic equations, sample problems that the students complete online, and email or phone assistance from tutors. The teacher wants to know whether the program has improved the students' ability to solve algebra problems. The teacher forms the following research question: *What effect has the online tutorial program had on my students' ability to solve algebraic equations as measured by the algebra achievement test?* To answer this research question, the teacher must now select the appropriate quantitative data collection instruments. In this instance, a paper-and-pencil achievement test would be the most appropriate. Throughout this book, we have discussed at length the purpose of achievement assessments, how to construct an assessment that is valid and reliable, and the best practices when administering an assessment. Therefore, we will not go to any additional explanation here. Instead, we will now turn our discussion to another type of instrument commonly used in education action research to collect quantitative data.

Questionnaires. Administering a questionnaire consisting of closed-ended questions to a group of individuals is an efficient method to gather factual, demographic information. It is also an efficient method to determine the opinions and attitudes of the respondents. Common uses in action research include questionnaires that measure students' satisfaction with a course, teachers' attitudes toward a new school policy, or parents' involvement in school activities, to name a few. When carefully crafted, a good questionnaire can provide usable data that, for example, informs teachers about their teaching strengths and areas needing improvement or aids administrators when making decisions about changes to education materials and programs. Below are the steps necessary to develop good questionnaires.

1. **Identify the target population and the information desired.** The place to begin is to decide who should receive the questionnaire and the information that should be gathered. Obviously, these are important considerations since administering the questionnaire to the wrong audience or asking the wrong questions will yield useless data, if the questionnaire is completed and returned at all. The researcher should first ask himself or herself, "What do I want to know?" A teacher, for example, who is interested in how satisfied students are with his course, would want to know their reactions to his teaching style, the course materials, the assessment methods, and so on. These categories, then, provide a framework for the questionnaire.

The second question the researcher should ask is "Who is in the best position to answer the questions?" Students, for example, are in the best position to rate their satisfaction with a course, while parents are in the best position to rate their experiences with school admission and enrollment procedures. It is also important that the questionnaire not include unnecessary demographic questions. The questionnaire should seek only essential information that can't be obtained from another source. For example, parents should not be asked for information such as a student's age or the name of his or her homeroom teacher, which can be obtained from the student's records. Including them on the questionnaire only lengthens the amount of time required to complete it, thereby increasing the likelihood that the parent will throw the questionnaire out.

2. **Select the types of questions.** With the target population and desired information identified, the work of generating questions begins. Questions that require respondents to choose a response (e.g., "yes" or "no") are in closed-ended form, while questions that require respondents to write in a response are in open-ended form. The advantage of closed-ended questions is that they can be answered more quickly by the respondent and are easily scored by the researcher. Therefore, closed-ended questions are usually preferred. However, open-ended questions may yield more substantive information. For instance, a teaching evaluation questionnaire with only closed-ended questions will indicate areas of strength and areas needing improvement, but will not indicate how teaching could be improved. Depending on the information desired, both forms of question might be necessary.

A closed-ended question that seeks the opinion of the respondent will include a scale of responses to choose from. Two types of scales are the most common: the **Likert-type scale** and the **semantic differential scale**. The Likert-type scale is typically written in a form that requires the respondent to select his or her level of agreement or disagreement with a statement among five alternatives (i.e., strongly disagree, disagree, undecided, agree, strongly agree). For example, to rate the readability of a textbook the student may be presented with the following scale:

The textbook is easy to read. Strongly Disagree/Disagree/Undecided/Agree/Strongly Agree

For data analysis purposes, the researcher would then code each alternative with a number (e.g., strongly disagree = 1; disagree = 2; undecided = 3; agree = 4; strongly agree = 5).

The semantic differential scale requires the respondent to select a number that lies on a continuum between two semantically opposing adjectives such as "bad" and "good." Below is an example of a semantic differential scale to measure a student's opinion about the readability of the textbook:

Difficult 1 2 3 4 5 6 7 Easy

Each of these types of scales has its strengths. The strength of the Likert-type scale is that the results from the data analysis that would follow can be more easily interpreted than the results from a semantic differential scale. Specifically, because each number in the Likert-type scale is anchored by a descriptor (e.g., agree) easier interpretation is possible. If the mean rating of the readability of the textbook among a group of students is 4.1, then the researcher would conclude that, on average, students "agreed" that the textbook is easy to read. Because the numbers on the semantic differential are only anchored by descriptors at the extremes of the scale and not between the extremes, making a meaningful interpretation is difficult at best. A mean rating of 5.8, for example, would be difficult to interpret in absolute terms of "difficult" or "easy." However, the scale would allow for direct comparisons of ratings between students (e.g., Sally rated the textbook easier to read than Cindy). The strength of the semantic differential scale is that multiple scales can be efficiently presented to measure opinions of a single object. For instance, scales with additional opposing adjectives could be added to gather ratings of other characteristics of the textbook such as confusing–clear and useless–useful. Multiple scales provide the researcher with a more holistic view of opinions about an object.

3. Construct the questionnaire. A good questionnaire should begin with a clear and concise statement of its purpose. It is important that those who are asked to complete the questionnaire understand who is requesting this information, why this information is needed, why they are being asked to complete it, how the information will be used, and whether or not they will remain anonymous. Otherwise, they will be less inclined to take time to answer the questions. If the questionnaire will be sent by mail, then a cover letter should be included that provides this information, as well as a self-addressed stamp envelope.

Equally important, but often overlooked, are the directions. In order to reduce any potential confusion that respondents may have when answering questions, the directions must thoroughly explain how responses should be recorded. The researcher should never assume that the method of recording or changing responses will be obvious to others. A sample question should be provided that shows how a response is recorded.

Finally, the questionnaire should be visually appealing, easy to read, and organized properly. The questions using the same scale (e.g., Likert-type) should be grouped together and arranged in order from general questions to more specific questions. Closed-ended questions should precede open-ended questions, and demographic questions should always be last on the questionnaire. A researcher who includes the demographic questions first runs the risk of respondents quickly losing interest in the questionnaire.

4. Conduct a pilot test of the questionnaire. Before the questionnaire is administered, it is important that a pilot test be conducted. The pilot test involves administering the questionnaire to a small group of individuals who share the same characteristics as the target population. If the study will involve administering the questionnaire to a population of teachers at a school, then those in the pilot test should also consist of teachers who are not in the population pool, such as teachers from a neighboring school. The purpose of the pilot test is to verify that the questionnaire is free of any problems that may cause the population respondents to become confused. Table 13.3 lists some common problems with questionnaires that have not already been addressed in the previous section.

OTHER TYPES OF DATA COLLECTION INSTRUMENTS. Other types of instruments used in education action research include aptitude tests, career interest inventories, and measures of psychological constructs. Aptitude tests are instruments that measure not only previously acquired knowledge, but also the capacity to learn and master new information. For example, a person identified as having an aptitude for music would be expected to master musical composition more quickly and easily than others. These tests are used most often to identify an education track or vocational area in which an individual would likely excel given his or her specialized talents and predispositions.

Career interest inventories are commonly used in schools to help students make decisions about potential careers. These instruments identify a student's interests and the activities he or she enjoys, and then matches those to a related career. The inventory will not predict whether the student will perform well in the career. It will only suggest a career that the student would likely enjoy.

Measures of psychological constructs include instruments used to determine the personality types and traits of students. Of most interest to education researchers are those types and traits that are related to academic achievement. For instance, there are instruments that measure a student's intrinsic motivation to achieve academically. Another example is an instrument that measures a student's preferred learning style. Instruments such as these are used to create a personality profile of students who are academically successful compared with the profile of students who are not.

TABLE 13.3 Common Questionnaire Problems

Unfamiliar terms	Questions should be free from terms not familiar to respondents. If a word or phrase could be interpreted in multiple ways, then the questionnaire should include an explanation regarding how the word or phrase should be interpreted.
Lack of question clarity	Questions should be kept as brief as possible, and written at the proper reading level of the respondents. Also, ambiguous terms such as "frequently" or "occasionally" should be avoided because they may be interpreted differently by respondents.
Double-barreled questions	Two questions framed within a single question causes the respondent to not know how to answer. An example is "Do you feel the objectives were clear and realistic?" It is quite possible that the respondent may agree that the objectives were clear, but were unrealistic.
Lack of adequate options to select	When asking for demographic information, questions should include a comprehensive list of possible options to select from. For example, if the researcher wishes to know the ethnicity of respondents, then all possible ethnic groups should be included as options. It is also advisable to include an "other" option that asks respondents to write in a response if an option that pertains to them is not provided.
Takes too long to complete	As a rule of thumb, a questionnaire should take a respondent no more than 10 minutes to complete. Beyond 10 minutes, the respondent will likely lose interest in conscientiously completing the questionnaire.

Choose the Research Design

We now discuss the various research designs commonly used in experimental research. While not all of these designs are commonly used in action research, a discussion of the designs will help to illuminate the variety and purpose of each. These designs are presented within the categories of true experimental, pre-experimental, time-series, and single-subject designs. When illustrating these designs, we will be using the notational system developed by Campbell and Stanley (1966). The symbols and the descriptions are shown in Box 13.2.

BOX 13.2   Campbell and Stanley Notation System

R   indicates that subjects have been randomly assigned to a group or treatment

X   indicates the group that receives the treatment (intervention)

C   indicates the group that receives no treatment (intervention) or a placebo treatment

O   indicates that data has been collected through a measurement of some type

TRUE EXPERIMENTAL DESIGNS. These are considered the most effective in reducing threats to the **internal validity** of a study. Internal validity refers to whether it is appropriate to attribute group differences or a change in the dependent variable to the independent variable (e.g., the teacher's intervention). In other words, a study is considered to be internally valid when other explanations (i.e., **extraneous variables**) for the findings of the study have been ruled out. Consider, for example, an action research study in which a teacher wants to compare the achievement of students who complete her course face-to-face in a traditional classroom with another group of students who complete the same course with her in an online distance learning format. Specifically, she wants to know whether the method in which the course is delivered (in-class versus online) affects their test performance. The teacher formulates the following research question: *Is there a difference in test scores between the students who completed the course in the classroom and students who completed the course online?* Thus, the independent variable would be the method of course delivery (in-class versus online) and the dependent variable would be test scores.

At the end of the course, she administers the final exam and then compares the mean scores of the in-class students with the mean scores of the online students. She finds that, on average, the online students performed better. So, she concludes that online delivery is the better method to deliver the course. Is her conclusion valid? Are there any alternative explanations why the online students performed better, other than the method of delivery? It is quite possible there are if the teacher did not take measures to reduce or eliminate these alternative explanations during the design and implementation of the action research. For example, perhaps the online students were, on average, more academically gifted or motivated. Maybe the online students were allowed to take the test unproctored and online. Perhaps the online students began the course with more prerequisite knowledge. Maybe the online students had more females, and females tend to perform better in this course. We could go on. The point is that if the teacher did not conduct the research in a controlled manner, then these alternative explanations are threats to the internal validity of the study. The comparably better performance among the online students may have nothing to do with the method in which they took the course, and everything to do with these extraneous variables. When possible, the action researcher should use one of the true experimental designs discussed below.

Design 1: Two-Group Posttest-Only Design with Random Assignment

$$R \quad X \quad O$$
$$R \quad C \quad O$$

This design is appropriate when the action researcher wishes to make a comparison between two groups on a dependent variable. Applying this design to the example presented earlier, the teacher would first randomly assign (R) the students to the group who will receive the instruction online (X) or to the group who will receive the instruction in the classroom (C). **Random assignment** of subjects doesn't need to be a complicated procedure. It could be as simple as flipping a coin for each student in which heads results in the student being assigned to one group and tails to the other group. The value of random assignment is that it increases the likelihood that, on average, the two groups will be balanced on all salient characteristics. For instance, both groups will have roughly the same proportion of students who are male and who are female, the average intelligence and motivation levels of students in both groups will be roughly the same, and so on. Thus, many of those extraneous variables that are threats to the internal validity of the study are eliminated through random assignment. Once the groups have been formed, the independent variable is introduced (e.g., the online course and the in-class course). Afterward, the dependent variable (e.g., test scores) is measured (O) for each group so that a comparison of group means can be made.

Design 2: Two-Group Pretest-Posttest Design with Random Assignment

$$R \quad O \quad X \quad O$$
$$R \quad O \quad C \quad O$$

The second design has many of the same characteristics as the first. Both involve two groups, random assignment, and a posttest measurement. But, there is one important distinction with this design. Before the independent variable is introduced to the groups, a pretest measure is taken. The pretest must be identical to or an equivalent form of the posttest. The value of the pretest is, first, it allows the researcher to determine the nature and degree of difference in pretest and posttest scores. Nature refers to whether the posttest scores went up or down compared with the pretest scores. Degree refers to how much the scores changed. Applying this design to our example, the teacher would be able to compare the two groups on the average gains in knowledge by making a few calculations using the procedures shown in Box 13.3 The second value of the pretest is that it allows the researcher to determine whether the two groups are beginning the study essentially equal on the dependent variable measure. Earlier we mentioned that an imbalance between the groups on prerequisite knowledge is a potential threat to the internal validity of the study. Based on the laws of probability, randomly assigning subjects to groups should balance the groups on this salient characteristic. However, there is still a chance that it may not do so sufficiently. By incorporating a pretest into the study, the researcher will have added assurance that the two groups are balanced. After administering the pretest to all the subjects, the researcher would use a **matching cases approach** to randomly assign subjects. This involves pairing students who have similar pretest scores and then randomly assigning one of the students in each pair to the treatment group and the other to the control group.

BOX 13.3   Procedure to Calculate the Mean Change Score

1. For each subject, calculate the change score (Δ) by subtracting the pretest score from the posttest score.

$$\Delta_{\text{subject 1}} = \text{Posttest Score} - \text{Pretest Score}$$
$$\Delta_{\text{subject 2}} = \text{Posttest Score} - \text{Pretest Score}$$
$$\Delta_{\text{subject 3}} = \text{Posttest Score} - \text{Pretest Score}$$
$$\vdots$$
$$\Delta_{\text{subject } n} = \text{Posttest Score} - \text{Pretest Score}$$

2. Add the change scores (Δ) of the subjects in the treatment group (X) and then divide by the total number of subjects in the group (n) to calculate the mean change score.

$$\text{Mean of } \Delta_x = \Delta_{\text{subject 1}} + \Delta_{\text{subject 2}} + \Delta_{\text{subject 3}} \cdots \Delta_{\text{subject } n}$$

3. Repeat step 2 with the subjects in the control group (C).

$$\text{Mean of } \Delta_c = \Delta_{\text{subject 1}} + \Delta_{\text{subject 2}} + \Delta_{\text{subject 3}} \cdots \Delta_{\text{subject } n}$$

PRE-EXPERIMENTAL DESIGNS. These designs differ from true experimental designs in that they do not prescribe the random assignment of subjects to groups. Instead, there may be only one group of subjects participating in the study, or the study may include two groups that are similar but already intact, such as comparing the performance between students in two different sections of the same course. As noted during the discussion of true experimental design, random assignment reduces the threat to internal validity. Therefore, the weakness of pre-experimental designs is the failure to ensure the balance between groups that random assignment provides. Despite this weakness, it is often the case that randomization simply isn't possible or feasible in an action research study and, therefore, a pre-experimental design is used. As we will discuss next, though, some pre-experimental designs are stronger than others.

Design 1: Single-Group Posttest-Only Design

X O

The single-group posttest-only design is the weakest design that could be used in action research. As shown in the notation, there is simply a single group that receives the treatment and then a measure of the dependent variable is taken. The weakness of this design is that, first, there is no comparison group. A teacher may conclude from research using this simple design that the intervention was effective in raising test scores. However, without a comparison group, there is no way for the teacher to determine how effective the intervention has been compared with a different intervention or no intervention at all. Second, there is no way for the teacher to know the knowledge that students possessed before the intervention was applied. The students may have already had the knowledge needed to do well on the test, thereby rendering the treatment ineffective.

Design 2: Single-Group Pretest-Posttest Design

O X O

The addition of the pretest, as shown in this design, is an improvement over the single-group posttest-only design. The pretest allows the teacher to compare student performance on the pretest with performance on the posttest. The teacher would follow the procedures explained in Box 13.3 to calculate the mean change in scores among the students in the class. Still, this design has a weakness. Like the previous design, it does not include a comparison group.

The teacher may be pleased to see an improvement in posttest scores, but the question that remains is whether similar improvements would have occurred without the intervention.

Design 3: Two-Group Posttest-Only Design

X   O

C   O

The third design provides for an opportunity to compare the group that receives the intervention with a group that receives either no intervention or a different form of intervention. However, the lack of random assignment is a weakness that threatens the internal validity of the study. Further, the lack of a pretest draws attention to the question of whether the two groups were equivalent on the dependent variable prior to the intervention.

Design 4: Two-Group Pretest-Posttest Design

O   X   O

O   C   O

The final pre-experimental design that we will discuss is the two-group pretest-posttest design. This design is considered a quasi-experimental design because it approximates the internal validity controls of a true experimental design by including a pretest. The pretest is used to determine the equivalency of groups on the dependent variable before the intervention. However, the lack of random assignment still leaves the door open for the potential of alternative explanations for the findings. Among all of the pre-experimental designs we have discussed, this design is the strongest and should be used when random assignment is not possible or feasible.

TIME-SERIES DESIGNS.   So far, we have discussed designs that involve collecting data through a measurement at a single point in time prior to the intervention and/or after the intervention. Depending on the research question, it may be more appropriate to collect data over multiple points in time at regular intervals. For example, a teacher may wish to know how long students retain knowledge gained after implementing a new teaching method. Time-series designs are those in which multiple measurements ($O_1, O_2, O_3, \ldots O_n$) are taken to allow the action researcher to determine changes in the dependent variable measure over time. It is important to remember, however, that a meaningful interpretation of the findings from a times-series study requires that each measurement is taken at equal time intervals (i.e., days, weeks, months, etc.) and that the same methods are used each time to collect the data. Also, because this design will compare the average scores of a single group of students, or multiple groups, it is necessary that the group composition of students remains intact throughout the study. The absence of one or more students during one of the data collection periods will create a situation where the mean group score from that period can't be meaningfully compared with the group means collected during other points in time.

Design 1: Single-Group Pretest-Posttest Time-Series Design

O   O   O   O   X   O   O   O   O

As noted by the notation above, the intervention is preceded by four pre-tests and followed by four posttests that would be equally spaced apart in time (e.g., a week apart, a month apart). This notation represents just one of any number of configurations possible. For instance, another configuration might show only one pretest with multiple posttests. Such a configuration would make more sense when wanting to determine the length of time that students retain information. The single pretest will provide sufficient data indicating the knowledge that students possess prior to the intervention, and the multiple posttests will indicate any degradation of knowledge over time. However, when research calls for the measurement of attitudes or behaviors, a single "snapshot" approach may produce misleading results. In order to identify patterns of stability or change in attitudes and behaviors over time, data should be collected from multiple pretests and multiple posttests.

Design 2: Two-Group Pretest-Posttest Time-Series Design

O   O   O   O   X   O   O   O   O

O   O   O   O   C   O   O   O   O

The previous design would be strengthened by adding a comparison (C) group, as shown in this design. This design makes it possible for the teacher to determine, for example, changes not only in retention rates of student knowledge over time but also in retention rates for a group that received no intervention or an alternative intervention.

SINGLE-SUBJECT DESIGNS.   All of the designs presented so far have been group based. The data collected from individuals is combined and comparisons are made based on group averages. The final category of designs that we will discuss is referred to as single-subject designs. Here, the focus of the research is to determine the effects of an intervention on an individual. Consider the following hypothetical example. A teacher is experiencing daily disruptive behaviors from a student previously diagnosed with attention deficit hyperactivity disorder (ADHD). This student is taking medication for the disorder, but the teacher suspects that the prescription may be insufficient. Working with the student's parents, school nurse, principal, and the student's physician, the teacher records the daily frequency and nature of his disruptive behaviors over a period of four weeks. The teacher then provides this information to the school nurse, who then consults with the student's parents and his physician. After reviewing the information and conducting a thorough exam of the student, the physician prescribes a new medication that she believes may be more effective. She provides the student with enough daily medication to last a trial period of four weeks and asks the teacher to, again, record the student's daily classroom behavior and to report back to her at the conclusion of the trial period.

What is described in this hypothetical example is the A-B single-subject design. A represents the baseline measurements taken over a period of time without the intervention (X). The baseline serves to identify patterns in behavior when the intervention is absent. B represents the measurements taken during the intervention, over a period of time equal to that of the baseline. In this case, A is the teacher's daily observations of the student's behavior during the four-week period before he is given the new medication and B represents the teacher's daily observations during the four-week trial of the new medication (i.e., the intervention). The daily baseline measures would then be compared with the measures taken during the intervention to determine whether the intervention was effective in reducing disruptive behaviors.

As with the other designs we have discussed, single-subject designs can be configured in a number of different ways as necessary. For example, the A-B-A design would be used when the researcher wishes to determine the effect of removing the intervention. Does the undesirable behavior return to the baseline position once the intervention is removed? If the findings indicate that the answer is yes, then obviously the intervention should continue on a permanent basis.

GUIDELINES FOR CONDUCTING ACTION RESEARCH

Poorly planned and/or implemented action research will likely yield questionable findings. The validity of the findings from action research lies in the thoughtful identification of the problem, selection of an appropriate intervention, and administration of the correct methods and tools used to gather and interpret the data. Box 13.4 provides a summary checklist to guide the action researcher.

BOX 13.4   Checklist for Conducting Action Research

1. Has the problem been correctly identified?
2. Does existing literature support the selected intervention as a viable solution to the problem?
3. Is the research question stated in clear and measurable terms?
4. Given the research question, is the data collection method (quantitative or qualitative) appropriate?
5. Will the data collection instrument yield the information desired by the researcher?
6. Will the study produce enough data necessary to answer the research question?
7. Given the research question, is the research design appropriate?
8. Besides the intervention, are there any alternative explanations for the study results?

Summary of Points

1. Education action research is conducted to determine whether an intervention effectively solves a problem local to a classroom or school.
2. Action research is generally more simplistic in research design, review of literature, and data collection methods.
3. Quantitative research involves the objective collection and statistical analysis of numbers to determine the differences between groups based on certain characteristics or the relationship between variables. Qualitative research involves basing conclusions on observations, interviews with subjects, or examinations of existing documents.

4. A population is a group of individuals that shares a common element. A sample is a group of individuals selected from the population in such a way that they are representative of the population.

5. Simple random sampling, systematic sampling, and stratified random sampling are all sampling techniques common in research to allow generalization of sample results to the population. Nonprobability sampling provides no assurance that the sample shares the characteristics of the population and, therefore, generalizations are generally inappropriate.

6. Conducting action research requires identifying the research problem, stating the research question, selecting the methods to collect data, choosing the research design, and analyzing the results.

7. Common methods to collect qualitative data are observation, interviews, questionnaires, and reviews of existing documents. Action researchers should use multiple data collection methods to triangulate the findings.

8. Common types of instruments used to collect quantitative data are achievement assessments, questionnaires, aptitude tests, career interest inventories, and measures of psychological constructs.

9. Internal validity refers to whether the manipulation of the independent variable is the cause for the change in the dependent variable. Alternative explanations that are not controlled and, therefore, threaten the internal validity of a study are referred to as extraneous variables.

10. True experimental designs are those in which subjects have been randomly assigned to a control group or treatment group. These designs are considered the most sound because random assignment produces a control group and treatment group that are equal on those characteristics that threaten the internal validity of the study results.

References and Additional Reading

Best, J. W., & Kahn, J. V. *Research in Education*, 10th ed. (Boston, MA: Pearson, 2006).

Campbell, D. T., & Stanley, I. C. *Experimental and Quasi-experimental Designs for Research*. (Chicago: Rand McNally, 1966).

Gall, M. D., Gall, J. P., & Borg, W. R. *Education Research: An Introduction*, 8th ed. (Upper Saddle River, NJ: Pearson, 2007).

McMillan, J. H., & Schumacher, S. *Research in Education: Evidence-based Inquiry*, 7th ed. (Upper Saddle River, NJ: Pearson, 2010).

Self-Assessment

MULTIPLE CHOICE

DIRECTIONS: Select the best answer for each item by circling the corresponding letter.

1. The variable that defines the condition or characteristics that the action researcher manipulates or controls is referred to as the
   (a) dependent variable
   (b) extraneous variable

    (c) mediating variable
    (d) independent variable

2. Which of the following is a feature of a simple random sample?
    (a) Subjects are chosen from the population in such a way that each has an equal chance of being selected
    (b) Choosing one subject increases the probability of another subject being chosen
    (c) Subjects within a subpopulation are randomly chosen to ensure that each subpopulation is adequately represented
    (d) Subjects consist of those who are available to participate in the study

3. In research, the population refers to
    (a) the pool of individuals from which subjects were randomly drawn
    (b) the subjects actually participating in the experiment
    (c) only those subjects in the control group
    (d) only those subjects in the treatment group

4. Internal validity refers to whether the manipulation or control of the independent variable has a genuine effect on the dependent variable in
    (a) a controlled setting
    (b) an uncontrolled setting
    (c) other settings
    (d) none of the above

DIRECTIONS: Use the following to answer questions 5 through 9.

A debate coach in a large high school wants to know whether having her students watch videotapes of high school debates will improve the performance of the team. She randomly assigns half the team to watch videotapes of five debates prior to the first debate of the season, while the other half does not watch any debates. She will then compare the performance of group A, those who watched the debates, and group B, those who did not watch the debates.

5. In order to test her hypothesis, the coach should have which group watch the debates?
    (a) The best debaters
    (b) The poorest debaters
    (c) The treatment group
    (d) Those who volunteer

6. The control group would be those who
    (a) watch the debates
    (b) do not watch the debates
    (c) are willing to participate in the study
    (d) do well in their debate

7. The design of the study would be classified as a
    (a) single-group pretest-posttest design
    (b) two-group pretest-posttest design with random assignment
    (c) two-group posttest-only design with random assignment
    (d) two group pretest-posttest time-series design with random assignment

8. The independent variable is
   (a) watching debates
   (b) debate performance
   (c) the size of the school
   (d) the class ranking of the debaters

9. The dependent variable is
   (a) watching debates
   (b) debate performance
   (c) the size of the school
   (d) the class ranking of the debaters

Restricted-Response Essay

10. Explain in your own words why the true experimental design is the strongest design to use in action research. Confine your answer to one page.

APPENDIX A

Revised Edition of Bloom's Taxonomy of Educational Objectives

The Taxonomy Table

The Knowledge Dimension	The Cognitive Process Dimension					
	1. Remember	2. Understand	3. Apply	4. Analyze	5. Evaluate	6. Create
A. Factual Knowledge						
B. Conceptual Knowledge						
C. Procedural Knowledge						
D. Meta-Cognitive Knowledge						

These tables are from Lorin W. Anderson & David R. Krathwohl (eds.), *A Taxonomy for Learning, Teaching, and Assessing: A Revision of Bloom's Taxonomy of Educational Objectives,* © 2001. Published by Allyn and Bacon, Boston, MA, copyright © 2001 by Pearson Education. Used by permission of the publisher.

The Knowledge Dimension

Major Types and Subtypes	Examples
A. Factual Knowledge—The basic elements students most know to be acquainted with a discipline or solve problem in it.	
Aᴀ. Knowledge of terminology	Technical vocabulary, musical symbols
Aʙ. Knowledge of specific detail and elements	Major natural resources, reliable sources of information
B. Conceptual Knowledge—The interrelationships among the basic elements within a larger structure that enable them to function together	
Bᴀ. Knowledge of classifications and categories	Periods of geological time, forms of business ownership
Bʙ. Knowledge of principles and generalizations	Pythagorean theorem, law of supply and demand

Major Types and Subtypes	Examples
Bc. Knowledge of theories, models, and structures	Theory of evolution, structure of Congress
C. Procedural Knowledge—How to do something, methods of inquiry, and criteria for using skills, algorithms, techniques, and methods	
Ca. Knowledge of subject-specific skills and algorithms	Skills used in painting with watercolors, whole-number division algorithm
Cb. Knowledge of subject-specific techniques and methods	Interviewing techniques, scientific method
Cc. Knowledge of criteria for determining when to use appropriate procedures	Criteria used to determine when to apply a procedure involving Newton's second law, criteria used to judge the feasibility of using a particular method to estimate business costs
D. Metacognitive Knowledge—Knowledge of cognition in general as well as awareness and knowledge of one's own cognition	
Da. Strategic knowledge	Knowledge of outlining as a means of capturing the structure of a unit of subject matter in a textbook, knowledge of the use of heuristics
Db. Knowledge about cognitive tasks, including appropriate contextual and conditional knowledge	Knowledge of the types of tests particular teachers administer, knowledge of the cognitive demands of different tasks
Dc. Self-knowledge	Knowledge that critiquing essays is a personal strength, whereas writing essays is a personal weakness; awareness of one's own knowledge level

The Cognitive Process Dimension

Categories and Cognitive Processes	Alternative Names	Definitions and Examples
1. Remember—Retrieve relevant knowledge from long-term memory		
1.1 Recognizing	Identifying	Locating knowledge in long-term memory that is consistent with presented material (e.g., Recognize the dates of important events in U.S. history)
1.2 Recalling	Retrieving	Retrieving relevant knowledge from long-term memory (e.g., Recall the dates of important events in U.S. history)

The Cognitive Process Dimension (Continued)

Categories and Cognitive Processes	Alternative Names	Definitions and Examples
2. Understand—Construct meaning from instructional messages, including oral, written and graphic communication		
2.1 Interpreting	Clarifying, paraphrasing, representing, translating	Changing from one form of representation (e.g., numerical) to another (e.g., verbal) (e.g., Paraphrase important speeches and documents)
2.2 Exemplifying	Illustrating, instantiating	Finding a specific example or illustration of a concept or principle (e.g., Give examples of various artistic painting styles)
2.3 Classifying	Categorizing, subsuming	Determining that something belongs to a category (e.g., concept or principle) (e.g., Classify observed or described cases of mental disorders)
2.4 Summarizing	Abstracting, generalizing	Abstracting a general theme or major point(s) (e.g., Write a short summary of the events portrayed on a videotape)
2.5 Inferring	Concluding, extrapolating, interpolating, predicting	Drawing a logical conclusion from presented information (e.g., In learning a foreign language, infer grammatical principles from examples)
2.6 Comparing	Contrasting, mapping, matching	Detecting correspondences between two ideas, objects, and the like (e.g., Compare historical events to contemporary situations)
2.7 Explaining	Constructing models	Constructing a cause-and-effect model of a system (e.g., Explain the causes of important 18th-century events in France)
3. Apply—Carry out or use a procedure in a given situation		
3.1 Executing	Carrying out	Applying a procedure to a familiar task (e.g., Divide one whole number by another whole number, both with multiple digits)

Categories and Cognitive Processes	Alternative Names	Definitions and Examples
3.2 Implementing	Using	Applying a procedure to an unfamiliar task (e.g., Use Newton's Second Law in situations in which it is appropriate)
4. Analyze—Break material into its constituent parts and determine how the parts relate to one another and to an overall structure or purpose		
4.1 Differentiating	Discriminating distinguishing focusing, selecting	Distinguishing relevant from irrelevant parts or important from unimportant parts of presented material (e.g., Distinguish between relevant and irrelevant numbers in a mathematical word problem)
4.2 Organizing	Finding coherence, integrating, outlining, parsing, structuring	Determining how elements fit or function within a structure (e.g., Structure evidence in a historical description into evidence for and against a particular historical explanation)
4.3 Attributing	Deconstructing	Determine a point of view, bias, values, or intent underlying presented material (e.g., Determine the point of view of the author of an essay in terms of his or her political perspective)
5. Evaluate—Make judgments based on criteria and standards		
5.1 Checking	Coordinating detecting, monitoring, testing	Detecting inconsistencies or fallacies within a process or product; determining whether a process or product has internal consistency; detecting the effectiveness of a procedure as it is being implemented (e.g., Determine if a scientist's conclusions follow from observed data)

The Cognitive Process Dimension (Continued)

Categories and Cognitive Processes	Alternative Names	Definitions and Examples
5.2 Critiquing	Judging	Detecting inconsistencies between a product and external criteria, determining whether a product has external consistency; detecting the appropriateness of a procedure for a given problem (e.g., Judge which of two methods is the best way to solve a given problem)
6. Create—Put elements together to form a coherent or functional whole; reorganize elements into a new pattern or structure		
6.1 Generating	Hypothesizing	Coming up with alternative hypotheses based on criteria (e.g., Generate hypotheses to account for an observed phenomenon)
6.2 Planning	Designing	Devising a procedure for accomplishing some task (e.g., Plan a research paper on a given historical topic)
6.3 Producing	Constructing	Inventing a product (e.g., Build habitats for a specific purpose)

APPENDIX B

Self-Assessment Answer Key

Chapter 1

1)	d	6)	t
2)	c	7)	t
3)	a	8)	f
4)	b	9)	f
5)	b	10)	Individual response

Chapter 2

1)	d	6)	f
2)	b	7)	t
3)	a	8)	f
4)	b	9)	f
5)	t	10)	Individual response

Chapter 3

1)	a	6)	f
2)	d	7)	f
3)	a	8)	t
4)	a	9)	t
5)	t	10)	Individual response

Chapter 4

1)	b	6)	.66
2)	d	7)	.90
3)	a	8)	2.91
4)	a	9)	80.9 to 85.91
5)	a	10)	Individual response

Chapter 5

1)	a	6)	c
2)	d	7)	.55
3)	d	8)	.3
4)	b	9)	.74
5)	b	10)	Individual response

Chapter 6

1)	b	6)	t
2)	b	7)	f
3)	c	8)	f
4)	c	9)	f
5)	f	10)	Individual response

Chapter 7

1)	b	6)	f
2)	b	7)	t
3)	d	8)	f
4)	b	9)	f
5)	t	10)	Individual response

Chapter 8

1)	a	6)	t
2)	c	7)	f
3)	b	8)	t
4)	d	9)	t
5)	t	10)	Individual response

Chapter 9

1)	d	6)	b
2)	a	7)	t
3)	a	8)	t
4)	a	9)	t
5)	b	10)	Individual response

Chapter 10

1)	a	6)	t
2)	a	7)	f
3)	c	8)	f
4)	d	9)	f
5)	c	10)	Individual response

Chapter 11

1)	b	6)	f
2)	a	7)	f
3)	d	8)	t
4)	a	9)	f
5)	a	10)	Individual response

Chapter 12

1)	b	6)	amodal
2)	a	7)	11.3
3)	d	8)	32
4)	80.2	9)	60.44
5)	80.5	10)	Individual response

Chapter 13

1)	d	6)	b
2)	a	7)	c
3)	a	8)	a
4)	a	9)	b
5)	c	10)	Individual response

GLOSSARY

This glossary of assessment terms focuses primarily on the terms used in this book.

Achievement Assessment A procedure that is used to determine the degree to which individuals have achieved the intended learning outcomes of instruction. It includes both paper-and-pencil tests and performance assessments, plus judgments concerning learning progress.

Achievement Test An instrument that typically uses sets of items designed to measure a domain of learning tasks and is administered under specified conditions (e.g., time limits, open or closed book).

Action Research A study conducted to solve a local, specific problem.

Alternate Forms Two or more forms of a test or assessment that are designed to measure the same abilities (also called *equivalent* or *parallel forms*).

Alternative Assessment An assessment procedure that provides an alternative to paper-and-pencil testing.

Analytic Scoring The assignment of scores to individual components of a performance or product (e.g., Evaluate a writing sample by using separate scores for organization, style, mechanics, etc.).

Anecdotal Record A brief description of some significant student behavior, the setting in which it occurred, and an interpretation of its meaning.

Applied Research A study conducted to test a theory that is generalizable.

Asynchronous Occurring at different points in time.

Authentic Assessment An assessment procedure that emphasizes the use of tasks and contextual settings like those in the real world.

Basic Research A study conducted to advance knowledge, but there is no immediate, practical application of what is learned.

Battery of Tests Two or more tests standardized on the same sample of students, so that performance on the different tests can be compared using a common norm group.

Checklist A list of dimensions of a performance or product that is simply checked present or absent.

Content Standard A broad educational goal that indicates what a student should know and be able to do in a subject area.

Convenience Sampling A nonprobability sampling method in which subjects are selected to participate in a study based on accessibility and availability.

Correlation Coefficient A statistic indicating the degree of relationship between two sets of test scores or other measures.

Criteria A set of qualities used in judging a performance, a product, or an assessment instrument.

Criterion-Referenced Interpretation A description of an individual's performance in terms of the tasks he or she can and cannot perform.

Dependent Variable The variable in an experimental study that changes when the independent variable is manipulated or controlled by the researcher.

Descriptive Statistics Mean, median, mode, standard deviation, range, frequency, correlation, percentile rank, and standardized scores.

Difficulty Index Percentage of individuals who obtain the correct answer on a test item or task.

Discrimination Index The degree to which a test item or task discriminates between high and low scorers on the total test.

Expectancy Table A twofold chart that shows the relationship between two sets of scores. It can be used to predict the chances of success on one measure (the criterion) for any given score on the other measure (the predictor), and it can be used for obtaining criterion-related evidence of validity.

Extraneous Variable A variable not controlled by the researcher that serves as an alternative explanation for the findings of an experimental study.

Field Notes Records of behavior collected through observation of subjects.

Generalizability The extent to which an assessment procedure provides comparable results over different samples of similar tasks, different settings, and different administrations.

Grade Equivalent Score A derived score that indicates the grade level at which an individual's score matches the average score (e.g., a grade equivalent score of 4.5 indicates the raw score matches the average score of students in the middle of the fourth grade).

Hawthorne Effect A phenomena in which people behave differently than normal when they know they are being observed.

Holistic Scoring The assignment of a score based on an overall impression of a performance or product rather than a consideration of individual elements. The overall judgment is typically guided by descriptions of the various levels of performance or scoring rubrics.

Independent Variable The variable in an experimental study that is manipulated or controlled by the researcher.

Inferential Statistics A group of statistics calculated for the purpose of making inferences to a population from data collected from a sample.

Informal Interview An interview that is conducted in a conversational manner, without predetermined questions formulated.

Internal Validity Refers to the appropriateness of attributing changes to the dependent variable on the manipulation or control of the independent variable.

Item Analysis Traditionally, a method for determining the difficulty and discriminating power of test items. It can also be used to determine the responsiveness of test items to instructional effects.

Kuder-Richardson Formula 20 (KR-20) A method for estimating reliability based on the internal consistency of a test (i.e., on the extent to which the test items correlate with each other).

Likert-type Scale A scale requiring subjects to select a response indicating their level of agreement with a statement.

Mastery Test An assessment method used to determine whether an individual has met some predetermined level of performance.

Matching Cases Approach Subjects are randomly assigned to groups by matching subjects who have similar characteristics.

Mean The arithmetic average that is determined by adding together a set of scores and dividing by the number of scores.

Nonprobability Sampling A sample that is not randomly selected from a population.

Normal Curve A symmetrical bell-shaped curve based on a precise mathematical equation. It is widely used in interpreting standardized test scores because of its fixed mathematical properties (e.g., when standard deviations are plotted along the baseline of the curve, each portion of the curve contains a fixed percentage of scores).

Normal-Curve Equivalent Score A normalized standard score that ranges from 1 to 99 with a mean of 50. It is used for reporting performance on standardized achievement tests.

Norm-Referenced Interpretation A description of an individual's performance in terms of how it compares to the performance of others (typically those in a norm group).

Norms Data that describe the performance of individuals in some reference group (e.g., national norms, local norms). Norms represent average or typical performance and are not to be interpreted as standards.

Objective Test A test that can be consistently scored by equally competent scorers (i.e., they obtain the same scores). This contrasts with subjective tests where the scores are influenced by scorer judgment (e.g., essay tests).

Percentage-Correct Score The percentage of items that an individual answers correctly on a test, or the percentage of tasks an individual performs correctly on a performance assessment.

Percentile Band A range of percentile ranks that sets reasonable limits within which an individual's true score is likely to fall. It takes into account the inconsistency of obtained scores due to errors of measurement (also called an *error band* or *confidence band*).

Percentile Rank The percentage of individuals in a group scoring at or below a given score. Not to be confused with the percentage-correct score.

Performance Assessment A procedure that requires individuals to perform tasks and the process or product of the performance is judged using prespecified criteria.

Population A group of individuals that shares common elements that are the focus of research.

Portfolio Assessment A preplanned collection of samples of student work, assessment results, and other data that represent the student's accomplishments. It is viewed by some as a basic type of performance assessment and by others as merely a convenient method for accumulating evidence of student performance.

Purposeful Sampling A nonprobability sampling method in which subjects are selected to participate in a study based on a particular characteristic they possess.

Qualitative Research A study that involves the collection of non-numerical data through observation, interviews, and document analyses.

Quantitative Research A study that involves the collection and statistical analysis of numerical data.

Random Assignment The assignment of subjects to groups based on chance.

Range The difference between the highest score and the lowest score in a distribution of scores.

Rating Scale A systematic procedure for guiding and recording judgments concerning the degree to which the characteristics of a performance or behavior are present.

Raw Score The score that is obtained when first scoring a test or performance task (also called an obtained score). The raw score is frequently converted to some type of derived score for interpretation (e.g., percentile rank or standard scores).

Reliability The degree to which assessment results are consistent from one measurement (or assessment) to another. Reliability estimates typically indicate the consistency of scores or judgments over different forms, different time periods, different parts of the instrument, or different raters. High reliability indicates greater freedom from error.

Sample An individual or group of individuals selected from a population using a random sampling technique.

Scoring Rubric A set of scoring guidelines that describe the characteristics of the different levels of performance used in scoring or judging a performance.

Semantic Differential Scale A scale consisting of a continuum of data points anchored at each end by polar opposite adjectives.

Semi-structured Interview An interview conducted without predetermined questions, but general topics are predetermined.

Standard A prespecified level of performance that is considered satisfactory for the use to be made of the assessment results (e.g., minimum standards, mastery standards).

Standard Error of Measurement A method of expressing reliability that estimates the amount of error in test scores. It is the standard deviation of the errors of measurement and is used to compute the error bands (e.g., percentile bands) used in interpreting test scores.

Standard Score A term used to describe a variety of derived scores that convert raw scores to a standard scale for a more useful interpretation of test results.

Standardized Achievement Test A test constructed to fit detailed specifications, administered under prescribed conditions to selected groups, and scored using definite rules of scoring. Published standardized tests typically include a test manual that contains rules for administration and scoring, norms for interpretation, and validity and reliability data.

Stanine A standard score that ranges from 1 to 9 with a mean of 5. Each stanine is one-half of a standard deviation wide, except 1 and 9 at the ends of the distribution.

Structured Interview An interview that is conducted with predetermined questions formulated, with questions asked in a precise order.

Synchronous Occurring simultaneously.

***T*-Score** A standard score with a mean of 50 and standard deviation of 10.

Table of Specifications A two-way chart that specifies the number or proportion of test items (or assessment tasks) to be designed for each area of content and each type of intended learning outcome when planning a test (or other assessment procedure).

Task An assessment exercise that requires students to demonstrate a knowledge, skill, or combination of attributes, by means of a performance or product (see *performance assessment*).

Triangulation The use of multiple data sources to corroborate findings in a qualitative study.

Validity The extent to which inferences made from assessment results are appropriate, meaningful, and useful in terms of the purpose for the assessment. Validity is a unitary concept that depends on a variety of types of evidence, is expressed by degree (high, low), and refers to the inferences drawn (not the instrument itself).

INDEX